A MULTIPLE FAMILY GROUP THERAPY PROGRAM FOR AT RISK ADOLESCENTS AND THEIR FAMILIES

ABOUT THE AUTHOR

Susan T. Dennison, ACSW, LCSW, is a well-known group consultant, lecturer, professor, and social worker. She is currently an associate professor at The University of North Carolina at Greensboro in the Department of Social Work. Susan has had an extensive practice background working with at risk families and their children for over 10 years. She has spent the past 20 years providing group training and consultation to a wide variety of settings across the country. Susan has authored six earlier books on groups with at risk children and adolescents. She has been married for 32 years and has one adult age son.

A MULTIPLE FAMILY GROUP THERAPY PROGRAM FOR AT RISK ADOLESCENTS AND THEIR FAMILIES

By

SUSAN T. DENNISON, ACSW, LCSW

Illustrations by
John N. Secor, Jr.

CHARLES C THOMAS • PUBLISHER, LTD.
Springfield • Illinois • U.S.A.

Published and Distributed Throughout the World by

CHARLES C THOMAS • PUBLISHER, LTD.
2600 South First Street
Springfield, Illinois 62704

ISBN 0-398-07553-0

Library of Congress Catalog Card Number: 2004058051

With THOMAS BOOKS *careful attention is given to all details of manufacturing
and design. It is the Publisher's desire to present books that are satisfactory as to their
physical qualities and artistic possibilities and appropriate for their particular use.*
THOMAS BOOKS *will be true to those laws of quality that assure a good name
and good will.*

Printed in the United States of America
SM-R-3

Library of Congress Cataloging-in-Publication Data

Dennison, Susan T.
    A multiple family group program for at risk adolescents and their fami-
lies / by Susan T. Dennison ; illustrations by John N. Secor.
        p. cm.
    Includes bibliographical references.
    ISBN 0-398-07553-0 (pbk.)
    1. Group psychotherapy for teenagers. 2. Adolescent psychotherapy. 3.
Family psychotherapy. I. Title.

RJ505.G7D463 2004
616.89'15'0835--dc22

                                                            2004058051

This book is dedicated to all families who struggle to cope with life's challenges and those families who reach out to help and support them. As a result of my professional and personal experiences I have come to appreciate the incredible power of families healing families.

CONTENTS

A MULTIPLE FAMILY GROUP THERAPY PROGRAM FOR AT RISK ADOLESCENTS AND THEIR FAMILIES

Chapter 1

INTRODUCTION

Multiple Family Group Therapy (MFGT) has been utilized as an approach to treatment for the past four decades in this country. However, in spite of this long history, the popularity of this approach had initially been among a relatively small group of clinicians. In the past 20 years there has been a steady, increased interest in MFGT with professionals across a number of different settings utilizing this unique approach to treat the problems of at risk families. What is so interesting about this shift in emphasis is that many group facilitators today who use this treatment modality are passionate about its impact on families. And, of particular interest, many of the families being treated are often ones who have had long histories of chronic problems that have not been successfully addressed by other more traditional approaches to treatment (e.g., family therapy, group therapy). Moreover, families who have been recipients of this innovative service are just as positive in their feedback, often noting that this is the first intervention that elicited positive changes in their entire family system.

The purpose of this book is to provide the reader with a practice model for conducting effective multiple family group therapy with at risk adolescents and their families. This model provides practical guidelines for setting up, planning, and facilitating MFGT with a particular focus on the latter at risk population. In addition, a wide variety of interventions for each of the three phases (i.e., initial, middle, and termination) of this group model are provided along with related task forms. These intervention suggestions are the heart of the book since four of the ten chapters are devoted entirely to these group technique ideas.

This book is intended to serve as a "how to do it" manual for those helping professionals who are experienced group workers. Such individuals could include social workers, counselors, or psychologists who have had course work, supervision, and ongoing training in group work. Professionals who have had a specific background in MFGT will most benefit from the material in this book because they should be able to easily utilize the treatment interventions in their current group programs. Also, these professionals should be able to adapt, modify, and change some of the techniques so they can be more effectively utilized with their specific client population.

Even though the primary intention of this book is to provide an intervention-based practice model for MFGT, this author felt that readers would benefit from knowing the history and major studies that have been conducted on this unique approach to treatment. Therefore, Chapter 2 provides a literature review of MFGT with an emphasis on practice-based implications from studies and an identification of research still needed on this treatment modality. In addition, this chapter contains extensive literature resources that should provide readers with research and/or treatment programs on client populations or settings that may be similar to their own targeted client groups.

Chapter 3 outlines the Dennison Group Practice Model for MFGT, which provides a suggested framework for utilizing the interventions contained in Chapters 5 through 8. This model has been developed and refined by this author for the past 20 years. For some readers, who are experienced group workers, this group model will provide a new and somewhat different view of the group treatment modality. Many students and practitioners who have been trained on this approach report that it delineates specific goals for the initial, middle, and termination phases such that facilitators have very clear guidelines for planning and facilitating their groups. Readers are strongly encouraged to review this chapter before using the interventions contained in the following intervention chapters. The intent for providing this group practice model is not that professionals have to adhere to it strictly. Instead, readers should find that they will be able to more easily plan and facilitate their groups with a greater understanding of what makes a group an effective treatment modality.

Chapter 4 focuses on the pregroup phase and provides practical suggestions for setting up, composing, planning, and facilitating MFGT with at risk adolescents and their families. These guidelines are based on findings from studies on MFGT, focus groups with both facilitators and participants, and field notes from this writer's training of practitioners involved in this treatment approach. Group facilitators will find that the material in this chapter outlines in very clear terms some of the essential tasks that should be completed before beginning a MFGT program. In addition, some related forms (e.g., planning session form) are contained in this section of the book so readers will not have to design forms related to some of the setup suggestions.

Chapter 5 contains relationship-building interventions that should be used throughout the group phases but with particular emphasis in the initial phase of a MFGT. Relationship building is so important and critical for MFGT that there are significantly more techniques provided in this chapter when compared with the number contained in the other three intervention chapters (i.e., Chapters 6, 7, and 8). It is hoped that the many different techniques provided in this chapter for building both relationships and trust among members of MFGT will provide readers with a wide variety of intervention ideas. Group facilitators are encouraged to modify and add to these technique suggestions so their interventions can be individualized to both their client population and their own style.

Chapter 6 contains psychoeducational interventions for the therapeutic instruction of both parents and teens in MFGT. These techniques, typically used in the initial group phase, provide instruction to group members through a variety of teaching approaches. Readers should again consider modifying these techniques so they can be the most effective for their particular group. These interventions are intended to provide nonthreatening yet educational methods for teaching families more effective ways to handle their presenting problems.

Chapter 7 contains problem discussion interventions that are intended for use in the middle phase of a MFGT. These techniques serve four purposes for members of MFGT: 1) increasing problem awareness, 2) increasing knowledge of alternative coping responses to problems, 3) providing group members opportunities to try out new coping responses, and 4) helping members integrate new coping responses into their repertoire. Again, readers are encouraged to change and modify these techniques to maximize their effectiveness for any particular group.

Chapter 8 contains interventions for the termination phase of a MFGT and these techniques address three goals: 1) to help members validate their progress in the group, 2) to assist members in acknowledging the value of the group and grieve its ending, and 3) to increase members' awareness of other people and places in their lives that can support and reinforce the changes they have made in the group. These techniques are critical to providing a therapeutic closure to the group experience. Hopefully, family members will end a MFGT with increased confidence that they can more effectively address problems that were focused on in the group.

Chapter 9 provides the reader with an overview and implementation guidelines for setting up and facilitating a parallel/conjoint group that is a modified form of multiple family group therapy. Since this text is specifically targeting at risk families and their teens, this author felt it important to introduce this type of MFGT. This approach to group treatment can be the treatment of choice for families where there are serious levels of conflict and intense feelings among its members. In this chapter readers are provided a sample 12-session plan where the interventions in Chapters 5 through 8 are delineated for each group session, including parent groups, adolescent groups, and MFGT. Facilitators should review this chapter before setting up MFGT because this may be a more effective approach with some at risk families and their adolescents.

Chapter 10 provides the reader guidelines for conducting research and program evaluation of MFGT. Also, specific standardized scales are provided with publishing information so facilitators can more easily identify measures that could be used to evaluate their particular multiple family therapy group. Moreover, this chapter highlights some of the current evaluation needs in regard to this treatment modality. The message in this chapter is that facilitators these days need to have more than just passion and a feeling that multiple family group therapy is effective. It is essential that these feelings and beliefs are validated with rigorous studies that can demonstrate the effectiveness of this very unique approach to family treatment.

This "how to do" manual should easily become group facilitators' daily resource for both planning and conducting MFGT. Readers will find the material has been presented in a user-friendly format so that setup guidelines and intervention ideas can be easily understood and duplicated in most therapeutic settings. It is hoped that the interventions suggested will elicit other creative ideas from readers such that this innovative approach to treatment will be further refined and improved.

CAUTIONARY NOTES

Many of the interventions presented in this text may appear to be fun techniques that could be used in any number of settings. However, the attractive presentation of these interventions is intended primarily to encourage family members to participate in group treatment exercises. Readers should not use these techniques for nontherapeutic purposes. Rather, this material should only be used by experienced group workers who have credentials in a helping-related profession like social work or counseling. In the case of an inexperienced group worker or student, use of these interventions should only be done under the supervision of an experienced group therapist, particularly one who has a specific background in MFGT.

Chapter 2

OVERVIEW OF MULTIPLE
FAMILY GROUP THERAPY

HISTORICAL ROOTS OF MULTIPLE FAMILY GROUP THERAPY

A group of schizophrenic girls and their mothers, addressing issues of symbiosis, was the first group of clients treated utilizing the Multiple Family Group Therapy (MFGT) approach (Abrahams & Veron, 1953). Detre, Kessler, and Sayers (1961) and Hes and Handler (1961) continued using this approach with psychiatric patients and their families, reporting more positive changes when compared to more traditional treatment approaches (e.g., family therapy and group therapy with patients). However, it is Laqueur (Laqueur & LaBurt, 1962) who is usually considered the creator of MFGT and whose initial work using this approach was on an insulin treatment ward where the patients and their families were treated together due to a staffing shortage. Much of the early work using this treatment modality was with inpatients and their families, primarily in psychiatric settings and somewhat fewer in medical units. In addition, the beginning use of this approach tended to be more pragmatic than theoretical (McFarlane, 2002), which may be one of the reasons why the development of the underlying theory and definition of MFGT has subsequently been slow and continues to need further work.

In spite of the lack of rigorous studies on this approach in the 1960s, the response from several client population groups was so positive that it was used in a variety of settings. These early trial-and-error attempts of using MFGT included use with outpatients in community mental health centers (Donner & Gamson, 1968; Jarvis, Esty, & Stutzman, 1969), prisoners, (Ostby, 1968; Wilmer, Marko, & Pogue, 1966), alcoholic couples (Burton & Young, 1962), drug addicts (Klimenko, 1968), and at risk adolescents (Julian, Ventrola, & Christ, 1969; Kimbro, Taschman, Wylie, & Machennan, 1967). Hes and Handler (1961) noted that even though these early groups were formed in somewhat unorthodox ways, the marked changes in patients and their families were almost always noted by facilitators and ward staff. Interestingly, these reports of dramatic changes in group members that had not been attained by any traditional treatment methods have continued even today as practitioners report their experiences in using this unique approach. However, there is still a need to know what is different about the changes attained by this intervention and why this treatment modality appears to work more effectively with some of the most challenging client populations and their families.

From the late 1960s to the late 1980s, MFGT continued to be used in a greater variety of settings but with a new emphasis on practice applications around the effective set up, composition, and facilitation of these groups (Dennison, 1999). Open versus closed models were attempted (Gritzer & Okun, 1983; Matthews & Cunningham, 1983; Pattison, 1973; Raasoch, 1981; Reiss & Crostell, 1977), composition of these groups was reported in more detail (Gould & DeGroot, 1981; Leichter & Schulman, 1968; Matthews & Cummingham, 1983; Singh, 1982), number of therapists per group was discussed (Anderson, et al., 1986; Bowen, 1972; Laqueur, 1980; Pellman & Platt, 1974), and facilitator styles were delineated with advantages and disadvantages (Laqueur & Wells, 1969). In addition, the ideal number of families per group was considered with the range from three per group (Parker, Hill, & Miller, 1987; Singh, 1982) to as many as thirteen per group (Reiss & Castell, 1979). Moreover, short-term MFGT (Anderson, 1983) versus longer-term MFGT (McFarlane, 1983) was debated and discussed.

Comprehensive reviews of the literature on MFGT were conducted by both Strelnick (1977) and O'Shea and Phelps (1985). These latter examinations of related studies and treatment program descriptions provide the reader with excellent overviews of the early years involved in the development of this treatment approach. Also, the entire November 1989 issue of *Social Work with Groups* was devoted to articles on MFGT, which provides a sampling of the types of settings where this unique treatment modality was being attempted after being in use for almost 30 years.

In summary, the initial use of this innovative approach to treatment was related more to pragmatic issues than a belief in its underlying theory or therapeutic value. However, almost from the start experienced clinicians and related staff found the client and family changes elicited from this approach to be dramatic when compared to the treatment outcomes from more traditional forms of therapy (i.e., family therapy, individual therapy, or client group therapy). These latter observations were particularly noteworthy since many of the targeted client populations had very challenging, chronic, and serious problems. During the first 30 years of applying and refining this approach, the MFGT model was used increasingly with a wider variety of client populations and in many different treatment settings. By the close of the 1980s practice application guidelines were delineated for clinicians such that they had more specifics on how to effectively set up, compose, and facilitate these groups. However, the theory development of this model and related research clearly remained lacking (Cassano, 1989).

THEORETICAL BASIS, DEFINITION AND GOALS OF MFGT APPROACH

The conceptualization of MFGT that has evolved over the past four decades has included a wide spectrum of theoretical bases, treatment approaches, and interventions (Meezan & O'Keefe, 1998). The delineation of a clear theory base that is agreed on by most of the leading proponents of this approach has been very challenging and difficult to achieve. Part of the reason for the lack of progress in articulating a clear underlying theory seems to be a result of MFGT being a hybrid of group therapy and family therapy (O'Shea & Phelps, 1985). There has been some ongoing controversy as to whether the influence of group therapy or family therapy should be viewed as equal in contributing components to MFGT. However, most researchers do agree that MFGT is a blend of both treatment modalities and thus, appears to be based on theories from each approach.

A combination of family systems theory, structural family theory, strategic family theory, social learning theory, and social group work theory have been reported in the literature as forming the current theoretical basis for this unique treatment approach (Meezan, O'Keefe, & Zariani, 1997; Meezan & O'Keefe, 1998; O'Shea & Phelps, 1985). However, the degree to which each theory contributes to MFGT is still unclear and needs further study. The articulation of these theories has, however, guided some of MFGT's early development and is at least a step toward forming a better understanding of its underlying theory base. From a positive perspective, one of the advantages of this treatment modality is that it appears to combine the strengths of several theories and resulting therapeutic approaches.

A wide variety of treatment approaches are reported in the literature as being used when practitioners conduct MFGT (McKay, Gonzales, Stone, et al., 1995; Meezan & O'Keefe, 1998). These approaches, like the underlying contributing theories, appear to be endorsed to varying degrees depending on the individual style of the group facilitator. Interventions based on the following therapeutic approaches have been successfully used within this treatment approach: social network, psychoeducation, behavioral management, solution-focused, group therapy, cognitive-behavioral, and problem solving (Dennison, 1999; McFarlane, 2002; Meezan & O'Keefe, 1998; O'Shea & Phelps, 1985; Springer & Orsbon, 2002). Here again is another example of what may be the reason why MFGT has had such positive results reported by practitioners, clients, and family members. A more eclectic approach has evolved such that the strengths of several approaches have been combined within this one treatment modality. As more rigorous studies of MFGT are conducted we may very well discover that this is one of the reasons why this approach is so much more effective with chronic long-term presenting problems of clients and their families.

Various definitions of MFGT have been presented over the years in the related literature. Papell and Rothman (1989) have described multiple family groups, based on the work of O'Shea and Phelps (1985), as:

> (consisting) of the members of two or more families, representing at least two generations in each family and present for all or most of the sessions. The explicit focus of the meetings is on problems or concerns shared by all of the families and pertaining to cross-generational interaction. Patterns of interfamilial interaction are emphasized. Actual or potential alliances among members of different families based on similarities of age, sex, focal problem or family role are fostered for therapeutic purposes...the intensity of family focus differentiates multiple family group practice from other group work involving similar populations and problems. (p. xi–xii)

This definition appears to show the blend of family therapy with group therapy and yet delineate the uniqueness of this particular treatment approach. In addition, this working definition provides some important guidelines and requirements on what constitutes multiple family group therapy. This writer selected this definition because it lays out for the practitioner the dual focus of these groups on both individual family problems but also problems shared by all family members of any one multiple family group.

The goals articulated for MFGT have also been varied and, in many cases, unclear and ambiguous (O'Shea & Phelps, 1985). Some of the difficulty in forming clear goals has been related to this approach being a blend of both family and group treatment. Moreover, several reports in the literature have indicated that this approach is often offered simultaneously to families with other treatment modalities (e.g., individual family therapy), which also makes the delineation of clear and distinct goals challenging. Strelnick (1977) summarized in his review of the literature some of the early goals formulated for MFGT that included: decreasing family alienation and isolation, improving family communication, increasing family members' awareness of their interactions, clarifying marital and family roles, and a variety of educational goals often related to the targeted family population. O'Shea and Phelps' (1985) later review of the literature noted that goals for this approach had still not been differentiated from goals common to other treatments such as family therapy. These writers went on to note that part of the problem may be that there are interlocking or overlapping treatment goals across related therapy approaches. Parloff (1976) discussed such goals in individual treatment and distinguished mediating goals from the ultimate goals of treatment. Gurman and Kniskern (1981) later applied this differentiation of goals to family therapy outcomes.

Studies in the past decade on MFGT have continued to either not report specific treatment goals or indicate goals in very general terms. An example of such a goal would be Meezan and O'Keefe's (1998) articulation that "the primary goal of MFGT is behavior change in family members through altering interfamilial patterns and increasing the responsiveness of family members to each other" (p. 330). Unfortunately, such goals are difficult to measure and do not address goals related to the process of a group (e.g., increasing cohesiveness among members, increasing participation of members, and establishing an attractive supportive setting).

McFarlane (2002), who has done the most extensive work using MFGT with schizophrenics, addresses goals related to psychoeducation, development of a social network within the group, and coping skill training. It is clear that this latter researcher and others delineate goals differently depending on the targeted client and family population being served. However, even though the treatment goals may vary between MFGT programs, there needs to be a clear formulation of process goals (or curative factors) that are consistent across groups that use this approach. Such goals would accomplish differentiating MFGT from both traditional family therapy and other forms of group therapy that has consistently been indicated in the literature as yet undeveloped for this approach.

POPULATIONS TREATED WITH MFGT APPROACH

During much of the 1960s and the early 1970s MFGT was used primarily with inpatients and their families either in a psychiatric setting or a medical unit. In the past 25 years this approach has not only been used increasingly in outpatient settings but with a wider variety of client groups (O'Shea & Phelps, 1985). Interestingly, in spite of the need for further theory development and more rigorous studies, practitioners across programs have been motivated to utilize this treatment intervention with their particular client population. Also, of particular note, many of these clinicians consistently find that the treatment outcomes attained are far superior when compared to traditional family treatment or group therapy. There appears to be three major types of client groups that have been the most frequently treated and reported in the literature. These groups include: 1) clients dealing with psychiatric problems, 2) individuals facing medical difficulties, and 3) at risk families dealing with a wide array of problems usually related to their children.

The psychiatric population was the initial group that was treated most extensively with MFGT and, as such, it served as the basis for the early development of this approach (Strelnick, 1977; Benningfield, 1978). Some of the beginning researchers in these settings were actually surprised by the outcomes they observed in some of their most chronic psychiatric patients (Abrahams & Veron, 1953; Detre, Kessler, & Sayers, 1961; Hes & Handler, 1961; Laqueur, Wells, & Agreti, 1969). Subsequently, practitioners working with both inpatient and outpatient psychiatric patients have repeatedly used and found success with this intervention method (Anderson, 1983; Brennan, 1995; Fallon, et al., 1981; McFarlane, et al., 1995). The extensive experimentation of this model with this population has surfaced some of the most informative data regarding setup, facilitation, expected outcomes, benefits, and challenges of MFGT. Not surprisingly, the first book on this approach has been recently published and based on McFarlane's (2002) long-term studies using it with clients having severe psychiatric disorders. The positive treatment outcomes that have been attained with this very challenging and often difficult to treat client population has probably been the impetus for practitioners in other settings to experiment with this intervention with their respective client groups.

The second group of clients that MFGT has effectively treated are those individuals dealing with serious medical problems and the related issues for their family members. Laqueur's first attempts to use this model were with an insulin-dependent inpatient population and his initial motivation was based more on pragmatics (i.e., staff shortage) than a belief in its therapeutic value (Laqueur & LaBurt, 1962). Since those early trial and error years MFGT has been increasingly used in both inpatient and outpatient medical settings. Some of the presenting problems addressed have included: chronic illness (Goldmuntz, 1990), kidney failure (Steinglass, et al., 1982), cancer (Parsonnet & O'Hare, 1990; Wellisch, Mosher, & Van Scoy, 1978), AIDS (Pomery, 1984), sickle cell disease (Nash, 1990), severe burns (Bauman & James, 1989), dementia (Dziegielewski, 1991), medical problems resulting in nursing home placement (Cox & Ephross, 1989), and life-threatening illnesses (Duhatscheck-Krause, 1989). The success this model has had with clients and their families dealing with a wide variety of medical problems is probably somewhat predictable. Studies with the psychiatric populations over the past 40 years have found particular improvements noted by families around their communication skills, increased knowledge and understanding of a disorder, and a decreased sense of isolation in their coping (McFarlane, 2002). These same areas of functioning would be typical problems for clients and their families facing a major medical problem.

The third population group that has been successfully treated with MFGT has involved a wide range of at risk families who are dealing with problems either with their young children or teenagers. This latter group is the most relevant to the focus of this book and the related studies demonstrate how this approach has been adapted to this population. In fact, even during the first decades that MFGT was applied and evaluated, several successful applications were attained with at risk adolescents (Durrell, 1969; Kimbro, et al., 1967; Powell & Mohahan, 1969). Moreover, Hardcastle (1977) conducted one of the first better designed studies of MFGT, using it with families who had school-related problems with their latency age children. In this latter study, the researcher evaluated a combination of MFGT and group therapy with a no-treatment control group. The results supported the effectiveness of the combined treatment approach when compared to the control group. The parents of this group reported an increase in positive behaviors among their children and a decrease in negative behaviors.

In the past 20 years this approach has been applied to a wider range of issues that at risk families face. Problem areas that have been targeted include: attention deficit disorders (Arnold, Sheridan, & Estreicher, 1986), adopted adolescents (Lang, 1993), multiproblem families (Aponte, et al., 1991), battered women and their children (Rhodes & Zelman, 1986), urban children with behavioral problems (McKay, Gonzales, Quintana, et al., 1999), inner city families (McKay, Gonzales, Stone, Ryland, & Kohner, 1995), African-American families (Boyd-Franklin, 1993; Foley, 1982), substance abusing adolescents (Springer & Orsbon, 2002), clients of family agencies (Gritzer & Orkum, 1983), parent-child relationship problems (Cassano, 1989), children at high risk for out of home placement (Zarski, et al., 1992), abusive and neglectful parents (Meezan, O'Keefe, & Zariani, 1997), stepfamilies (Mandell & Birenzweig, 1990), and children in public care (Tunnard, 1989). It is noteworthy that since the early 1980s consistent applications of this approach have been successfully made with a variety of presenting problems of young families. Again it is obvious that some of the at risk families targeted have had some of the most challenging and difficult to treat problems (e.g., attention deficit disorder, substance abuse with teens, abusive or neglectful families) that have not been as effectively addressed through traditional treatment methods.

There have also been some modifications of MFGT for other settings and population groups. For example, a parallel/conjoint format of this model has been found effective with children experiencing moderate behavior and emotional problems (Parmenter, Smith, & Cecic, 1987) and teens coping with family life changes (Dennison, 1995). Even though there have been limited studies using this modified form of MFGT, the few studies and reports on program models have shown promise particularly with families that are experiencing high levels of conflict. For this reason, Chapter 8 in this book outlines an example of a parallel/conjoint group for addressing issues related to at risk adolescents and their families.

BENEFITS AND CHALLENGES OF MFGT

Almost from its initial application, MFGT has been reported as providing a number of unique therapeutic benefits. Some of the strengths of this treatment approach are similar to those noted in more traditional forms of therapy but some are also quite different. Again, the reader is reminded that many of the studies on MFGT have been based on client populations and their families that have been the most challenging, having serious and long-term chronic problems. Not only have the facilitators of these groups been quite impressed with the treatment outcomes but also many staff members who interact with these clients in residential settings or schools. Observational reports and clinical impressions have repeatedly noted that targeted clients and their families attain levels of change that far exceed those accomplished by any earlier forms of traditional treatment. It is unfortunate that we still do not have the rigorous studies to validate these observations since they seem to be consistent across most clinical settings.

As indicated earlier, the predominant client population that initially received MFGT was psychiatric patients and their families. In many cases, these were inpatients that had experienced such regression in their functioning while living with their family that hospitalization was required. Schaffer (1969) noted in his study of this client group that significant changes regarding improved ward sociability were observed by the hospital staff over those clients in a control group. Paul and Bloom (1970) found that group members in MFGT function more as "therapists" and families could see their own maladaptive behavior better by observing it in other families. Strelnick (1977) reported a similar point when he noted that many studies of MFGT found that members of these groups provided more support to one another when compared to studies on conjoint treatment. Laqueur (1972) pointed out from his experience in these groups that there is "learning by analogy" where members gain insight through observation of others. Berman (1966) added to this list of therapeutic benefits when he found at a 12-month follow-up of VA patients who had received MFGT that their recidivism rates had dropped. Harrow et al. (1967) pointed out in their work that these group participants were much more verbal during treatment sessions when compared to similar clients in traditional treatment modalities. Laqueur and LaBurt (1964) also noted that when they compared clients in MFGT with those in patient only groups, they found that the former treatment modality offered more reality testing since the clients were mixed with healthier functioning family members.

Even though MFGT was conducted less frequently with nonpsychiatric populations in the early years, there were still some studies on such client population groups. For example, Anton et al. (1981) conducted an outcome study on drug addicts and found that they showed more prolonged compliance to taking medication and following the treatment regimen. Wellisch, Mosher, and Van Scoy (1978) used this approach with patients and their families dealing with cancer and found attendance was significantly better when the treatment shifted to a more MFGT format. It appears that, similar to the psychiatric client population, many researchers found this treatment modality elicited more positive changes both during the treatment sessions and at follow-up.

There were also some early studies of MFGT with at risk children or adolescents and their families that surfaced some promising positive outcomes. Kimbro et al. (1967) found in a group for at risk adolescents and their families that a unique benefit was the opportunity for extrafamilial adult-adolescent support. This treatment modality, unlike any other type, offers family members a chance to both parent one another's teens and teens to teach other teens' parents. In addition, these latter researchers found that therapists reported that they had less problems with "taking sides with family members" when they conducted MFGT as compared to conjoint family treatment. Leichter and Schulman (1972) went on to find in a group with at risk children and their families that this approach helped the youngsters to better cope with their families' pathology. Gould and Glick (1977) studied the use of MFGT with young adult and teen schizophrenics and found that at a 1-year follow-up these clients had better social and role functioning. Hardcastle (1977), who conducted one of the more rigorous early studies of MFGT, found that there was a reduction in negative child behavior and an increase in positive behaviors with these youngsters.

In the past decade there has been a continuing study of MFGT with psychiatric patients with several benefits identified that both validate and add to the earlier studies. For example, McFarlane, Link, and Dushay (1995) found that MFGT participants experienced extended remissions, had enhanced functioning, and had substantial reductions in their risk of relapse. McFarlane (2002), who has been identified as one of the leading researchers of MFGT with psychiatric patients, provided a summary of the advantages of this approach with this population is his recent book on this topic. The strengths of this approach noted in his publication include: improved social functioning of identified clients, all members experience the benefits of a support system, indirect learning by family members so there are opportunities for cross-parenting, improved role functioning within families, better communication among family members, expanded problem-solving capacity, and education provided reduces families' feelings of shame and guilt. Interestingly, McFarlane (2002) also points out that this treatment modality provides more individuals to absorb the anxiety created by a psychiatric illness, which subsequently reduces the stress level and related problems for the families. Moreover, this same researcher notes the benefits of MFGT to addressing boundary issues within families when he states, "The social structure of the multifamily group provides a nonintrusive alternative to the problem of family overinvolvement" (McFarlane, 2002, p. 43).

At risk families have been the other targeted clients studied most extensively in the past 10 years with some very positive outcomes noted when MFGT was utilized. McKay, Gonzalez, Stone et al. (1995), for example, reported their observations that these groups provided more support for parenting, exposure to new parenting skills, multiple sources of parenting feedback, cross-parenting opportunities, and a setting where families could practice their newly learned skills. Meezan, O'Keefe, and Zariani (1997) studied the use of this approach with abusive and neglectful parents and found better attendance, more members were helping out one another, less expensive treatment for high risk families, and this method appears to be as effective as in-home treatment. McKay, Gonzalez, Quintana et al. (1999) have researched this treatment with low-income minority families and found better attendance, fewer dropouts, and a reduction in children's disruptive behavior. Even though Springer and Orsbon (2002) did not conduct a formal study of MFGT with substance-abusing adolescents, they provided a clear rationale for its use along with a delineation of advantages for this particular challenging population. These researchers' initial work indicates that further study of MFGT with this population could prove very informative.

A number of benefits have surfaced from studies where MFGT has been utilized with a wide variety of client populations and their families. Many of these advantages have been noted in research from even the earliest years when this approach was first applied to clients' presenting problems. In addition, some of the benefits of this treatment modality are particularly relevant to our current times with the reduction in both staff time and services to at risk populations. Some of the particular advantages of this approach that address these issues include: it is time-efficient, the total family is the focus of treatment, a wealth of coping ideas can be shared, both education and resource information can be provided to a greater number of clients, and many of these groups can easily continue on as self-help groups or, at the very least, informal social networks for families experiencing chronic and serious problems (Dennison, 1999).

While there have been a long list of benefits noted with clients involved in MFGT, some specific challenges or implementation issues have also been recognized. For example, McKay, Gonzalez, Stone et al. (1995) delineated specific challenges in regard to the need for particularly well-trained facilitators who can effectively run these very large groups. In addition, these same researchers note that these groups usually involve members of diverse developmental levels that can make planning more difficult, particularly when the facilitator is attempting to achieve balanced participation. Cassano (1989) also addressed this same issue when she pointed out that both verbal and nonverbal activities must be planned so members at various age levels can be easily engaged in the treatment process. The other challenge indicated by several researchers has been the noise level or disruption sometimes present in these groups due to the size and the presence of younger age children (McKay, Gonzalez, Stone, et al, 1995; Cassano, 1989).

Most researchers would agree that there is a need for more rigorous studies of MFGT so that the many impressive observations and initial findings can be further studied and validated. However, there is no doubt that clinicians, using this unique approach from the very beginning years, have noted its many benefits over more traditional treatment methods. At the same time, there has also been a recognition of the challenges of this treatment modality that must be considered when utilizing this approach. When one considers the high at risk clients who have been effectively treated by MFGT, the benefits of this treatment method are even more noteworthy. Knowledge of the advantages of this approach over other approaches provides some insight as to why so many clinicians who have used MFGT are passionate about its impact.

PRACTICE IMPLICATIONS

MFGT is such an unusual approach to treatment that some of its challenges are related to implementation issues. Researchers who have studied this treatment method have identified and discussed some of these practice implications that are critical to effectively setting-up, planning, and facilitating these groups. Over the past 40 years clinicians have contributed to the following list of program implementation issues that have evolved as this treatment approach has been utilized, examined, and studied:

- Open-ended versus close-ended MFGT
- Short-term versus long-term MFGT
- Number of families served in any one group
- Ideal number of therapists per group
- Length of sessions
- Voluntary versus mandatory participation
- Composition of these groups
- Seating arrangement of groups
- Delineation of treatment goals
- Most effective facilitation style
- Single treatment approach or in combination with other treatment

• Specific methods of intervention.

The issue of open- versus close-ended groups was addressed early on as MFGT was being applied to practice (Pattison, 1973). During much of the 1980s several researchers appear to have reached an agreement that open-ended groups seem to work best in residential settings (Raasoch, 1981; Reiss & Costell, 1979; Singh, 1982) and close-ended was ideal for nonresidential settings (Gritzer & Okun, 1983; Matthews & Cunningham, 1983; Parker, Hill, & Miller, 1987). However, McFarlane (1983) still promoted close-ended groups with MFGT that targeted psychiatric inpatients and their families. Also, in more recent years, Springer and Orsbon (2002) supported the use of open-ended MFGT for substance-abusing teens and their families. Similar to the literature on group therapy, there seems to be mixed opinions about which type of group is ideal when following this treatment approach. As a result, this variable needs to be studied further to determine if one type of group is superior to the other.

There also appears to be differing views on the ideal length of MFGT with some practitioners promoting lengths as short as one session to others endorsing as long as two years. McFarlane (1983) has strongly supported long-term groups whereas Anderson and his associates (Anderson, 1983; Anderson & Reiss, 1982) have advocated for short-term MFGT. It may very well be that the type of client population targeted will determine the ideal length of treatment time. However, this is another implementation variable that needs to be studied further since it is critical that we know what length of treatment maximizes the impact of this approach.

The very nature of MFGT has required close examination of the ideal number of families served in any one group. Since its early years of development researchers have addressed this issue with some promoting as many as 13 families per group (Reiss & Castell, 1979). Other authors have advocated for smaller groups, indicating that no more than three families should be seen in any one group since otherwise the size is too large (Parker, Hill, & Miller, 1987). In more recent years the suggested number of families per group has seen closer agreement with Brennan (1995) advocating for six to nine families, Meezan and O'Keefe (1998) suggesting six to eight families, and Springer and Orsbon (2002) indicating that four to five families seems most ideal. The difficulty with this setup issue has been that many researchers have not reported the number of families seen in their MFGT. Furthermore, there have been no studies to date that have specifically examined this composition question, which is particularly relevant to the issue of cost-effective treatment. Not only do we need to know what size of MFGT is ideal for this format but also what types of families are most effectively treated.

The ideal number of facilitators per group was addressed during the initial years of applying this approach (Pellman & Platt, 1974; Bowen, 1972) with Kimbro et al. (1967) providing the most detailed definition of facilitators' roles. Unfortunately, there has been ongoing disagreement regarding this setup variable with some researchers promoting two cofacilitators (Manchester Berger, 1984; Anderson, et al., 1986) while others have advocated for many more therapists per group (Laqueur, 1980; Matthews & Cunningham, 1983). More recently practitioners have suggested teams of four facilitators per group when working with abusive and neglectful parents (Meezan & O'Keefe, 1998). This is another implementation question that needs further study particularly because it may be very relevant to both treatment impact and cost-effectiveness.

The length of each MFGT session has also been addressed almost from the beginning with Strelnick (1978) finding in his review that most practitioners were advocating 75 minutes to 90 minutes per group session. Since the initial two decades of utilizing this approach, most researchers today suggest between 1.5 hours to 2.5 hours per session (Meezan & O'Keefe, 1998). It may very well be that the type of problems being addressed in a group and the number of families served determines the most ideal length of meeting time.

Voluntary versus mandatory participation is a particularly important variable because eliciting several families into treatment can be challenging. Similar to most group treatment programs, it is usually more energy-consuming to identify and obtain a commitment from all potential members then it is to actually facilitate a group. This author has found from informal reports that many residential programs today require family participation if MFGT is one of the treatment approaches being utilized. Other authors have indicated that voluntary participation works just as effectively with outpatient substance-abusing adolescents and their families (Springer & Orsbon, 2002). Interestingly, Brennan (1995) supported the participation of family members in his

MFGT program even when the bipolar patient refused to participate. It could prove most informative to find out if there are any differences in treatment outcomes when participation is voluntary versus mandatory. Moreover, it would be important to study any differences in the process of treatment when families join voluntarily as opposed to being required to attend.

Which client groups and their families most benefit from MFGT? This question has been examined and studied since the 1960s with many of the findings based on experimentation with various client population groups (Leichter & Schulman, 1968; Strelnick, 1977). Interestingly, several population groups have been effectively treated over the years with this approach (Durrell, 1969; Hardcastle, 1977; Gould & DeGroot, 1981; Matthews & Cunningham, 1983; McFarlane, 1983; Anderson, 1983; Steinglass, et al., 1982; Cox & Ephross, 1989; Aponte, et al., 1991; Rhodes & Zelman, 1986; Meezan, O'Keefe, & Zariani, 1997; Springer & Orsbon, 2002). Benningfield (1978) supported the guideline that only families with one symptomatic member should be treated in these groups, which would limit, to some degree, the problems focused on in MFGT. Related to this point, Raasoch (1981) strongly advised eliminating clients who were acutely psychotic or markedly passive and withdrawn. On the other hand, O'Shea and Phelps (1985) in their literature review found that this treatment modality appears to be ideal for families experiencing boundary issues, feeling socially isolated, addressing psychologically or physically debilitating problems, and coping with difficulties that have not been effectively treated with traditional approaches. The last group mentioned is of particular interest since it relates to one of the benefits of this approach, eliciting positive changes among clients who have experienced chronic and long-term problems. During the past four decades MFGT has been used with an increasingly wider array of client groups with many of the related studies surfacing positive treatment outcomes. As more rigorous research is conducted on this treatment approach, it will be interesting to see if some groups do, in fact, benefit more from this unique intervention method.

Composition of these groups also relates to which members of a family should be included in this treatment. Luber and Wells (1977) were some of the first researchers to support the involvement of the index client, his or her parents, and siblings in order for the group to truly follow the MFGT approach. This same point was made by O'Shea and Phelps (1985) when they articulated their definition of a multiple family therapy group, which was a void in the literature they had identified from their comprehensive review. Another related issue has been the involvement of younger children, which Leichter and Schulman (1972) strongly supported since they too are experiencing the same problems. Almost 20 years later, Cassano (1989) concluded from her study of the interactions in MFGT that the involvement of very young children still needs to be further studied since there were differences in interactions when they were present in these groups. Some practitioners have indirectly addressed this point when they report that families should be directed to take responsibility for keeping their children on task and under control in MFGT.

Seating arrangement of these groups has rarely been addressed in the literature on MFGT. It could be assumed that some clinicians allow group members to freely determine where they want to sit each session since articles on this topic usually do not delineate any guidelines regarding this issue. However, Reiss and Costell (1977) found in their study that when clients were left to sit where they wanted, they almost always sat with their peer group (i.e., parents with parents and teens with teens) and continued to stay in that position throughout the life of the group. This finding is particularly important because it could mean that by allowing seating selection by members, facilitators run the risk of having two separate groups rather than a group that is addressing family-wide problems and issues. This author has found from informal conversations with clinicians that they ultimately decided to require that all family members sit together because otherwise the focus shifts from the family units to the peer groups. In addition, these same group facilitators have found that when family members do not sit together they have increased problems with keeping the group on task and an increase in disruptive behaviors among younger members or the index clients.

The delineation of goals for MFGT has not been clearly or consistently articulated in the development of this approach. Some researchers believe that part of the reason for this lack of clarity around treatment goals is related to the fact that this approach is a blend of both family therapy and group therapy (O'Shea & Phelps, 1985). At the same time, the other difficulty is that often MFGT is provided simultaneously with other treatment approaches, which has made a delineation of the unique goals of this approach very challenging. During the early years of applying this approach some common general goals surfaced that involved improving family communication, providing support to the family, reducing feelings of alienation and shame, and focusing on family roles (Strelnick, 1977). McFarlane (1983) further refined these goals when he indicated that the goal for nonpsychotic patients is the active restructuring of family interactional patterns whereas the goal for psychotic patients is to reduce social isolation and establish a supportive social network. Anderson, Hogarty, and Reiss (1980) were some of the first researchers to strongly advocate for the didactic goals of MFGT. Some of these same goals have been reported in later studies with additional ones noted in terms of improving parenting skills, clarifying responsibilities of various family members, sharing coping skill ideas, and practicing newly learned skills (McKay, Gonzalez, Stone, et al., 1995; McKay, Gonzalez, Quintana, et al., 1999; Meezan & O'Keefe, 1998). Dennison's (1999) review of the MFGT literature resulted in a listing of the 12 most common goals reported by researchers. Clearly there is a need to further study this aspect of MFGT particularly since it connects directly to the expected treatment outcomes of this therapeutic approach.

The variable of group facilitation style was addressed on a very limited basis during the first decades when this approach was utilized with clients (Laqueur & Wells, 1969). Cassano (1989) later noted the wide array of practice skills required of facilitators running these groups. In addition, several researchers have noted indirectly the skills required of MFGT facilitators when they have delineated some of the challenges in conducting these unique groups (McKay, Gonzales, Stone, et al., 1995; Cassano, 1989). Unfortunately, there have been few studies that have reported any specifics regarding the facilitation style utilized with particular multiple family groups. McFarlane (2002) has been one of the few proponents of this approach that has provided guidelines for facilitators to follow when conducting MFGT in each stage of the group's development. Furthermore, this same researcher has outlined specific suggestions for handling problems that arise in these treatment groups. This is one of the implementation issues that probably has been the least articulated in terms of any specific descriptions of facilitation styles and, thus, has not been studied to any degree. It will be important that future studies on this approach target programs that more clearly delineate facilitators' interaction methods such that successful multiple family group programs can be replicated.

The utilization of MFGT either as a single treatment approach or in combination with other approaches has also been an implementation issue. When O'Shea and Phelps (1985) conducted their literature review they found that the majority of studies since Strelnick's (1977) review indicated that MFGT was used in combination with other treatment methods. Typically these treatment approaches were provided simultaneously to targeted clients and could include individual counseling, peer group therapy, or traditional family treatment. In fewer studies MFGT has been utilized in a temporal sequence of treatment approaches like the transition between inpatient and outpatient treatment phases (Kaufman & Kaufmann, 1979). One of the difficulties with this format of combining MFGT with other approaches is that evaluating which treatment outcomes were a result of this particular method of intervention can be quite challenging. Also, there are no recent statistics on how many current multiple family group therapy programs are utilizing this modality as a sole approach or in combination with others. Moreover, O'Shea and Phelps (1985) noted in their review that there is some concern as to the benefit of this approach when it appears that most clinicians feel it must be combined with other methods of intervention. Clearly this setup variable requires further study in order to determine the most effective way to provide this treatment. Moreover, such research must address concerns about the therapeutic worth of MFGT that have surfaced over the years.

The last implementation issue that has been addressed in the literature involves the specific types of interventions used in MFGT. In the early years only a few studies reported actual interventions being used in these groups like role-playing and psychodrama (Coughlin & Winberger, 1968) and role assignments (Barcai, 1967). Bloomfield (1972) was one of the first researchers to identify four stages of MFGT where he then described suggested methods of interventions based on each treatment phase. These stages included: an introduction and information-gathering stage, a second stage where more peer-group support emerges, a working period where problems surface, and a final stage of termination. In these initial years, studies tended to provide general guidelines for interventions based on the treatment stages that various authors endorsed. Unfortunately, there were limited studies that provided any details regarding actual interventions used. When O'Shea and Phelps (1985) conducted their review they noted that there seemed to be no preferred clinical interventions for this approach and most of the techniques were from a combination of other approaches.

In the past decade, studies on MFGT have begun to report more details about the types of interventions being used in these groups. For example, McKay, Gonzalez, Stone et al. (1995) provided the goals and plans for each of the eight sessions in their MFGT program that targeted inner city children and their families. Meezan, O'Keefe, and Zariani (1997) described in detail a treatment protocol for a parallel/conjoint form of MFGT that addressed the needs of families involved in the child welfare system. Brennan (1995) provided session by session plans for MFGT that addressed bipolar patients and their families. Springer and Orsbon (2002) were not as specific in their actual interventions but indicated they had used two techniques (the scaling question and the miracle question) from solution-focused therapy (Berg & de Shazer, 1991) for substance-abusing adolescents and their families. Dennison (1999) provided specific planning guidelines and an 8-week session by session plan for a parallel/conjoint MFGT program that targeted divorced parents and their teenage children.

McFarlane (2002) has done the most extensive work on interventions for MFGT with clients having severe psychiatric disorders. His latest book publication (McFarlane, 2002) provides the reader with a delineation of MFGT treatment into four stages and then outlines some guidelines for facilitating each of these stages. In addition, this same researcher describes in detail several interventions that can be used in these groups and the rationale for each. There appears to be a shift in the literature on MFGT with more studies that provide readers with details regarding the interventions that were used. This delineation is important since it will greatly assist in the replication of particularly effective programs. Moreover, the more detail with which interventions are described, the easier it will be to both study these groups and then compare various types of multiple family groups with one another.

Several implementation issues have been identified as relevant and important to the setup, planning, and facilitation of MFGT. Some of these variables have been studied in more depth than others. However, all 12 of the implementation issues listed here require further study and such research will be critical for several reasons. First of all, a clearer understanding of these variables will increase practitioners' knowledge as to how to effectively set up and conduct MFGT. Second, with the mixture of opinions from leading proponents regarding these setup or planning variables, clinicians need more clarity on such issues as what is the ideal number of families per group or the ideal number of therapists. And third, in order to conduct more rigorous studies of MFGT, researchers must be able to describe in more detail specifics regarding variables like the composition of these groups, the actual interventions used, goals of the group, length of the treatment, and setup procedures.

CURRENT STATUS OF RESEARCH AND
FUTURE EVALUATION NEEDS

Since Strelnick's (1977) initial review of the studies on MFGT there has been tremendous clinical support for this treatment approach but little empirical support. In spite of the fact that there have been so few controlled studies of this therapeutic modality, clinicians' praises on the dramatic changes attained with some of the most challenging clients have continued for the past 40 years. And, even though many of these findings have been based on observations and less than ideal research designs, the fact that this unique approach continues to grow and expand to more areas of practice speaks to its therapeutic worth. O'Shea and Phelps (1985) make this point particularly when they stated, "This attests to the strength of MFT's signals and renders MFT both deserving of and overdue for controlled, rigorous, clinical, and scientific scrutiny" (p. 579).

The consensus among most proponents of this approach is that there are many aspects of MFGT that still require further study. Some of this research needs to be of a more rigorous type while other evaluation can utilize some of the data typically available in clinical reports (O'Shea & Phelps, 1985). Examples of these latter data could include rehospitalization rates, other treatments provided to client, academic performance, acting out behaviors or regressive functioning, and changes in adaptive social and role behavior. O'Shea and Phelps (1985) in their review addressed the difficulties regarding the study of MFGT and suggested that some of the guidelines for conducting family therapy research could be applied to the evaluation of this method. Several factors have contributed to the lack of progress in researching MFGT including no clear well-developed theory base, it is a blend between family therapy and group therapy with no specific identity of its own, it is often provided in combination with other approaches, a lack of consistent and measurable goals, and inconsistency in terms of how these groups are setup, composed, and facilitated.

Recent studies of MFGT have surfaced potential areas for future research of this unique treatment approach. For example, Cassano (1989) found from her assessment of interaction patterns in MFGT that this needs to be studied further particularly because of the large number of clients involved and the diversity of age levels in any one group. Meezan, O'Keefe, and Zariani (1997) noted in their work, applying this method to abusive and neglectful parents, that more follow-up studies are needed to see if changes are maintained. McKay, Gonzalez, Stone et al. (1995) in their work with inner-city children and their families pointed out the need to evaluate "the usefulness of MFGT in relation to other, more established treatment modalities" (p. 54). This suggestion is particularly relevant to the study of MFGT since it is often either combined simultaneously or in a treatment sequence with other therapeutic interventions. Furthermore, Dennison (1999) noted the need to provide more consistent training of facilitators for these groups so that similar levels of skills could be maintained when conducting further research.

Recent research on this approach has surfaced some additional reasons why further study is warranted. Meezan and O'Keefe (1998) addressed the value of studying MFGT more rigorously because there is less money available for child protective services and managed care is forcing programs to conduct more cost-effective services that are outcome based. Furthermore, Springer and Orsbon (2002) found from their clinical observations that this approach seems to work more effectively with substance-abusing adolescents and their families. These researchers noted that this population has been very challenging to treat and with little success from more traditional approaches. Another very difficult to treat population has been clients with severe psychiatric disorders and McFarlane (2002) strongly supports the need for more rigorous studies of MFGT with this population. This researcher has conducted the most extensive studies on MFGT with this group of clients for the past 20 years. The results of his research "provides unusually consistent evidence for its efficacy and feasibility for the younger, community-based, relapse-prone patient suffering from schizophrenia" (McFarlane, 2002, p. 70).

Clinical evidence regarding the therapeutic value of MFGT has continued to grow and expand to new treatment settings in the past decade. As more and more practitioners sing their praises of the dramatic positive changes elicited from this innovative treatment approach, there is even more reason to validate these observations with more rigorous research. Both quantitative and qualitative research will be necessary in order to identify the specific impact of this treatment method. The nature of MFGT is such that some of the expected changes will be similar to those indicated from research on both family therapy and peer group therapy. However, some of the clinical reports have indicated that very different changes are being elicited that may not be identified by more standardized measures. As a result, future research should include the use of both standardized measures and assessment methods like focus groups. Moreover, future study of this approach needs to focus on both treatment outcomes and process outcomes so practitioners will be able to easily replicate more successful programs. Also, it will be imperative that some studies focus on follow-up so that researchers can see if the changes made during the group experience are maintained. In summary, there is agreement among most proponents of this approach that more well-designed and rigorous studies are needed on MFGT. This is particularly warranted in view of the strong and consistent clinical evidence of positive treatment outcomes across increasingly diverse client settings.

Chapter 3

DENNISON GROUP PRACTICE MODEL

BACKGROUND AND UNDERLYING PRINCIPLES OF
DENNISON GROUP PRACTICE MODEL

The primary purpose of this chapter is to provide the reader with a group practice model that provides the rationale and timing of the interventions contained in the following four chapters. In addition, this model delineates a treatment paradigm for setting up, planning, and facilitating multiple family group therapy programs for at risk adolescents and their families. Readers are strongly advised to review this chapter in detail before utilizing the interventions in the following chapters. Even experienced group facilitators should take the time to understand this approach to group treatment because it is a somewhat different perspective from traditional practice models on group work. This model has been developed and refined by this author over the past 25 years. One of the unique features of its development has been that much of the model's refinement has been based on applying it to a wide array of groups including children, adolescents, parents, and multiple family therapy groups.

As noted in Chapter 2, there has been much clinical support for MFGT but limited empirical support. Even though more well-designed studies on this innovative treatment approach are definitely needed, there is an equally important need for more consistency in how these group programs are set up, planned, and facilitated. By providing a clearly defined treatment paradigm, such as the one outlined in this chapter, research of this approach should be easier to design and conduct. In addition, if positive outcomes are surfaced by groups that follow this model then replication of effective MFGT programs can then be attained. Moreover, it is hoped that this group practice model will further the development of the underlying theory for this approach and the resulting practice implications.

As a background to the material in this chapter, it will be important for the reader to understand some of the major findings identified after applying, modifying, and refining this model to a variety of practice situations. Consistent observations, self-reports from group members, and feedback from facilitators have guided the development of this treatment paradigm. As a result, the current state of the model is based both on small group theory and feedback/observations from treatment settings where facilitators have followed it with their groups. This author has had the opportunity to conduct focus groups with facilitators in training programs that have been held across the country. This audience has afforded this author a unique opportunity to hear firsthand how following this model has impacted different treatment groups in a variety of settings, both in terms of the types of agencies and geographic locations. As a result of repeatedly hearing similar feedback about what parts of this model seem to relate to effective group treatment, this author felt compelled to develop a group practice model that would further expand small group theory.

The following ten critical components of effective group treatment have been provided to this author over the past two decades of further refining and developing this group practice model. This feedback, gleaned from repeated clinical applications, serves as the major underlying principles for this group practice model.

1. Joining and increased bonding of members is therapeutic in and of itself.
2. Group treatment requires a longer period for building trust among its members (as compared to individual therapy).
3. Every group should follow two sets of goals: 1) process goals that are consistent for all groups and whose attainment helps create a therapeutic environment (i.e., also known as curative factors for a group), and 2) treatment goals that are individually determined for each group and encompass the problems focused on in treatment.
4. Most short-term groups (eight sessions or less) typically remain in the initial phase of group development and thus address primarily the process goals and with the treatment goals of secondary emphasis.
5. Balanced participation must be established early on in a group and be maintained throughout the group's length of treatment.
6. A variety of interventions should be utilized both within each session and across sessions so learning and growth can be stimulated via many different techniques.
7. Session plans and interventions should be carefully determined and be based on the

goals of the group's phase of development, the individualized treatment goals, developmental levels and interests of group members, and the individual preferences of facilitators.

8. "In vivo" learning (i.e., learning by actually performing a new behavior in a group) seems to be the most potent way for group members to acquire healthier coping responses.

9. Following a format in group sessions provides many advantages to a group's development.

10. The facilitator's most potent intervention, particularly in the initial phase, is therapeutic use of self through modeling openness, warmth, a nonjudgmental attitude, genuine concern for others, and a sense of humor.

Some of these principles are similar to the effective components of group treatment that have been developed from small group theory. However, some of these points highlight new variables that have not previously been given the same level of importance. Further details regarding these ten principles will now be delineated so the reader can better understand how each contributes to the current group practice model. In addition, this further explanation will assist practitioners in applying these guidelines to group treatment programs.

This first principle, the therapeutic value of joining and bonding, may explain why MFGT has had such a significant impact on some of the most challenging client populations. Even though group workers have acknowledged that developing trust among group members is important, the degree to which this variable contributes to an effective group has rarely been addressed. Furthermore, there is limited literature on specific interventions for joining and helping groups increasingly bond with one another.

This author is passionate about the critical role this variable plays in the development of an effective group. In fact, from her experience, some group participants actually gain more from this part of the group treatment than even the problem-solving opportunities. Facilitators seem to forget that part of the problem for clients being seen in groups is they have become isolated in their problems or have never had the skills to share their difficulties with others. This latter situation is compounded by our current times where isolation and watching out for oneself have become norms in our society.

It is unfortunate that we have not conducted enough follow-up studies on group treatment because this author is convinced that clients who have developed trust in a therapeutic group continue to make positive changes even after this experience. In some cases, the changes gained after treatment may even surpass those acquired while in a group. We as practitioners and researchers have greatly underestimated the importance of joining and increasingly bonding group members. As indicated earlier, this may very well be one of the key reasons why MFGT is more effective than other treatment modalities. These groups afford at risk families the opportunity to feel validated, less isolated, and less ashamed. And, what is particularly different compared to traditional group treatment, clients' entire family system is being impacted by the creation of this therapeutic community. Interestingly, the studies on MFGT noted in Chapter 2 have again and again surfaced this same finding.

The second principle underlying this model is group treatment takes a longer period of time to establish trust among its members. When one steps back and thinks about this point it makes sense in that it would take longer to trust seven other people in a group as opposed to a single therapist when individual counseling is provided. And why is it so critical to make this point? The reason is that it has tremendous practice implications. Too many times this writer has observed group facilitators pushing groups to move into a middle or problem-solving phase of a group when they were not ready. This type of intervention can be antitherapeutic for several reasons. First, groups cannot be moved to the middle phase; they are either ready or not. Some groups may never be ready for the middle phase, which is not to say that they have not made therapeutic gains from being in the initial phase of a group (first assumption addressed in this section is relevant to this point). Second, it restricts the attainment of the first phase goals (i.e., the process goals), which limits the degree to which a group can and will address the treatment goals in the middle phase. Third, this response conveys a message that the facilitator is not moving a group based on their needs but rather based on time pressures or expected outcomes.

The development of a trusting relationship among group members clearly takes longer than establishing trust with an individual therapist. However, once group members trust one another the potential changes elicited from this treatment modality far exceed those often attained in individual treatment. In addition, the establishment of a therapeutic community (i.e., the group) provides a tremendous learning experience for participants who often lack the skills in creating such a social network for themselves. Once this type of support is experienced, most group members are more motivated to establish similar relationships outside a group and have acquired the beginning skills to accomplish this task.

The third principle noted as being important to establishing an effective group is the delineation of two sets of goals. First, the process goals that should be consistent for all groups and are sometimes termed the curative factors of a group. These goals address those aspects of a group that must be attained in order to establish an attractive group, a setting that elicits participation by members, and an environment where trust is increasingly developed among the membership. The means by which these goals are attained will vary depending on the age level of group participants and the presenting problems. The treatment goals are the second set of goals and these are individualized for each group since they address those problems that are the focus of a group.

Why is this delineation of two sets of goals so important for the development of an effective group? Group treatment by its very nature requires a longer period for addressing process goals and typically the attainment of these goals is more challenging in this modality. Facilitators must realize that their planning and facilitating should be directly related to the set of goals being emphasized in each phase of a group. So, for example, if a group is in the initial phase then the session plans and facilitation style should be determined by the process goals that are of primary emphasis in this phase. This point will be further explained when the group practice model is presented later in this chapter. By delineating these two sets of goals and indicating which are of primary emphasis in each of the three phases (initial, middle, and termination), facilitators can more easily plan and run effective groups.

The fourth principle of this model is the recognition that most short-term groups (eight sessions or less) typically only complete the initial phase of a group. This point is particularly important because it has major implications for the planning and running of these short-term groups. As indicated earlier, groups take longer to establish a trusting relationship among the membership and as a result usually require several sessions to successfully attain the process goals of this phase that are of primary emphasis. In addition, this realization in no way reduces the therapeutic value of a short-term group but rather reinforces the importance of establishing a trusting relationship among group members and validates that this is very therapeutic for most participants. Here again, readers are reminded that groups cannot be pushed into the middle phase but must show signs that they are ready to move into this stage of development. Interestingly, several practitioners have noted to this author over the years that once they accepted this fact their groups proceeded much more smoothly. This point might be related to the rationale behind many programs providing MFGT simultaneously with other treatments like family therapy. Short-term MFGT could be providing an important setting where families start to bond to one another and form a therapeutic community. Traditional family therapy could be the treatment setting where these same families address more pressing problems that they need to resolve quickly.

The fifth principle places importance on the establishment of balanced participation early on in a group and the maintenance of it throughout a group's time in treatment. Balanced participation means that equal participation occurs among all members such that the group develops increasing levels of trust and cohesiveness. This component of group is a critical one because it ensures the development of a cohesive group, one of the unique strengths of this treatment modality. Too many times facilitators conduct therapy with a few members at a time while the rest of the group observes. This situation is not a therapeutic group but rather individual counseling with an audience. The establishment of balanced participation is not typically a skill within the repertoire of most helping professionals. As a result, it is important that group facilitators receive training on this skill and learn how it relates directly to the effective planning and facilitating of group sessions. Readers will be provided more details on this aspect of groups when the practice implications of the group model are delineated later in this chapter. Also, it is important to point out that establishing and maintaining balanced participation in MFGT is even more challenging because of the number of participants and the diverse age levels.

The sixth underlying principle of this model emphasizes the utilization of a variety of interventions both within each session and across sessions. Group participants can be of different age levels, have varying interests, and differ in their learning styles. As a result, facilitators need to make sure their plans take all of these issues into account so their interventions can be attractive to members, engage their full participation, and elicit maximum learning and growth. One of the unique experiences this author had in her work history was the task of developing a group program for high at risk children. This experience confirmed the importance of relying on more than just verbal discussions for group session plans. Unfortunately, the literature on group therapy contains limited information on various types of intervention ideas for specific groups. Facilitators, as a result, have to often develop their own techniques for groups so that they can respond to the different age levels, interests, and learning styles of their members. It is also imperative that the interventions planned for a group are directly related to the group's phase of development and the related goals. More guidelines in regard to such planning will be provided later in this chapter when the practice implications of the group model are addressed.

Group sessions must be carefully planned is the seventh principle regarding the effective setup and planning of groups. This point is related to the earlier one because the types of interventions chosen should always be individualized for each group. The selection process should take into account the following: age and interests of group members, the group phase of development, the treatment goals of a particular group, and the preferences of the facilitators. Effective treatment rarely just happens because group members have been brought together in this modality. Rather, group leaders need to carefully plan sessions, particularly in the initial phase, so that the positive impact of treatment can be maximized. This point is particularly relevant to MFGT because of the diverse age levels and the size of these groups.

The eighth principle is the importance of "in vivo" learning, which involves members actually practicing newly learned behaviors in the safety of the group setting. One of the unique parts of the group modality is that it provides a setting where clients can see how they feel and behave when they attempt different coping responses. For this reason, it is essential that facilitators plan their sessions with this learning opportunity in mind. Group members will be more likely to try new behaviors outside the group once they have been able to practice them in a supportive and accepting setting. In addition, it is imperative that practitioners understand that some of this "in vivo" learning is taking place as members observe one another in the group. So, for example, as a member works through some of their negative thought patterns and how they connect to their behavior, other members learn by watching this process of change and growth. Here again, this point is particularly relevant to MFGT. Several studies, as indicated in Chapter 2, have found that many participants in these groups report that some of the most beneficial parts of MFGT have involved this "indirect learning." Families sometimes need to see one of their problems resolved by another family before they even realize it has been a problem for them.

The establishment of a consistent format or routine to sessions is the ninth underlying principle of the Dennison Group Practice Model. This guideline serves many important purposes for a group. First, it addresses the attention span of group members particularly because many groups are held in the late afternoon or evening hours. By planning changes of routine throughout group sessions, facilitators are able to more easily keep members' attention. The latter issue is particularly relevant to groups that involve young children as is the case in MFGT. Second, following a routine provides a sense of security for members, which is helpful because therapeutic groups often initially elicit a level of anxiety from participants. Routine is something that is predictable and as such, creates a more comfortable and nonthreatening setting. Third, the use of routines provides an easy framework to follow so a variety of interventions can still be planned but within a consistent format. In addition, facilitators who follow a routine in group report that they are often better able to maintain their opening and closing group times.

The tenth principle emphasizes the potency of facilitators' modeling and sharing of themselves with groups. It is interesting that many studies that have compared various group approaches have often found that effective treatment was less dependent on the approach utilized and more on the personal qualities of the facilitator. Studies on the qualities and facilitation styles of effective group leaders are clearly lacking. Facilitators need more guidance in knowing how to therapeutically use themselves in the group treatment process. Moreover, these practitioners require specifics on how to change their facilitation in response to a group's phase of development or in response to problems that surface. Guidelines for these purposes will be provided later in this chapter under the practice implications of the group model.

DENNISON GROUP PRACTICE MODEL

The Dennison Group Practice Model (originally published in 1998 by Charles C Thomas Publishers in *Activities for Adolescents in Therapy*) is

Table 3.1

Dennison Group Practice Model

Group Phase	Primary Goals	Secondary Goals	Interventions	Timing
Initial	**Process Goals** 1. To create an attractive group setting. 2. To initiate balanced participation among members. 3. To build a trusting relationship among members.	**Treatment Goals** 1. To delineate more specific treatment goals that are common to the membership. 2. To provide psychoeducation on targeted treatment areas of functioning.	**Chapter 5:** Relationship Building **Chapter 6:** Psychoeducational	8 sessions total= 7 initial 12 sessions = 7 initial 16 sessions= 7 initial
Middle	**Treatment Goals** 1. To increase members' awareness of their specific problems in regard to targeted treatment areas of functioning. 2. To increase members' awareness of alternative responses to problems. 3. To assist members in selecting alternative responses to their problems and integrating those into their repertoire.	**Process Goals** 1. To continue building an attractive group setting. 2. To increase member-to-member participation and maintain balanced participation. 3. To continue developing member trust and a cohesive group unit.	**Chapter 5:** Trust Building **Chapter 7:** Problem Solving	8 sessions total= 0 middle 12 sessions = 4 middle 16 sessions= 8 middle
Termination	**Process Goals** 1. To have members acknowledge value of group and grieve its ending. 2. To have members acknowledge progress they have made in group. 3. To have members identify other sources that will support the changes they have made in group.	**Treatment Goals** 1. To have members acknowledge attainment of treatment goals in groups. 2. To have members develop a relapse prevention plan for maintaining positive treatment gains.	**Chapter 5:** Relationship Validation **Chapter 8:** Termination and Closure	8 sessions = 1 termination 12 sessions= 1 termination 16 sessions= 1 termination

introduced for two major purposes. First, it provides a treatment paradigm for practitioners to follow when conducting MFGT. Second, this model provides a planning guide for the utilization of the interventions in Chapters 5 through 8. This model builds on small group theory by delineating goals in such specific terms that facilitators will be able to more easily plan and conduct successful multiple family group therapy programs. Most of the ongoing development of this model has been based on data gleaned from practice application with a wide variety of groups that have been diverse in terms of problem focus, age of participants, client population served, type of agency setting, and geographic location. As a result, practitioners should find the resulting paradigm is applicable and effective with many different types of groups, not just MFGT. In fact, this model was originally developed for group treatment with at risk adolescents and children. It was later modified to be used with parent groups and then adapted to parallel/conjoint MFGT.

There are five major components of the Dennison Group Practice Model that are provided on Table 3.1. First, similar to many group theorists' beliefs, group treatment is viewed as going through three phases: initial, middle, and termination. The purposes and goals of these phases will be described in more detail later in this chapter. However, it is important to note that one major difference in the delineation of these three phases relates to the second component of the Dennison Model, treatment time in each phase. As readers will see on Table 3.1 in the far right column of each phase there is a timing guide for MFGT programs that breaks down session lengths for 8, 12, and 16 sessions. This breakdown of the typical number of sessions spent in each phase was included as part of this model because it introduces a very different view of group treatment; particularly in terms of expected treatment time in the initial phase. The third component of the model is the delineation of two sets of goals: process goals and treatment goals. As the reader will note on Table 3.1, these two sets of goals are seen as being addressed in each of the phases but with some modifications for each phase. Moreover, the fourth component of this model, the delineation of primary and secondary goal emphasis, provides clear guidance as to which set of goals are of primary emphasis in each of the three phases. The fifth component of the model is the coordination of interventions to each phase and related set of goals. As readers will note on Table 3.1, the interventions from Chapters 5 through 8 are indicated under the relevant group phase. It is hoped that practitioners who chose to develop their own intervention ideas or use ones originated by other writers, can determine the timing of such techniques by following the model's planning guide.

Practitioners who choose to follow the Dennison Group Practice Model will find that one of its strengths is the very detailed guidelines provided for both planning and facilitating sessions. In addition, the model differentiates individual treatment from group treatment in two major ways. First, this is accomplished through the delineation of both process and treatment goals, which are articulated specifically for group treatment. Second, the timing of treatment by phase provides practitioners a clearer understanding of the contrast between group treatment and individual work with clients. Typically, clients seen for individual therapy will go through the initial phase of treatment much more quickly than a group's treatment pace in this same phase. This author made a conscious effort to develop the model in a way that helps practitioners better understand some of the differences between individual therapy and group treatment. Observations of many groups over the past 25 years have convinced this writer that many facilitators, even today, continue to plan and facilitate groups based on an individual treatment approach. Many group leaders seem to lack formal training on groups such that they are not knowledgeable and/or skilled in this specific treatment modality. The latter point is even more relevant to MFGT where facilitators must also have a clear understanding of these unique group programs. They must also be skilled at handling much larger groups with very diverse age levels represented.

PHASING OF GROUP TREATMENT

Although the delineation of group treatment into three phases (initial, middle, and termination) is not a new concept, it is a very important one. The focus of treatment changes from the initial phase of joining and bonding group members to the problem-solving phase (i.e., middle phase) to the termination of treatment phase. This delineation of the group modality provides practitioners critical insight into the primary thrust of treatment in each phase. In addition, the model's primary and secondary goal emphasis guide clearly shows how this shift takes place in terms of the primary goal focus for each phase.

The two sets of goals, process and treatment goals, for each phase also provide guidance in terms of group planning and facilitating. On Table 3.1 the reader can see that in the initial phase the process goals are of primary emphasis that directs the facilitator to concentrate his or her efforts on creating an attractive setting, eliciting balanced participation from the membership, and increasingly build group trust. Addressing the treatment goals of a group should only take place in this phase for two purposes. First, to further delineate the groupwide treatment goals that will be the focus of the middle phase. And, second, to provide some therapeutic instruction to the members that is related to the treatment goals. In addition, this latter instruction should only require members to share their problems via anonymous or other non-threatening methods. As a result, such psychoeducation should provide validation to all members that they share similar problems and increase their knowledge of how to more effectively address these shared difficulties.

In the middle phase the goal emphasis shifts to the treatment goals that are the problems that will be the focus of a group's problem-solving efforts. Following this model, groups are not moved to this phase but instead indicate signs that they are ready for this stage of treatment. It will be critically important that a level of group trust and cohesiveness has been established before a group moves to this phase. At this point in the group members are ready to both share their problems and explore other ways of responding to these same problems. Most members should indicate by their verbal and nonverbal behaviors that they feel comfortable sharing this type of disclosure. Moreover, the establishment of trust among the members should assist participants in being able to openly help one another in their problem-solving efforts. This is the working stage of the group where members are able to share their strengths such that problem resolution ideas come from across the membership.

By the termination phase the emphasis shifts back to the process goals as noted on Table 3.1. Groups enter this phase for one of two reasons: 1) a group's time has run out and so the facilitator spends the last session or two addressing closure issues, or 2) a group has successfully moved through the initial and middle phases of the group and is ready to address closure. Regardless of the reason, groups should move into this phase, even if only for a session, before the group ends. It is at this time in a group that members need to acknowledge the value of the group, the progress they have made, and other ways they can maintain their changes. In addition, facilitators may have to directly elicit grieving from the members regarding the ending of the group so they can experience a healthy closure from the group. It is not unusual that group leaders find themselves having to be more directive with groups in this phase. Members will often resist having to address termination and closure issues and may want to just ignore that the group is ending. This is an opportunity for a corrective experience around healthy closures for members and can prove important even in terms of the degree to which members maintain changes.

TREATMENT TIMING IN EACH PHASE

The timing of treatment in each phase of a group is probably one of the critical contributions this model has made to the practice of this modality. This component of the Dennison Group Practice Model most clearly conveys the importance and necessity of developing a trusting and cohesive group before any in-depth level of problem disclosure or resolution takes place. For this reason, readers will see on Table 3.1 that an 8-session MFGT program could function primarily in the initial phase and then terminate in the last session. Furthermore, this is one of the ways the model emphasizes the therapeutic value of just joining and increasingly bonding members. In the past, many group approaches have neglected this part of group treatment. Many theorists and practitioners view this initial phase as merely a brief period in treatment when members get to know one another and then the important work happens in the middle phase when problems are addressed. This author, due to her extensive experience in both conducting groups and training practitioners, sees this phase of group quite differently. In fact, for some members this may be the phase that provides the most learning and growth. Related to this point, many of the studies on MFGT have found that families often report the most beneficial part of their experience was getting to know other families and finding out that they too share some of the same problems and concerns.

The other important point about the timing of group treatment in

45

each phase is that there is no right or consistent pace that groups move through each of the three phases. In addition, this author has found that no matter how long some groups stay together they may never be ready to move to the middle phase. Any number of reasons could account for why this happens, but, many times it seems to be related to the composition of the group. Some group memberships are not able to establish a level of trust and cohesiveness as a unit such that they can open up about their problems. However, in accordance with this model, this does not mean that such a group has not gained from this therapeutic experience. Rather this group may have prepared clients for future treatment where they will be able to open up about their problem areas.

DELINEATION OF TWO SETS OF GOALS: PROCESS GOALS AND TREATMENT GOALS

After many years of studying group work concepts and facilitating groups, this writer had a lightbulb experience. It became crystal clear one day in an adolescent group that there were, in fact, two different types of goals that needed to be addressed in this modality of treatment. Group theorists like Yalom (1985) have long recognized that there are important group variables, which he terms curative factors, that significantly contribute to the overall effectiveness of a group. In the Dennison Group Practice Model these therapeutic factors have been termed process goals because this author has found that without this designation practitioners do not realize their tremendous value to the group treatment process. Yalom (1985) made this same point when he stated, "From the patients' point of view, group cohesiveness was seen not only as necessary for perpetuation of the group but as in itself of great therapeutic value" (p. 73). Furthermore, placing these therapeutic factors on the same level as treatment goals conveys the critical importance of attending to their attainment both in the initial and termination phases where they are of primary emphasis.

The other important part of this goal delineation is the modification of each set of goals for the three phases. As the reader will see in Table 3.1, both the process goals and treatment goals have been differentiated for each group phase so facilitators will understand the main thrust of these goals as groups proceed through treatment. For example, the process goals whose focus is on the development of a therapeutic environment are further delineated in each phase. In the initial phase (column to the right of initial phase on Table 3.1) these goals are addressing the creation of an attractive nonthreatening setting, initiation of members' participation, and the development of a trusting relationship among members. Then in the middle phase (second column to right of middle phase on Table 3.1) these goals shift slightly such that facilitators are now maintaining the attainment of these goals rather than initially working on them. By the termination phase (see column to the right of termination phase on Table 3.1), however, these goals change more significantly. The focus now for the process goals is on having members acknowledge their progress in the group, the value of the group for them, and other sources of support so they can maintain the changes made in treatment. These goals continue to address those parts of the group that make it a therapeutic setting and provide some closure to that experience.

The process goals remain constant for all groups since the attainment of these goals is essential for the establishment of a therapeutic group. What does vary is the means by which these goals are attained. In terms of MFGT programs, facilitators can either select interventions from Chapter 4 or techniques from other sources as ways to attain these process goals. The selection of interventions to address these goals should be based on variables such as age levels represented in the group, common interest areas of participants, and individual preferences of facilitators. Practitioners will often find that with new groups it will take a period of trial and error to find out which interventions are most effective with a particular combination of families.

On the other hand, the treatment goals of a group address those problem areas that are the focus of a group. These goals will vary with each group since they are intended to target areas of functioning that resulted in families' referral to a MFGT program. As the reader will see on Table 3.1, there is also some shifting in the focus of these goals for each phase. In the initial phase (second column to right of initial phase on Table 3.1) the treatment goals are of secondary emphasis and should focus on either 1) the further delineation of the groupwide treatment goals or 2) psychoeducational goals that address the problem focus of the group. By the middle phase (column to right of middle phase on Table 3.1) these goals are of primary emphasis since the process goals have been solidly attained in the initial phase. At this point in the group these goals will be consistently addressed in each session and, typically, to more and more depth. As indicated on Table 3.1, the general focus of these goals is: 1) to increase family units' awareness of their own difficulties in regard to the problem focus of the group, 2) to increase families' knowledge of alternative coping responses in terms of their problem areas, 3) to assist members and families in their selection of healthier coping responses, and 4) to assist members and families in the integration of new coping responses to their repertoire. Then in the termination phase (second column to right of termination phase on Table 3.1) the treatment goals are only addressed in terms of validating members' progress and increasing their awareness of sources outside the group that will support their changes. Again, the specific delineation of treatment goals in each phase of a group has been developed so facilitators can more easily plan and facilitate their group programs.

PRIMARY AND SECONDARY GOAL EMPHASIS GUIDE

As the Dennison Group Practice Model evolved over the years it became clear that facilitators needed more specific guidelines on which goals should be emphasized in each phase of a group. Otherwise, practitioners have found themselves simultaneously addressing both treatment and process goals with no understanding of which goals should be of primary importance in the three phases. As the reader will note on Table 3.1, the primary and secondary emphasis guide is provided for each of the three phases of group. In the initial phase the goal focus should primarily be on the process goals. Whereas, by the middle phase that primary focus shifts to the treatment goals and then by the termination phase the primary emphasis switches back to the process goals. These guidelines should help facilitators not feel as overwhelmed as to which goals they need to focus on in a group in any one session. In addition, this goal focus guide should clarify the primary thrust of treatment in each phase of a group.

COORDINATION OF INTERVENTIONS WITH GROUP GOALS

The Dennison Group Practice Model was developed specifically with practice application in mind. Therefore, this fifth component of the model involves the coordination of interventions with the goals of each phase of the group. The reader will see on Table 3.1 that the four intervention chapters (Chapters 5 through 8) are aligned with each of the three phases so practitioners will be able to easily plan effective interventions for their MFGT program that are based on the goals of each group phase. In addition, readers should find it easier to plan their own intervention ideas or techniques from other resources in such a way that they address the goals of a group's particular phase of treatment. One of the contributions of this model is that it provides a direct connection between group phases/related goals and intervention plans. Readers will want to use Table 3.1 as a guide initially when planning sessions for their MFGT program.

SUMMARY

In this chapter the Dennison Group Practice Model was presented as a treatment paradigm for practitioners to follow when planning and facilitating their MFGT programs. This model combines concepts from small group theory with some new perspectives that has resulted in a more practice-based group model. Some of the unique contributions of this model include group treatment being viewed as going through three stages (initial, middle, and termination) that address two sets of goals (i.e., process goals and treatment goals), a shifting of goal emphasis that takes place in each of these three phases, the importance of carefully pacing treatment in the initial phase is noted and endorsed, and a more direct connection between interventions and the goals of each phase is delineated.

Readers can use the material presented in this chapter to guide their selection and timing of interventions from Chapters 5 through 8. In addition, the practice model provided should provide some of the rationale for the pregroup phase guidelines presented in the next chapter. Even though this treatment paradigm is being presented here specifically for MFGT, it is a model that has been successfully followed when conducting groups with children, adolescents, parents, and parallel/conjoint forms of MFGT. Therefore, practitioners could easily use this same model to direct their group treatment programs with other client populations.

Chapter 4

GUIDELINES FOR SETTING UP, COMPOSING, PLANNING, AND FACILITATING MFGT

This chapter delineates important tasks that facilitators of MFGT need to address in the pregroup phase in order to establish effective treatment programs that utilize this approach. Readers should carefully review all the material in this chapter before beginning a multiple family therapy group. Even experienced group facilitators are encouraged to read the guidelines provided in this section of the book since much of this material is based on findings surfaced from research on MFGT. The intent of this chapter is to outline in an easy-to-follow format those implementation issues that need to be carefully addressed and planned before beginning this innovative group treatment program.

The development of the Dennison Group Practice Model, findings surfaced from focus groups with facilitators, and results from previous studies of MFGT have provided important practice implications for this group treatment approach. Data surfaced and observations noted from the latter sources have resulted in the delineation of guidelines for the setup, group composition, planning, and facilitation of MFGT. These implementation suggestions are based on data from well-designed studies, feedback from facilitators of MFGT, focus group findings with participants, and this author's own field notes from training practitioners across the country. Therefore, many of the guidelines listed require further study so that practitioners of MFGT will have research that either validates these implementation suggestions or surfaces new ones. For this reason, extensive material on designing and conducting research on MFGT is provided in Chapter 10.

The following implementation issues will be discussed with specific suggestions provided in the remaining part of this chapter. These issues encompass the major parts of MFGT that have to be addressed in order to effectively setup, compose, plan, and facilitate these groups:

- Composition and screening of group including ideal number of families
- Ideal number of group facilitators and their roles
- Setup of meeting room, location, and other environmental issues to consider
- Seating arrangement of MFGT participants
- Voluntary versus mandatory membership of these groups
- Meeting days/times/frequency/length of sessions
- Unique treatment issues of at risk adolescents and their families
- Single or Combined Treatment Approach
- Planning of sessions including the use of a consistent format
- Facilitation styles and handling of problems that surface in groups
- Documentation notes on these treatment groups
- Evaluation design for MFGT programs.

Readers will find the guidelines for these implementation variables to be extremely helpful since they will ensure that key parts of these groups are carefully planned both in the pregroup phase and the later treatment phases. Moreover, the suggestions provided should reduce some of the facilitator's decision making in regard to designing, planning, and conducting these groups.

COMPOSITION AND SCREENING OF GROUP MEMBERS

There are several issues related to the composition and screening of group members for MFGT. Facilitators may not choose to follow the complete process of selecting group members outlined in this section. Since facilitators have individual preferences and different ways of composing groups, practitioners should regard the following as suggestions or points to consider when completing this part of their group setup. However, readers should review the complete list of suggestions to be assured that they have carefully considered all issues that impact this very important selection process. This author has found that the composition of a group can play a major role in the ultimate effectiveness of that treatment program.

First, consider having individual screening sessions with potential family units. These sessions will provide facilitators and families an opportunity to get to know one another in a more comfortable setting.

In addition, group leaders can probe to see if families are motivated to attend such a group, which members seem to be most committed to this process, and what problem focus would be of the most benefit for the family. Moreover, these sessions are excellent times to obtain individual family members' commitment on a written contract form that delineates the length of a group, meeting times and places, attendance policy, and basic rules of the treatment program. Readers will find in Appendix A an example of a sample contract form for a MFGT program. Even though it may seem to be a subtle point, this author has been surprised at MFGT participants' feedback that it was very comforting to know that all attending families had signed such a contract before joining a group. It appears that there is an initial sense that everyone joining a particular group has acknowledged they have a similar problem and they are making a commitment to work on that problem in the group. Also, many families appreciate having the rules of a group program reviewed with them ahead of time rather than taking up time in the group sessions.

Secondly, it is very important to determine which members of a family will attend a MFGT program. Some of these decisions may be based on family members' interest and motivation to be involved. Also, some parents may feel that some children are too young to keep on task in such a group setting. There have been many conflicting opinions on this latter point in the literature on MFGT. Some researchers have promoted the value of having all family members present while others have noted that only family members over the age of 5 should be allowed to attend. This is an individual decision for each facilitator and may be best made after experimenting with various composition plans.

Readers are reminded of the definition of MFGT that is provided in Chapter 2, which is the one utilized for material in the current text. In order to compose a true MFGT program it is important to have the index client (i.e., the at risk adolescent) present along with that individual's parents and siblings. This sounds all clean and neat but the reality today is that many adolescents do not live in traditional family units. So the other issue to consider is who else related to the index client should be invited. These family members could include grandparents (some of whom have raised the teen), stepparents, boyfriends or girlfriends of the teen's parents, foster parents, or half brothers or half sisters. The additional difficulty with many at risk adolescents is they may even live between two households as a result of either joint custody issues or problems related to parenting the teenager. Therefore, group leaders will have to often make these decisions on a case-by-case basis due to the wide variety of family units often involved with at risk teens' lives. It will, however, be important that as much as possible the same inclusion criteria are used for all families who join the same multiple family group. Otherwise, families could begin to feel that special considerations are being made for particular family units.

The third important issue related to group composition relates to screening out entire family units or excluding individual family members that fall into the following categories: clients who are not consistently connected to reality and who have regular periods of psychotic behaviors that are not controlled with medication, overly needy family units who are unable to share and take turns in a group modality, and families who are in a crisis situation that requires more intense treatment services. Here again facilitators will have to use their own expertise in determining to what degree family units or individual family members are functioning at a level that makes them not a good candidate for this type of treatment. The added challenge with this issue is that even to date we have very few studies that have surfaced findings regarding the ideal composition of groups.

IDEAL NUMBER OF GROUP FACILITATORS AND THEIR ROLES

As noted in Chapter 2, there are conflicting opinions in the MFGT literature as to the ideal number of facilitators for a MFGT program. Some researchers have recommended as few as two while others have suggested teams of up to four facilitators. Some of this particular setup issue may be dependent on the size of the group and the availability of professionals to work in this role. Typically larger multiple family groups will require more facilitators but we still do not have studies that have clearly identified the ideal ratio of group members to group leaders in these treatment programs. Here again, facilitators will have to make their own individual decisions based on any or all of the earlier mentioned variables. Furthermore, it may require a trial and error approach to this setup issue since this is often the best test as to how many facilitators are required for a particular MFGT program.

The other issue related to the number of facilitators is the roles assigned to those professionals who co-lead a group. There is wide variation in the roles of MFGT facilitators partly due to the fact that the literature on group treatment in general promotes several styles of co-facilitating. For example, some group leaders endorse the equal role of facilitators while others believe that one facilitator must be primary with the others in a secondary role. Readers will have to determine which facilitating roles work best for them and their targeted client group. The important point is that all facilitators of the same group must be clear on their roles ahead of time and may even need to review this point regularly as they process group sessions.

SETUP OF MEETING ROOM, LOCATION, AND OTHER ENVIRONMENTAL ISSUES TO CONSIDER

There are several things to prepare and plan regarding the physical setting for a MFGT program. First, these are typically large groups and so a room with enough space to comfortably handle all the group members should be arranged for sessions. In addition, it will be important to make sure such a space is free of outside auditory noises and physical distractions in the room. Facilitators must remember that often young children are members of these groups and maintaining their attention on the tasks of the sessions will be more difficult due to their developmental levels. Attractive materials in the room that are unrelated to the group session will be tough to compete with in terms of keeping these youngsters' attention. In addition, even noise from other rooms can easily distract these younger children from the tasks of the group. Often a large room with almost no visual stimuli in the room is the best choice of setting for these groups.

The second issue regarding the physical setting is the arrangement of seating for group members. Usually, due to the larger size of these groups, facilitators utilize chairs arranged in a circle so all members have a full view of one another. This arrangement also allows the facilitators a clear view of all the interactions in the group and eye contact with one another. A very large conference table or several tables placed together could be also included but often times such tables put too much physical distance between members.

The third issue to consider and plan is the location of the group meetings. There may not be much decision making involved in this setup variable because some facilitators may have no choice but to use a room in their program's office building or at the residential setting. If there are other available options for locations of these groups then some consideration should be made for the most ideal location for the group. Group leaders should consider issues like the most convenient location for the majority of participants, locations that are the safest to be in during and after the group meeting times, and availability of public transportation if members will have to use this service.

Another part of the environment that should be considered during this pregroup phase is the provision of drinks or snacks for participants. Here again, some of this decision may be dependent on the availability of funds to cover the cost of such items. However, if at all possible, it is strongly recommended that both drinks and small snack food be made available at each session. By providing this type of treat members will feel more welcomed and after sessions may be even more inclined to visit informally with one another as they enjoy drinking and eating together. Facilitators will want to also determine if such snacks and drinks will be available throughout the sessions or just at a particular point, like the beginning or ending of the group. One disadvantage of making such things available throughout group sessions is that this setup can cause regular disruptions in sessions as members walk back and forth to a snack table. Furthermore, if funding is a problem, facilitators may want to ask families to take turns providing the drinks and snacks. By making this suggestion families may feel more ownership of a group program because of this added role.

A last point about the physical setup is that facilitators may want to discuss with a multiple family group if they would like to plan a special ending session. Such an event could involve a potluck supper or all the families going out to dinner at a local restaurant. Planning this type of ritual can be an excellent way for group members to celebrate their progress in a group program. Also, by the facilitators making this suggestion families are directly shown a healthy response to hard work and attaining accomplishments. Many at risk adolescents and their families need to experience this type of modeling since many may have few such rituals as part of their family lives.

Readers are reminded that the physical setting, location, and provision of drinks and snacks may seem like small parts of the setup of a MFGT program. However, from this writer's experience, these parts of a treatment program can have tremendous positive impact on a group and should never be underestimated in their value to the therapy process. Participants of these groups often feel a sense of shame and guilt about the problems their family is facing. By providing a warm, comfortable, and inviting setting facilitators convey a feeling of respect for the participants. In addition, such an environment is very welcoming to new group members who are usually feeling somewhat anxious in the initial sessions.

SEATING ARRANGEMENT OF MFGT PARTICIPANTS

As noted in the literature review in Chapter 2, there are conflicting opinions about the seating arrangement of MFGT programs. Some practitioners promote allowing all group members to decide where they want to sit each session. Others endorse the policy of requiring that all family members sit together as a unit, with the seating within the family left to their choice. One of the difficulties with allowing group members the choice of seat location, particularly in MFGT that focuses on at risk adolescents, is that many clinicians have informally reported that peer subgroups tend to form so that parents end up sitting with other parents and teens with other teens. As such a group continues to meet, facilitators report that they have more problems keeping members on task (particularly the at risk adolescents) and eventually feel like they have two separate groups. Moreover, by not requiring family members to sit together there is less tendency for parents to take responsibility for keeping their children on task, which can be more problematic with younger children. Furthermore, some facilitators have reported to this writer that when families do not sit together in these groups they begin to see such treatment as focusing less and less on familywide issues. Considering the disadvantages of allowing members free choice as to where they sit, it is strongly recommended that group leaders consider the policy that all family members must sit together as a unit. As a somewhat related point, it is suggested that name tags be created for group members that can be picked up as they enter the sessions each week and left with the facilitators as they leave. These groups are so large that most practitioners have found it very helpful to have everyone wear name tags, which assist with the relationship building among the membership.

VOLUNTARY VERSUS MANDATORY MEMBERSHIP OF THESE GROUPS

Facilitators will have to decide if they are going to require a targeted client population and their families to attend a MFGT program or allow for voluntary participation. In some cases this decision may also be determined by administrative staff or other professionals involved with setting up the treatment program for a particular at risk adolescent population. Sometimes this issue on the participation policy may be dependent on whether the clients are in a residential or nonresidential setting. It appears from the literature review that a higher number of residential settings require participation while outpatient settings tend to have a policy of voluntary participation. In addition, if there are some legal decisions around the custody of such teens, then programs may want to require participation in MFGT as a means for determining if parents are able to handle the responsibility of a particular teenager.

An additional point related to this issue is the attendance policy for families who are participants in a MFGT program. Usually it is a good idea to put such an attendance policy in a contract form that all families sign before starting the treatment sessions (see an example of a contract in Appendix A). Related to this issue, facilitators need to be ready for the possibility that some family members may attend some sessions that other members choose not to attend. Of course, there can be valid reasons for such absences but members might also miss sessions due to a lack of motivation to be involved with a group experience. Facilitators will have to decide how they want to handle such situations, either in the group or with family units separately. Also, practitioners have noted informally that if the at risk adolescent or one of the parents are the family members absent from sessions then group leaders may have to decide if the family can continue in a MFGT program. The reason for this latter caution is that the absence of key family members can have a significant negative impact on their treatment services. Furthermore, when these groups are targeting at risk adolescents, there is a higher probability of a domino effect in the group. So, for example, if one teen decides not to attend, a facilitator may quickly find a number of other teen members are missing sessions.

MEETING DAYS/TIMES/FREQUENCY/LENGTH OF SESSIONS

Before establishing a meeting day, time, and session length, it is suggested that facilitators obtain potential families' feedback on what will work best within their schedules. By obtaining this information group leaders will accomplish two purposes. First, families will appreciate that they are being treated with enough respect to consider their schedules and other demands. Second, this feedback will be extremely helpful in establishing meeting days and times that will have the highest probability of working with the targeted families' schedule. Of course, with busy lives today, obtaining a 100 percent agreement from members on these setup details will be challenging, if not impossible. Therefore, facilitators should determine the best days and meeting times that work for the greatest percentage of participants.

When reviewing the literature on these implementation issues, one finds that most MFGT programs meet once a week primarily because the logistics of getting all the members of a family together more often is difficult. From these same studies, we find that the length of sessions reported varies from as short as 1.5 hours to as long as an entire day. Typically the latter time length is used in MFGT programs that only meet once or twice and then the treatment service is completed. Also, these programs often focus mainly on psychoeducation as the primary goal for their treatment intervention. Researchers have also noted that the size of a MFGT program will also determine how long such groups meet.

Facilitators will have to consider several variables (e.g., availability of meeting space, participants' schedules, group leaders' schedules, etc.) when determining the length of meeting time of their MFGT programs. Informally, this writer has found that most groups that average 20 to 25 members at each session require about 2 hours of meeting time. One important issue related to this setup variable is that it is extremely important that facilitators make sure MFGT programs begin and end on time. Families will feel they are being treated with respect and appreciation for their other responsibilities when group leaders make sure groups keep to a posted schedule.

UNIQUE TREATMENT ISSUES OF AT RISK ADOLESCENTS AND THEIR FAMILIES

Since the focus of this book is on MFGT targeting at risk adolescents and their families, it is important to discuss some of the treatment issues more unique to this population. Obviously the types of problems that adolescents are experiencing can vary widely. These are youngsters who often still have difficulties related to growing up and yet might have already been involved in some pretty serious problems. Some of the presenting problems of these teens could include substance abuse, sexual promiscuity, delinquency, aggressive acting out behaviors, sexual identity issues, gang involvement, depression and withdrawal, onset of psychiatric disorders, school-related problems, and difficulties in getting along with peers or adults. This is not an exhaustive list and yet delineates some of the more common problems with this population, along with the level of seriousness with some of the presenting difficulties.

In addition to teens' more individual specific problems, most of these youngsters are also dealing with typical developmental issues related to growing up. As many theorists have noted, adolescence is a time of almost continual crisis such that other problems just add to the already high stress level for this age group. Moreover, as clinicians know, this developmental period is also a common onset time for psychiatric problems and serious levels of depression. Furthermore, family members will struggle as they cope with a teen's difficulties along with some of their other problems. As a result, facilitators should expect that these teens and their families will enter a group with several problems that they are dealing with simultaneously.

Facilitators should expect that the combination of individual problems, developmental issues, and family-related difficulties often result in these families having some very serious levels of conflicts and intense feelings. As most of us know adolescence is not a time we would choose to relive again and, in the case of parents, not a stage of parenting most would like to go through again. Therefore, it is extremely important that facilitators be sensitive to the high levels of stress many of these teens and their families are facing. For this reason, MFGT may be best provided to this population in combination with other approaches like peer group therapy, individual counseling, or family therapy. In addition, the parallel/conjoint MFGT program has been provided in Chapter 9 since readers may find that this approach is more the treatment of choice for a particular targeted group of families.

From a more positive perspective, it is understandable that MFGT has been utilized with this population for many years and with more frequency in the past decade. There are a number of benefits this approach has been found to have with at risk teens and their families. First, this type of group has been found to impact and improve family communication, which is often an issue for this group of families. Moreover, several studies have found that MFGT effectively addresses boundary and roles issues within families. This is very relevant area of functioning to this population since most of the families will be struggling with difficulties related to role changes for both teens and parents. The other strength of this approach is that it offers teens an opportunity to be in a group with other teens, which is usually more attractive and less threatening. These youngsters typically want to spend all their time with their peer group, which is why teens will often be more inclined to participate in MFGT, as opposed to traditional family therapy. Furthermore, with such intense feelings and conflicts often present, these family units will benefit from the cross-parenting opportunities that this approach offers. Parents in these groups have been found to reach another parent's adolescent because they do not have the same level of emotionality involved and the same history of problems. In addition, some of teens will be able to help other teens' parents hear a point of view that otherwise was missed due the nature of the relationship and other problems within the family.

There are clear challenges when working with at risk adolescents and their families in MFGT. However, this approach offers several unique benefits that are particularly relevant to this population. Also, this modality of treatment has the potential of preventing further deterioration of a parent and teen's relationship, which speaks to some of the preventive contribution of this approach. And, as with any client group, the probability of at risk teens maintaining their changes is increased when their entire family system has been involved in the change process.

SINGLE OR COMBINED TREATMENT APPROACH

There have been limited studies comparing MFGT as a single treatment approach with MFGT used in combination with other treatment. Also, such additional treatment has sometimes been provided simultaneously with MFGT, whereas in other settings a sequencing of treatment approaches has been used. As a result of this lack of research on this implementation issue, we cannot state with confidence whether a single or combined approach is more effective. Therefore, facilitators will have to individually determine which treatment format they will use with a particular population. It should be noted, however, that a greater percentage of studies have reported that they combined MFGT with other simultaneous treatment. With this latter point in mind, group leaders may want to carefully consider offering at risk adolescents and their families other types of treatment in combination with MFGT. Such additional approaches could include parent groups, teen groups, traditional family therapy, or individual counseling. The choice of treatment offered with this group approach could be dependent on a number of issues. Facilitators will have to examine the following before making this decision: availability of other treatment services, family participants' willingness to be involved in additional treatment, nature of targeted clients' problems, and individual preferences of group leaders.

This writer has been given some informal feedback on this implementation issue from various facilitators. These group leaders have noted that many times at risk teens and their families are in such a state of crisis that they benefit both from MFGT and traditional family treatment. The latter modality provides these families a setting where they can deal with more intimate and possibly sensitive issues that need to be addressed in a timely manner. MFGT often does not afford this same treatment outlet because these groups take some time to become trusting cohesive units. In addition, the larger size of these groups precludes most families from being able to probe into a difficult problem to any depth. Readers are cautioned not to think that this latter point means that MFGT does not serve an important therapeutic value to these families. In fact, many facilitators working with this population state that it is this combined approach that keeps most of these families in treatment and provides an increased sense of hope that they can resolve their problems.

PLANNING OF SESSIONS AND USE OF A CONSISTENT FORMAT

It is unclear from much of the research on MFGT if these treatment programs are carefully planned or if a more spontaneous approach is used. Related to this point, more recent studies have reported in detail (see literature review in Chapter 2) the session by session plans for various types of MFGT. Also, McFarlane (2002), who has recently written the first book on multiple family group therapy, provides specific interventions and session formats when using this approach with clients having serious psychiatric problems. Facilitators will have to make their own individual decisions around the planning of these groups. However, readers are reminded that obtaining more empirical support for MFGT requires that programs studied provide more details around the format, planning, and interventions used. Otherwise, it will be difficult if not impossible to replicate programs that have been successful.

This author, based on her many years of both facilitating groups and consulting, strongly promotes the careful planning of every MFGT session. In addition, readers are encouraged to consider following a format in their sessions. Formats provide a routine for groups such that members report being more comfortable in such settings. Most clients come to treatment with a level of anxiety, and by creating a predictable format, facilitators will find that participants are less anxious and more inclined to participate from the onset of a group. The type of format planned is less important; the critical point is that there be a consistent routine to these sessions. Moreover, facilitators will also find that younger children function better with such routines that are similar to their experience in a classroom setting. Furthermore, following a set format will assist group leaders (in these larger groups) in maintaining members' attention, stimulating learning via several intervention methods, and ensuring that groups address their full agenda for each session.

Following is an example of a format for a MFGT program that can serve as a guide as facilitators plan their own routine for their groups:

I. Warm-Up Question

Directions. Facilitator goes around the circle in seating order and asks each member to respond to a disclosure task or question that is intended to help group members get to know one another better. These questions should be factual or positive in the beginning sessions so that participants establish a level of relationship before they open up about problems or more difficult parts of their lives. It is important that facilitators be the first to share their response to these questions both as a way of modeling for the members and also so they too become part of the trusting group relationship. The relationship-building interventions contained in Chapter 5 are intended to be used in this part of a MFGT program.

Time Required. Depends on the size of a group but hopefully should be completed in about 30 minutes.

II. Main Theme of Session with a Related Intervention

Directions. Facilitators will have to determine the theme or objective of each session and then select an intervention from Chapters 5 to 8 to utilize. Themes and techniques planned should be based both on the presenting problems of the targeted client population and the phase of the group. Readers are referred to Chapter 3 for more information on this latter point.

Time Required. Most of the group session time should be spent during this part of the format. Therefore, the time required for this task will be dependent on the size of the group and the total length of meeting time.

III. Positive Closure

Directions. At the end of each group session facilitators go around the circle and ask each member to share something they enjoyed about the session, they found helpful, they felt like a lightbulb went off for them, or they acquired some significant learning. This last task actually serves as a way of having members process sessions by primarily sharing what they enjoyed or found helpful. If members have negative feedback about their group experience, it is suggested that they be asked to share that information with the facilitator after the group meeting. The reason for this recommendation is that beginning groups need lots of positive reinforcement about the benefits of the group. Later on, as groups develop, facilitators may feel that members are ready to share both positive and negative feedback about sessions.

Time Required. Usually about 10 to 15 minutes.

This format example shows how a group can follow a consistent routine while at the same time allowing a facilitator to plan a variety of interventions. Also, readers are reminded that the major focus of this book is on interventions due to this author's belief that effective treatment groups have to be planned. Furthermore, it is important to make sure all members participate in the interventions planned since the creation of balanced participation is a critical element of a therapeutic group. Practitioners should keep in mind that planning of MFGT also requires that the age levels represented in a group be carefully considered. For this reason, interventions for various ages of clients have been provided in Chapters 5 to 8.

Readers should review the "MFGT Planning Sheet" provided in Appendix B that shows one method for carefully planning each group session. It will be essential that facilitators determine their session plans based on a group's phase of development (see Chapter 3 material on phasing of group treatment), members' ages, total length of the meeting time, needs of participants, and preferences of facilitators. In regard to the last variable, this author learned over the years that it is important to consider the preference of the facilitator. Group leaders have a tremendous impact on groups by their modeling and the enthusiasm with which they participate in sessions. The feeling created by facilitators is very contagious and therefore considering interventions that one enjoys contributes to the therapeutic atmosphere of a group.

In Appendix C the reader will find a master listing of the techniques from Chapters 5, 6, 7, and 8. This overview of the interventions contained in this book should assist facilitators in individualizing their MFGT planning based on the needs of their particular group.

FACILITATION STYLES AND HANDLING OF PROBLEMS THAT SURFACE IN GROUPS

What is the most effective approach to facilitating of MFGT? There is currently very limited data to answer this question. We do know that this is one of the aspects of MFGT, and group treatment in general, that future research needs to target. This is a particularly important question to answer because common sense tells us that that skills required of MFGT facilitators are different. Unfortunately, we do not know specifically in what ways the skills to run these groups vary from those required when facilitating other more traditional types of group treatment. Regardless, facilitators will still need to carefully think through how they will conduct these very unique groups. In particular, co-facilitators will have to be clear on their respective roles in this group and process after each session to ensure that the facilitation approach used is being effective. Moreover, for purposes of further developing the study of MFGT, facilitators should keep detailed notes on the approach they use in conducting their groups. It would even be helpful for group leaders to document even subtle changes in their approach as a group moves through each of the three phases of development (see Chapter 3 for specifics on these phases).

Readers will see on Table 4.1 guidelines for facilitating groups through each of the three phases, initial, middle, and termination. This chart was developed for group treatment in general, specifically when such groups follow the Dennison Group Practice Model (see Chapter 3). Much of this information is relevant to the facilitation of MFGT and as such, practitioners should review the suggestions provided. As the reader will note on Table 4.1, there are specific changes that need to take place in how facilitators conduct groups based on the phase of development and the goals related to that period in the treatment process. This author advises readers to mainly review the guidelines that are related to their group's phase of development. In this way, practitioners can concentrate on those guidelines most relevant to their group situation.

The other issue related to the facilitation approach is the handling of problems as they arise in these groups. As most experienced group workers have learned, there are any numbers of problems that can arise in a group. It is extremely important, first of all, that co-facilitators be

Table 4.1

Guidelines for Facilitation of Groups in Each Phase

Initial Phase	Middle Phase	Termination Phase
Warm, friendly, and accepting	Warm, friendly, and accepting	Warm, friendly, and accepting
Disclose with members for relationship building	Do not disclose your problems in group unless already fully resolved and being used as examples to assist members	Disclose with members re: ending of group feelings and progress of members
Have a sense of humor and model	Reinforce members' modeling of positive behaviors to one another	Model group termination sharing
Keep disciplining in group at a minimum	Laugh, share, and model same	Laugh, share, and model same
Take a directive role	Pose some problems of group to membership to discuss and resolve	Keep disciplining at a minimum
Consistently reinforce and compliment members' participation	Transition role of keeping group on task to membership	Take more directive role again
Use backup plans when intervention is not working	Usually can go with plans made for sessions	Reinforce members' overall progress
Any gamelike tasks should always be group competitive	Any gamelike tasks should now be team competitive	Plan tasks that address termination phase goals
Be ready with lots of energy for these sessions	Validate importance of enjoying time in group	Any gamelike tasks should now be individually competitive
Create enjoyable and nonthreatening setting	You should not need as much energy for these sessions	Elicit discussions on other supports outside the group that will help maintain changes
		Often these sessions will require more energy from you

67

clear on how they will handle problems and if either one is to take the lead in this role. Usually when problems do arise in a group, co-facilitators will have to thoroughly process those sessions afterwards with one another. Even though McFarlane (2002) has conducted most of his research on the use of MFGT with psychiatric patients, in his latest publication he outlines some excellent suggestions for handling problems that arise in these groups.

Identification of the typical problems that arise in MFGT and potential ways to respond to those issues clearly requires further study. However, facilitators can contribute to the research of this model by keeping detailed field notes on this aspect of their groups. In addition, any research that examines this issue could significantly help in the development of effective techniques to use in response to problems that arise in these groups. Furthermore, readers will find that by following the Dennison Group Practice Model and related practice implications outlined in Chapter 3, the incidence of problems will be greatly reduced. Moreover, it is always good practice to either receive regular supervision on one's work with a MFGT program or process after each session with all involved co-facilitators.

DOCUMENTATION NOTES ON THESE TREATMENT GROUPS

Most treatment settings today require some type of documentation of services rendered to clients and their families. Therefore, it is important that facilitators determine in this pregroup phase a method of meeting this requirement. Sometimes this decision must be made within the administrative policy on documentation already in place for a program. Other times, practitioners will be able to have more input as to how notes and progress on group participants are indicated in the agency's records. Regardless of the type of notes maintained, it is critical that there be some documentation of members' progress throughout a group treatment program.

Since most members of MFGT are in these groups because of an identified problem with an adolescent, all notes on the family unit could be indicated in this individual's records. This recording method will make documentation easier, particularly since the family is the focus of this treatment approach. With this point in mind, it will be important that facilitators remember that whenever they document an entire family's progress in one client's record, then all members of that family have a right to review such notes. Awareness of this familywide access right should guide the type of notes indicated in such files.

The other issue related to documentation involves the decision to use either a free-flowing progress note entry or a standard form developed specifically for this type of treatment program. This author has found the latter choice makes the maintenance of client records much less time consuming and ensures a more consistent documentation of clients' progress. For this reason, the reader will find in Appendix D (MFGT Progress Note Form) a note sample form that can be used as is or as a guide when developing a similar form, individualized to a particular program's group. As can be seen on this sample, the goals addressed in any client's (or family's note in the identified patient's file) record should always be the same for all members of the same MFGT. The rationale for this consistent goal focus is that, unlike individual therapy, group therapy addresses goals that are the same for the entire membership. In addition, these goals should correspond directly to the goals of the multiple family group. Following the Dennison Group Practice Model outlined in Chapter 3, readers should refer back to Table 3.1, which delineates the goals for each of the three phases of group when writing progress notes.

The last issue related to documentation is the frequency with which notes are entered into a client's or family's file. Here again, there may be an administrative policy already in place that requires that progress notes on clients be maintained on a specific schedule. However, if this is not the situation, then facilitators may want to follow the schedule utilized in the sample note form in Appendix D. As the reader will see on this sample, there are four different forms included that address: 1) clients' entry into a MFGT program and the initial phase goals of this group, 2) clients' completion of the initial phase of treatment with their group and the documentation of progress on those goals, 3) clients' completion of the middle phase of treatment with their goals and the documentation of progress on those goals, 4) clients' completion of the termination phase of a group with documentation of their progress throughout this treatment program. The rationale for having only a maximum of four times that notes are entered in clients' records is that, often in this type of treatment, such posting of progress will be sufficient to address individual families' response to treatment. Moreover, the reader will see on the forms contained in Appendix D a place for facilitators to indicate attendance records that most programs will require for both documentation purposes and in some cases for the filing of third party payment. Furthermore, attendance may have to be monitored on families when they have been mandated into such treatment.

Readers are also reminded when reviewing the note forms in Appendix D that consistent group phase goals should always be addressed in these documentations along with some indication of individual family progress. It is extremely important that practitioners understand that in group treatment the goals are the same for all participants due to the nature of this therapeutic modality. At the same time, it is understandable that some individualized documentation of families' progress should be made in progress notes, which is why there is a provision for these entries on the note forms provided in Appendix D. As an added caution, practitioners are reminded to be very careful not to indicate the names of other group members in any one client's record. Furthermore, any other identifying information about other participants should not be contained in any client's records since there would be no way of protecting such members' confidentiality. The only information about group treatment recorded in these notes should involve standard goals for the group and progress of the individual client or family.

EVALUATION DESIGN FOR MFGT PROGRAMS

Our current age of accountability requires that all treatment programs today have an evaluation design developed before the services are rendered to a targeted client population. In addition, there is increased motivation to evaluate MFGT programs because we have such limited empirical support for this treatment modality (see Chapter 2 on literature review). Therefore, it is essential that facilitators develop a plan to evaluate their MFGT program to both validate the treatment impact for their targeted client population and contribute to the further study of this innovative group approach. This implementation issue is so important that Chapter 10 in this book addresses this topic in detail. Due to the fact that extensive material on program evaluation is provided in Chapter 10, readers are strongly encouraged to review that part of the text in detail as they design of the evaluation of their MFGT program.

Readers are reminded that no matter how passionate they are as MFGT facilitators or enthusiastic clients are in response to this intervention approach, empirical evidence is needed to validate this treatment modality. In addition, there are many implementation issues in regard to MFGT that require further study. Surfacing such findings will help practitioners better understand how to setup, compose, plan, and facilitate more effective group programs. MFGT is a very unique approach to treatment that has not only survived but thrived over the past 40 years. The consistent and strong clinical support for this innovative treatment approach clearly warrants more empirical support.

SUMMARY

In this chapter, 12 implementation issues were delineated as important aspects of MFGT that require careful planning in the pregroup phase. Readers were informed of essential parts of each of these setup issues that must be considered before groups are started. In addition, specific suggestions were outlined for addressing each of these aspects of a MFGT program. Furthermore, sample forms related to these implementation issues were introduced and provided in the appendices. It is hoped that these examples will provide practitioners with more guidelines to follow when developing their own group setup forms. The material in this chapter was intended to provide facilitators with very specific suggestions for setting up, composing, planning, and facilitating MFGT programs. By following these recommendations, group leaders should find that their treatment flows more smoothly, with fewer problems, and with more positive treatment impact.

Chapter 5

INTERVENTIONS FOR RELATIONSHIP BUILDING

In this chapter the reader will be provided an overview of the initial phase of a multiple family group therapy program. The process and treatment goals of this phase will be reviewed so that clinicians can better understand the connection between these goals and the suggested techniques. In addition, general instructions for conducting the relationship-building interventions will be outlined so facilitators can easily duplicate these therapeutic tasks with their own groups. Twenty-five interventions with related task sheets are then delineated that compose the heart of this chapter. For each of these interventions the reader is provided the following: title of technique, timing in group, purpose, specific instructions, related task sheet if relevant, cautions, and possible modifications. These latter directions should increase the consistent application of these techniques to various multiple family group therapy programs. Readers are strongly urged to carefully review this chapter as they begin their MFGT because relationship building is a critical part of the therapeutic value of this treatment modality.

OVERVIEW OF INITIAL PHASE OF MFGT

As the reader may recall from Chapter 3, the process goals are of primary emphasis when following the Dennison Group Practice Model. These are the goals that are directed at creating a cohesive and trusting group. More specifically, these goals include creating an attractive group setting, initiating balanced participation among the membership, and building a trusting relationship among the participants. The interventions provided in this chapter are intended to address these three process goals along with the process goals in the middle and termination phases. As indicated in Chapter 4, these technique suggestions can be utilized for the warm-up part of each group session. For this reason, readers will find that the level of disclosure required from these interventions varies since they are to be selected and used at different points in a group's development. Every technique description contains a "timing in the group" section that will provide practitioners with guidelines on the phase for which techniques are most appropriate. The treatment goals (i.e., to delineate more specific treatment goals that are common to the membership and to provide psychoeducation on targeted problems), which are of secondary emphasis in this phase, are targeted with the interventions in Chapter 6.

It is critical that facilitators understand the importance of this phase of a group since the attainment of the process goals will directly impact the degree to which a group can address and resolve their problems in the middle phase (i.e., the treatment goals for the middle phase). In addition, multiple family group therapy involves a much larger number of participants who are usually of a greater age span than in traditional peer groups. For this reason, it typically takes these groups longer to form a trusting relationship such that the group becomes a potent unit for both eliciting and reinforcing positive changes. Moreover, such a cohesive group can also serve to confront members who either do not adhere to group rules or fail to work on their targeted problems.

The timing of this phase varies with each group but, as mentioned in Chapter 3, it would not be unusual for a multiple family group to require as many as seven sessions out of a total of eight sessions. Facilitators will have to use their knowledge and skills in determining when their particular group is ready to move into the middle phase. Each group varies in terms of the time they require in each group phase. Readers are again reminded that this timing guide is not intended to indicate that therapy is not occurring in this first phase. Rather, important parts of the therapeutic process are happening at this time in a group. For example, it may be that in MFGT there is important relationship building that takes place both between family units and within family units. Based on this author's research, families appear to find that in this phase they begin to experience some corrective relationship building within their family units or what might be termed some positive rebuilding of their relationships. This finding may be one of the reasons why families often report that this intervention has had a more positive impact on their entire family unit.

When addressing at risk adolescents and their families, practitioners are reminded that often these family units report feelings of shame or guilt that have resulted in increased levels of isolation. Many of these families find that this initial group phase affords them a critical opportunity to not feel so alone in their troubles. In addition, such family members often report that they no longer "feel crazy" or "so unusual" as they get to know other families dealing with similar problems. This initial phase can provide a much needed normalizing experience for these at risk families that will be essential before they can begin the change process.

It is unfortunate that we have limited follow-up research on MFGT or even groups in general. Such studies could surface some important findings regarding the value of this initial phase. For example, this author has found informally that members of particularly cohesive groups, that had only gone through the initial phase and then terminated, often report ongoing changes even after treatment ends. Could it be that members of groups that fully attain the goals of the initial phase are more motivated to resolve their problems? Also, could it be that participation in a cohesive and trusting group provides clients a corrective relationship building experience such that they are able to develop healthier support systems in their lives? These are important questions that need to be addressed in future follow-up studies because such findings could further delineate the therapeutic value of this initial phase of a group.

GENERAL INSTRUCTIONS FOR USE OF RELATIONSHIP-BUILDING INTERVENTIONS

The interventions in this chapter are intended to be used for the warm-up part of each group session. Readers will find that more interventions have been provided for initial phase groups since relationship building is the most important and critical time in a group's development. In fact, facilitators may decide to use two interventions from this chapter for their first few group sessions rather than selecting any techniques from Chapter 6 (i.e., psychoeducational interventions that address the treatment goals of the initial phase). When conducting MFGT leaders must be sensitive to the importance of creating a safe, nonthreatening, and comfortable environment where participants will spontaneously begin opening up about their presenting problems.

Specific instructions for each intervention include timing in a group, purpose of the task, directions on how to conduct the technique, reference to task sheet at end of chapter if relevant, cautions in regard to the use of this intervention, and suggestions for modifying the technique. This information should assist facilitators' understanding of how to plan and facilitate each of these interventions. Readers should feel free to duplicate the related task sheets found at the end of the chapter for use with their groups. (Duplication of these task sheets for other purposes (e.g., training) is prohibited and violates copyright.)

Unless otherwise indicated, facilitators should conduct these interventions in the same consistent manner at the onset of each group meeting. First, the intervention is introduced to participants and, if relevant, task sheets are passed out to each member. The group should be given some time to gather their thoughts or write down their responses on a task sheet before being requested to share with the group. It is strongly advised that the facilitator be the first to disclose in regard to the relationship-building task. Such disclosure can be done at the beginning of the membership's disclosure. Or the facilitator can share his or her disclosure as a way of explaining the task instructions. This method is more subtle but can be just as potent because it serves as a modeling to the membership. Typically clinicians will find that by being the first to disclose, similar levels of disclosure occur naturally and spontaneously by group participants.

After the facilitator has shared in regard to the relationship-building task, members are requested to go around the circle and share in a similar way. For some interventions, such sharing may be done by the family as a unit rather than by each individual family member. Leaders will need to decide how families determine who will do such sharing for the entire unit. In some groups the family member can be selected freely by the family whereas in other groups facilitators may want to have a set order as to who does the sharing for the family unit. Practitioners will need to use their skills and individual preferences in deciding which method they choose to use for this familywide sharing. The rationale for having some interventions that require a familywide response is such tasks will necessitate that family members share first with one another, which can serve as a corrective relationship building experience. In addition, this method of sharing requires less time in the session, which can be very helpful in these much larger groups.

It will be important that both during and at the completion of each intervention facilitators point out commonalities among the membership and reinforce participation. Such processing comments will contribute to the development of a cohesive and trusting group. Moreover, leaders may want to request the participants to process their response to the intervention after hearing all the membership's sharing. This request may surface some interesting and helpful feedback about the ongoing development of trust in a group.

The amount of time any particular intervention will require varies between groups. Such timing will depend on the size of the group, age span of participants, and amount of sharing that surfaces. Facilitators are cautioned to monitor both the amount and level of disclosure among participants. It is particularly important in the initial phase that balanced participation is established and maintained throughout the life of a group. Otherwise, clinicians will find themselves conducting individual or family therapy with an audience.

Modification of some interventions will be necessary due to the age span among members of any one multiple family therapy group. This author has attempted to design techniques that are relevant and developmentally appropriate for a wide span of ages. However, it is impossible to create interventions that will be effective for all possible ages of group participants. Therefore, readers are strongly encouraged to modify or change interventions so they will be effective for their particular MFGT program. Also, facilitators should feel free to ask family members to assist younger members who might have difficulty with some tasks. Such assistance can serve some important therapeutic value as family members relate more positively to one another. Or, another example might be a teen who only relates well to a younger sibling and such assistance provides some positive reinforcement for this family member.

Readers are reminded to always remember that one of the unique strengths of MFGT is the mixing of at risk family members with healthier members. Sometimes the strengths from these latter individuals can be used to increase the effectiveness of a particular intervention. For example, when the at risk teen cannot articulate what he does well in school, a sibling might be able to point out some strengths in his younger or older sibling. Facilitators of MFGT that focus on at risk adolescents and their families will find it immensely helpful to elicit feedback from other teens in the group. Adolescents are more likely to listen and respond to such teens who often have important strengths to share and model.

The remaining contents of this chapter will be a listing of relationship-building interventions with related task sheets. Readers are encouraged to review this entire chapter before planning their multiple family groups. In addition, the planning guidelines provided in Chapter 4 will serve as additional guidelines for the timing and facilitation of these interventions.

TECHNIQUE 1

Title of Intervention: Family Drawing
Timing in Group: Initial Phase
Purpose: To introduce families to one another and begin building a group relationship.
Specific Instructions: Pass out a large newsprint sheet to each family unit with a box of crayons. Ask each family to draw a picture of everyone who lives at their home and put the following next to each family member: age, grade in school or occupation, and hobby. Once every family has finished their picture ask that a member of each family unit volunteer to stand up and share their picture with the group. The facilitator should be the first to share with the group a picture they have drawn of their family members. Then the families begin sharing their pictures by going around the circle in order. After each person finishes showing their family drawing, members can be asked if they have any questions.
Related Task Sheet: Task sheet not required but will need newsprint and crayons for all families.
Cautions and Possible Modifications: This is an excellent technique to involve all age members of a family. Be sure to instruct families that

each person in attendance at the session must draw their own picture on the family drawing and answer the three questions about themselves. In order to avoid having the same family member volunteer each time to share for a family unit, it is a good idea to instruct families that different members must take turns sharing in future sessions. Facilitators can change the type of information requested by each person's drawing of himself or herself. It will be important that any different disclosure requested should be of a positive or factual nature due to the purpose of this intervention in the initial phase.

TECHNIQUE 2

Title of Intervention: Give Us the Family Rap!

Timing in Group: Initial Phase

Purpose: To provide more factual information on families and continue building a group relationship.

Specific Instructions: The task sheet titled *Give Us the Family Rap!* should be passed out to each family unit. Family members should be asked to take some time and complete this task sheet together. The group facilitator should be the first one to share their responses in regard to this task. Then a volunteer from each family should be requested to share the familywide response to the task sheet. Other group members should be allowed to ask questions or obtain clarification between family presentations. The sharing from each family unit should proceed around the circle in order.

Related Task Sheet: Give Us the Family Rap!

Cautions and Possible Modifications: This is an excellent technique for engaging teenagers who enjoy rap type of activities. It will be important that families are instructed at the outset to make sure every family member takes part in completing the task sheet. Facilitators should feel free to change the sentence completions on this rap sheet in order to elicit different types of disclosure. However, due to the timing of this intervention in the group, it will be important that such changes only require disclosure of a positive or factual nature.

Title of Intervention: What's in Style for Your Family Members?
Timing in Group: Initial Phase
Purpose: To increase relationship building and group attractiveness among the membership.
Specific Instructions: The task sheet titled *What's in Style for Your Family Members?* should be passed out to each family unit. Family members should be asked to take some time and complete this task sheet together. The group facilitator should be the first one to share their responses in regard to this task. Then a volunteer from each family should be requested to share the familywide response to the task sheet. Other group members should be allowed to ask questions or obtain clarification between family presentations. The sharing from each family unit should proceed around the circle in order.
Related Task Sheet: What's in Style for Your Family Members?
Cautions and Possible Modifications: This is an excellent technique for engaging teenagers who enjoy discussions about what is in style. It will be important that families are instructed at the outset to make sure every family member takes part in completing the task sheet. Facilitators should feel free to change the categories on this sheet in order to elicit different types of disclosure. However, due to the timing of this intervention in the group, it will be important that such changes only require disclosure of a positive or factual nature.

Title of Intervention: Your Family's Coat of Values
Timing in Group: Initial Phase
Purpose: To increase the level of disclosure between and within family units.
Specific Instructions: The task sheet titled *Your Family's Coat of Values* should be passed out to each family unit. Family members should be asked to take some time and complete this task sheet together. The group facilitator should be the first one to share his or her response in regard to this task. Then a volunteer from each family should be requested to share the familywide response to the task sheet. Other

group members should be allowed to ask questions or obtain clarification between family presentations. The sharing from each family unit should proceed around the circle in order.

Related Task Sheet: Your Family's Coat of Values

Cautions and Possible Modifications: This intervention may be more challenging for participants to complete because so often families do not talk openly about their values today. It will be important that families are instructed at the outset to make sure every family member takes part in completing the task sheet. Facilitators should feel free to change parts of this sheet in order to elicit different types of disclosure. However, due to the timing of this intervention in the group, it will be important that such changes only require disclosure of a positive or factual nature.

TECHNIQUE 5

Title of Intervention: Family Rituals at Your House

Timing in Group: Initial Phase

Purpose: To increase the level of disclosure and relationship building among the group membership.

Specific Instructions: The task sheet titled *Family Rituals at Your House* should be passed out to each family unit. Family members should be asked to take some time and complete this task sheet together. The group facilitator should be the first one to share their responses in regard to this task. Then a volunteer from each family should be requested to share the familywide response to the task sheet. Other group members should be allowed to ask questions or obtain clarification between family presentations. The sharing from each family unit should proceed around the circle in order.

Related Task Sheet: Family Rituals at Your House

Cautions and Possible Modifications: This intervention increases families' awareness of their daily, weekly, and yearly rituals. Facilitators can use this technique as an opportunity to emphasize the importance of rituals in developing more resilient families.

TECHNIQUE 6

Title of Intervention: Words that Describe Your Family
Timing in Group: Initial Phase
Purpose: To increase disclosure among the group membership.
Specific Instructions: The task sheet titled *Words that Describe Your Family* should be passed out to each family member. One family member should then be asked to collect each person's task sheet. The group facilitator should be the first one to share their responses in regard to this task. Then a volunteer from each family should be requested to share the familywide responses to the task sheet. Other group members should be allowed to ask questions or obtain clarification between family presentations. The sharing from each family unit should proceed around the circle in order.
Related Task Sheet: Words that Describe Your Family
Cautions and Possible Modifications: This can be a very effective intervention for family units to learn more about one another's perspective on their family. Facilitators will note that most of the words on the task sheet are positive and factual due to the group phase. Even though some group members may feel other words describe their families, it may be best to not allow or limit this type of disclosure. Responses to this technique have the potential of surfacing some conflicting feelings between family members. Therefore, facilitators need to proceed very carefully when conducting this intervention.

TECHNIQUE 7

Title of Intervention: Our Family Cartoon
Timing in Group: Initial Phase
Purpose: To increase more light-hearted disclosure among the group membership.
Specific Instructions: The task sheet titled *Our Family Cartoon* should be passed out to each family unit. Family members should be asked to take some time and complete this task sheet together. The group facilitator should be the first one to share their responses in regard to this task. Then a volunteer from each family should be requested to share the familywide response to the task sheet. Other group members should

be allowed to ask questions or obtain clarification between family presentations. The sharing from each family unit should proceed around the circle in order.

Related Task Sheet: Our Family Cartoon

Cautions and Possible Modifications: This intervention is intended to surface some of the humorous and light-hearted sides of each family's life. For some particularly troubled families, this task may be difficult so facilitators may have to offer encouragement and possible suggestions. Cartoon completions like this one can be easily modified but should always be changed keeping in mind the time in the group's development when this technique is being used.

TECHNIQUE 8

Title of Intervention: Good Times and Difficult Times in Our Family History

Timing in Group: Initial Phase

Purpose: To increase family background disclosure among the group membership.

Specific Instructions: The task sheet titled *Good Times and Difficult Times in Our Family History* should be passed out to each family member. One family member should then be asked to collect each person's task sheet. The group facilitator should be the first one to share their responses in regard to this task. Then a volunteer from each family should be requested to share the familywide responses to the task sheet. Other group members should be allowed to ask questions or obtain clarification between family presentations. The sharing from each family unit should proceed around the circle in order.

Related Task Sheet: Good Times and Difficult Times in Our Family History

Cautions and Possible Modifications: This intervention introduces the first direct request for family members to share their memories of both good and difficult times in their past history. It is important to allow each family member to first put together their graph and then have one member share the familywide view of this history. Often family members have very different recollections of what was a particularly happy time or what was a particularly tough period. Facilitators need to be sensitive to the possibility that this task may elicit the recall of some very difficult memories for some family members. Therefore, group members should be instructed that they need only share those memories they are comfortable disclosing with the group. On the other hand, surfacing this disclosure can provide some valuable background information on families that directly relates to current presenting problems. Surfacing such material can be helpful both within family units and between families in a multiple family group.

TECHNIQUE 9

Title of Intervention: It's on My Mind These Days!

Timing in Group: Initial Phase

Purpose: To increase members' disclosure of issues currently on their minds.

Specific Instructions: Facilitators will need to pass around different colored pipe cleaners to each group members. Then the group is instructed to use the pipe cleaners to make a symbol that relates to something that has been on their minds a lot lately. Typically it takes group members longer to respond to this type of symbolic task. However, as a result of the thinking elicited from this task, often the responses are gut level ones. Facilitators should be the first ones to share their pipe cleaner symbol and explain it as much as they choose. Then each group member is requested to go around the circle in order and do the same. Members should be allowed to ask questions or seek clarifications between members' sharing.

Related Task Sheet: No task sheet required but full selection of different colored pipe cleaners will be needed for this task.

Cautions and Possible Modifications: Symbolic tasks are excellent interventions to surface some of the more intimate levels of disclosures. This particular technique is usually appropriate for a wide age span, which adds to its beneficial use. Facilitators can change this intervention by either asking different types of questions (e.g., make the pipe cleaners into a symbol of what is particularly on your mind about school or work) or having members use a different material like clay, drawings, or painting.

TECHNIQUE 10

Title of Intervention: We Dial...for Support
Timing in Group: Initial Phase
Purpose: To increase members' disclosure of their current family support system.
Specific Instructions: The task sheet titled *We Dial...for Support* should be passed out to each family unit. Family members should be asked to take some time and complete this task sheet together. The group facilitator should be the first one to share his or her response in regard to this task. Then a volunteer from each family should be requested to share the familywide response to the task sheet. Other group members should be allowed to ask questions or obtain clarification between family presentations. The sharing from each family unit should proceed around the circle in order.
Related Task Sheet: We Dial...for Support
Cautions and Possible Modifications: By having each family unit complete this task sheet families can become more aware of their current support system or lack of it. It will be very important that families be instructed to elicit input for this task sheet from each member in attendance at the group session. Also, facilitators may find that a multiple family group spontaneously begins discussing ways to increase their respective support systems at the completion of this disclosure task.

TECHNIQUE 11

Title of Intervention: What's the Radio Playing at Your Home?
Timing in Group: Initial Phase
Purpose: To increase group members' level of disclosure.
Specific Instructions: The task sheet titled *What's the Radio Playing at Your Home?* should be passed out to each family member. One family member should then be asked to collect each person's task sheet. The group facilitator should be the first one to share his or her response in regard to this task. Then a volunteer from each family should be requested to share the familywide responses to the task sheet. Other group members should be allowed to ask questions or obtain clarification between family presentations. The sharing from each family unit

should proceed around the circle in order.

Related Task Sheet: What's the Radio Playing at Your Home?

Cautions and Possible Modifications: This is a type of symbolic task that often elicits more in-depth disclosure from group members. By having each family member select a song or make up a song that best summarizes their current life, families are able to obtain a better understanding of how everyone in their family is really feeling. Facilitators need to be prepared that some songs that are surfaced from this task may be difficult for families to hear and deal with in the group setting. Practitioners should use their skills in determining how much probing of such responses should be done in the group. In some cases, it may be necessary to meet with individual families after a group meeting to discuss and process such material further.

TECHNIQUE 12

Title of Intervention: Strengths of Our Family!

Timing in Group: Initial Phase

Purpose: To increase families' disclosure of their familywide strengths.

Specific Instructions: The task sheet titled *Strengths of Our Family!* should be passed out to each family unit. Family members should be asked to take some time and complete this task sheet together. The group facilitator should be the first one to share his or her response in regard to this task. Then a volunteer from each family should be requested to share the familywide response to the task sheet. Other group members should be allowed to ask questions or obtain clarification between family presentations. The sharing from each family unit should proceed around the circle in order.

Related Task Sheet: Strengths of Our Family!

Cautions and Possible Modifications: This is an effective technique for helping families formulate their strengths as a family. It is very important to instruct families from the onset that they must make sure they include strengths from each family member. Also, families should be reminded that some of their strengths are a result of how they function as a unit rather than just what they draw from each individual member. This latter information should be included on the task sheet. By timing this intervention later in the initial phase it is hoped that family members can be more positive with one another as they develop the contents of this task sheet. Facilitators may want to use the disclosure that surfaces from this task as a springboard for a discussion on families' use of their unique strengths as coping skills.

TECHNIQUE 13

Title of Intervention: Tracking the Unique Me
Timing in Group: Initial Phase
Purpose: To increase group members' disclosure level particularly in regard to each family member's unique personality.
Specific Instructions: The task sheet titled *Tracking the Unique Me* should be passed out to each family member. Each family member is requested to complete this sheet and be prepared to share with the group. The group facilitator should be the first one to share his or her response in regard to this task. Then a group member begins by sharing his or her response to the task sheet. Similar sharing continues around the circle in order. Other group members should be allowed to ask questions or obtain clarification between members' presentations.
Related Task Sheet: Tracking the Unique Me
Cautions and Possible Modifications: This task provides individual members an opportunity to think and reflect on how they have acquired the traits that make up their personality. Often this sharing provides important insight between family members, which can increase mutual understanding and sensitivity. Facilitators will have to monitor this sharing because there may be some uncomfortable feelings that surface from this task.

TECHNIQUE 14

Title of Intervention: Family Problem Checklist
Timing in Group: Middle Phase
Purpose: To provide a comfortable means for families to begin sharing their problems from each family member's perspective.
Specific Instructions: The task sheet titled *Family Problem Checklist* should be passed out to each family member. As each family member

completes this sheet he or she should be requested to place it face down in a pile in the front of the family unit. The group facilitator should not share their responses in regard to this task since this intervention should be used in a middle phase group. Instead, the sharing begins with a volunteer from each family unit reading the task sheets that were anonymously placed in the family pile. Other group members should be allowed to ask questions or obtain clarification between family presentations. The sharing from each family unit should proceed around the circle in order.

Related Task Sheet: Family Problem Checklist

Cautions and Possible Modifications: This is a less threatening way at the onset of the middle phase to introduce family problem disclosure. Facilitators should caution family members who read the family's task sheets to be careful to not reveal the name of the family member even if they feel they know whose checklist is being read. Another way to handle this intervention is to collect all family members' checklists and then mix up the piles so members who volunteer to do the reading will not know which family unit they are reporting on from the task sheets. This modification can be far less threatening for families and yet still help the membership feel validated and normalized from such sharing.

TECHNIQUE 15

Title of Intervention: Good News/Bad News at Our Home this Past Week

Timing in Group: Middle Phase

Purpose: To increase members' disclosure of relevant problems in their families.

Specific Instructions: The task sheet titled *Good News/Bad News at Our Home this Past Week* should be passed out to each family member. One family member should then be asked to collect each person's task sheet. The group facilitator should not share his or her response in regard to this task since it is being used in a middle phase group. Instead, the sharing begins with a volunteer from each family sharing the family-wide responses to the task sheet. Other group members should be allowed to ask questions or obtain clarification between family presentations. The sharing from each family unit should proceed around the circle in order.

Related Task Sheet: Good News/Bad News at Our Home this Past Week

Cautions and Possible Modifications: This intervention is intended to surface some of the most relevant problems occurring for each family unit. Here again, if a facilitator feels a group would be more comfortable with anonymous sharing then this technique can be modified. The family members of each unit can place their sheets face down in one pile. The facilitator collects all the piles and mixes them up so volunteers from each family unit read a pile of task sheets they have no way of knowing which family unit is being reported. This modification is able to still provide validation to the membership and normalize some of their daily problems and stresses.

TECHNIQUE 16

Title of Intervention: Fantasy Family
Timing in Group: Middle Phase
Purpose: To increase members' awareness of what they ideally would like different so their family will be happier and healthier functioning.
Specific Instructions: The task sheet titled *Fantasy Family* should be passed out to each family member. One family member should then be asked to collect each person's task sheet. The group facilitator should not share their responses in regard to this task since it is being used in a middle phase group. Instead, the sharing begins with a volunteer from each family sharing the familywide responses to the task sheet. Other group members should be allowed to ask questions or obtain clarification between family presentations. The sharing from each family unit should proceed around the circle in order.
Related Task Sheet: Fantasy Family
Cautions and Possible Modifications: This technique is based on a solution-focused approach where family members are asked to create a fantasy of how they would like their families to look and function. Here again, if a facilitator feels a group would be more comfortable with anonymous sharing, then this technique can be modified. The family members of each unit can place their sheets face down in one pile. The facilitator collects all the piles and mixes them up so as volunteers from

each family unit read a pile of task sheets they have no way of knowing which family unit is being reported. This modification is able to still provide validation to the membership and normalize their feelings. After this task has been completed, facilitators may want to conduct a discussion on ways that members can attain some or all of their fantasy family. Such a discussion can surface some helpful alternative coping response material that families will benefit from learning. In addition, this information can be invaluable as families work toward resolving some of their presenting problems.

TECHNIQUE 17

Title of Intervention: What is Each Family Member's Mantra?
Timing in Group: Middle Phase
Purpose: To increase members' awareness of positive self-talk that can assist in their problem solving.
Specific Instructions: The task sheet titled *What is Each Family Member's Mantra?* should be passed out to each family member. One family member should then be asked to collect each person's task sheet. The group facilitator should not share his or her response in regard to this task since it is being used in a middle phase group. Instead, the sharing begins with a volunteer from each family sharing the family-wide responses to the task sheet. Other group members should be allowed to ask questions or obtain clarification between family presentations. The sharing from each family unit should proceed around the circle in order.
Related Task Sheet: What is Each Family Member's Mantra?
Cautions and Possible Modifications: This is an excellent method of introducing family members' individual responsibility to work toward resolving their problems. In addition, this intervention provides some nonthreatening education on the value of positive self-talk and the role it can play in developing better coping skills. Moreover, each family has an opportunity to see their familywide mantra, resulting in a reinforcement of each member's contribution toward improving their functioning as a unit. Also, group members are typically validated and further educated as they share their responses to this task.

TECHNIQUE 18

Title of Intervention: Rate Your Life

Timing in Group: Middle Phase

Purpose: To increase each group member's disclosure regarding their overall view of their lives.

Specific Instructions: The task sheet titled *Rate Your Life* should be passed out to each family member. Each family member is requested to complete this sheet and be prepared to share with the group. The group facilitator should not share his or her response in regard to this task since this technique is intended for use in the middle phase. Group members begin by sharing their responses to the task with similar sharing continuing around the circle in order. Other group members should be allowed to ask questions or obtain clarification between member's presentations.

Related Task Sheet: Rate Your Life

Cautions and Possible Modifications: This particular intervention provides individual families more insight into one another's overall view of their life. In addition, this sharing has the potential of validating other group members' responses to this task and providing some important learning about the ways people often rate or view their life. The sharing from this intervention may surface some new specifics regarding family units' presenting problems. Also, such disclosure can identify problems that need to be included in the treatment goals for various family units.

TECHNIQUE 19

Title of Intervention: If I Were the Parent/If I Were the Teen

Timing in Group: Middle Phase

Purpose: To increase parents' and teens' understanding of one another's role in the family.

Specific Instructions: The task sheet titled *If I Were the Parent/If I Were the Teen* should be passed out to each family member. Each family member is requested to complete this sheet and be prepared to share with the group. The group facilitator should not share his or her response in regard to this task since this technique is intended for use in the middle phase. Group members begin by sharing their responses to the task with similar sharing continuing around the circle in order. Other group members should be allowed to ask questions or obtain clarification between members' presentations.

Related Task Sheet: If I Were the Parent/If I Were the Teen

Cautions and Possible Modifications: This intervention is an excellent way for parents and teens in MFGT to increase their understanding of the responsibilities and challenges that come with each of their respective roles in the family. In addition, the uniqueness of this treatment modality affords many more opportunities for group members to learn from one another regarding these two roles. Here is where MFGT can provide many opportunities for parents to teach other teenagers and teenagers to teach other parents. In this modality group members are sometimes able to hear and learn more when there is less emotionality or history involved in relationships. Cross-parenting would be a good example of this point, which involves a parent working on a problem or another viewpoint with a teen from another family unit. The same would be true with teens helping other parents see a different point of view or understand another way of responding to a problem.

TECHNIQUE 20

Title of Intervention: Take a Walk in my Shoes!

Timing in Group: Middle Phase

Purpose: To increase family members' awareness of what life is like for each member of their unit.

Specific Instructions: The task sheet titled *Take a Walk in my Shoes!* should be passed out to each family member. Each family member is requested to complete this sheet and be prepared to share with the group. The group facilitator should not share his or her response in regard to this task since this technique is intended for use in the middle phase. Group members begin by sharing their responses to the task with similar sharing continuing around the circle in order. Other group members should be allowed to ask questions or obtain clarification between members' presentations.

Related Task Sheet: Take a Walk in my Shoes!

Cautions and Possible Modifications: This particular task provides families with the potential to better understand each of their lives. In addition, this intervention can increase group members' understanding and awareness of how they view their daily lives. Surfacing such disclosure can be invaluable in helping group members to resolve their targeted problem areas. Moreover, individual family members may become less rigid in their expectations of one another as they better understand what daily life is for one another.

TECHNIQUE 21

Title of Intervention: What is Becoming Extinct in Your Family?
Timing in Group: Middle Phase
Purpose: To increase family units' awareness of those aspects of their family that are becoming less and less a part of their daily lives.
Specific Instructions: The task sheet titled *What is Becoming Extinct in Your Family?* should be passed out to each family member. One family member should then be asked to collect each person's task sheet. The group facilitator should not share his or her response in regard to this task since it is being used in a middle phase group. Instead, the sharing begins with a volunteer from each family sharing the familywide responses to the task sheet. Other group members should be allowed to ask questions or obtain clarification between family presentations. The sharing from each family unit should proceed around the circle in order.
Related Task Sheet: What is Becoming Extinct in Your Family?
Cautions and Possible Modifications: This task can surface both positive and negative aspects of families' lives that are no longer part of their daily living. Such disclosure has the potential of surfacing and reinforcing decreases in stress level or tension within family units. In addition, this task can surface some positive aspects or strengths of a family that are no longer present but could be resurfaced. This intervention can serve as a type of strength-based technique where families can begin looking at earlier strengths they had as a unit that they may benefit from bringing back into their lives.

TECHNIQUE 22

Title of Intervention: Good-bye Group Letter Completion
Timing in Group: Termination Phase
Purpose: To elicit group members' sharing of the positive aspects of their group experience and the progress they have made.
Specific Instructions: The task sheet titled *Good-bye Group Letter Completion* should be passed out to each family member. One family member should then be asked to collect each person's task sheet. The group facilitator should be the first one to share his or her response in regard to this task. Then a volunteer from each family should be requested to share the familywide responses to the task sheet. Other group members should be allowed to ask questions or obtain clarification between family presentations. The sharing from each family unit should proceed around the circle in order.
Related Task Sheet: Good-bye Group Letter Completion
Cautions and Possible Modifications: This is an effective technique for group members to prepare for the ending of their group and beginning their grieving process. In addition, the disclosure surface from this task will often serve to validate and reinforce the changes that individual members and family units have made as a result of this treatment experience. Moreover, this intervention will often surface feelings that reinforce the value of the group and the critical role it played in members' progress.

TECHNIQUE 23

Title of Intervention: Family Poem Completion
Timing in Group: Termination Phase
Purpose: To have individual family units compose a poem that conveys their feelings about the MFGT experience.
Specific Instructions: The task sheet titled *Family Poem Completion* should be passed out to each family member. One family member should then be asked to collect each person's task sheet. The group facilitator is not able to share his or her response in regard to this task since it requires a familywide poem. A volunteer from each family should be requested to share the familywide poem that was developed

as a joint effort. Other group members should be allowed to ask questions or obtain clarification between family presentations. The sharing from each family unit should proceed around the circle in order.

Related Task Sheet: Family Poem Completion

Cautions and Possible Modifications: This intervention provides families an opportunity to share on a more intimate level their feelings about their participation in the group. It also serves as a more creative outlet for family members to share the value of the group experience from each of their individual perspectives. Even though poetry completions can take longer for members to develop, the disclosure surfaced is often at a more gut level and conveys some of the less easily shared feelings.

TECHNIQUE 24

Title of Intervention: This Group Has Been Like...

Timing in Group: Termination Phase

Purpose: To increase members' feelings about the value of the group experience for them.

Specific Instructions: The task sheet titled *This Group Has Been Like...* should be passed out to each family member. One family member should then be asked to collect each person's task sheet. The group facilitator should be the first one to share his or her response in regard to this task. Then a volunteer from each family should be requested to share the familywide responses to the task sheet. Other group members should be allowed to ask questions or obtain clarification between family presentations. The sharing from each family unit should proceed around the circle in order.

Related Task Sheet: This Group Has Been Like...

Cautions and Possible Modifications: This is a symbolic task since it requires group members to share their feelings about the group via other descriptive words. Sometimes members will be able to more accurately and honestly convey the meaning of the group to them by using other symbols. It will not be unusual for group members to take longer to complete this task sheet since it requires more careful thinking. However, the result is almost always the surfacing of disclosure that is quite intimate and very meaningful to the membership.

TECHNIQUE 25

Title of Intervention: Our Family Leaves this Group Feeling...
Timing in Group: Termination Phase
Purpose: To increase each family's awareness of how they are feeling as a unit with the ending of the group.
Specific Instructions: This intervention does not require a task sheet but rather requires the facilitator to pose a question to the group. The question is *What words best describe how your family as a unit is feeling as they leave this group?* Due to the nature of this question, facilitators do not participate in this sharing but rather reinforce, summarize, and point out commonalities that surface. As each family unit is ready, group members are asked to come up with one word that best describes how their family is feeling as they end their MFGT experience. This sharing continues around the circle with members being given opportunities to ask questions or make similar affirmations.
Related Task Sheet: None required for this intervention.
Cautions and Possible Modifications: This task provides individual family units an opportunity to validate their changes as a unit and reinforce the value of the group in their progress. In addition, some of the words shared may give families some insight into issues they need to continue to work on or ways they will want to monitor and respond to future problems as they arise.

SUMMARY

This chapter provides an overview of the initial phase of a MFGT program with particular attention to the primary and secondary goal emphasis. The importance of this phase was emphasized since the degree to which a group attains the process and treatment goals will determine their readiness to move to the middle phase. In addition, multiple family groups that become cohesive, trusting, and supportive units during these initial sessions will be more likely to effectively problem solve in the middle phase. Also, 25 interventions were delineated in this chapter for building groupwide relationships during all three phases of MFGT. Specific directions for each intervention, along with related task sheets, were provided such that readers should be able to easily utilize the suggested techniques with their particular groups. The details provided for each suggested technique in this chapter should also increase clinicians' ability to modify, change, and even create similar relationship-building interventions.

Give Us the Family Rap!

Instructions: Please complete the below requested information and then give it to the family member who has volunteered to share your entire family's responses to this task with the group.

Our name is the _____ family.

Our game is_____

_____

_____

Lately we have kept sane by _____

_____

_____

Some fame we have had _____

_____

_____

98

What's in Style for Your Family Members?

Instructions: Please complete the below requested information (from your viewpoint) and then give it to the family member who has volunteered to share your entire family's responses to this task with the group.

Clothing: _____

_____

Shoes: _____

_____

Music:_____

_____

_____

Free Time Interests/ Activities: _____

_____

_____

Hangouts or Places to Go: _____

_____

_____

_____

Other:_____

_____

_____

Your Family's Coat of Values

Instructions: Please write on the coat of armor below the four values you feel are taught and promoted in your family. When your are done please hand your sheet to the family member who has volunteered to share all family members' responses to this sheet with the group.

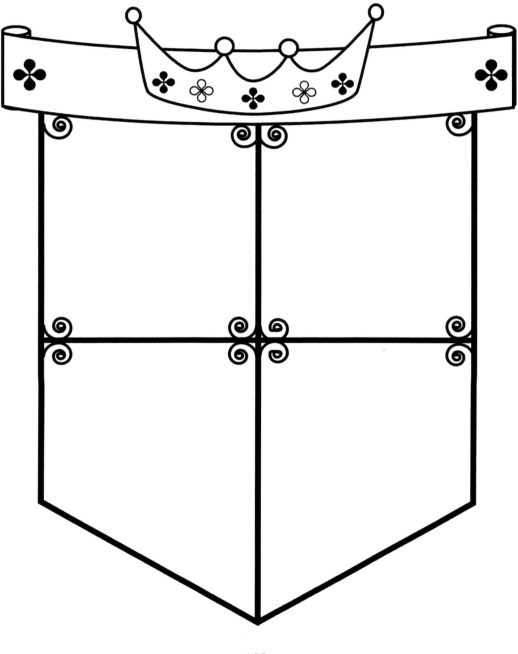

Family Rituals at Your House

Instructions: Please indicate with a check which family rituals or celebrations you have at your house and then hand this sheet to the family member who has volunteered to share all of your family's responses with the group.

Daily Rituals with Our Family

☐ A meal together at least once each day
☐ Family relaxation time together
☐ Completion of assigned chores
☐ Other _____

Weekly Rituals with Our Family

☐ A special meal together once a week
☐ A family outing or fun activity
☐ Attendance to a place of worship
☐ Completion of assigned chores
☐ Other _____

Celebrations or Yearly Events

☐ Parties for family members' birthdays
☐ Extended family get-togethers
☐ Family reunions
☐ Family trips or vacations
☐ Holiday celebrations every year
☐ Other _____

For me the best part about my family's rituals or celebrations is _____

_____

_____

One part of our rituals or celebrations I would like to change is _____

_____

_____

Words that Describe Your Family

Instructions: Please circle the words below that best describe your family. Add other words not listed and hand this sheet to the family member who has volunteered to share it with the group.

Our Family Cartoon

Instructions: Please do the cartoon completion below on some funny or light-hearted part of your family.

Good Times and Difficult Times in Our Family History

Instructions: Place Xs on the graph below to indicate good times and difficult times in your family history. When you are done please hand to the family member who has volunteered to share your family's response to this graph task.

	Early Marriage	Young Children	Teenagers
GOOD TIMES			
DIFFICULT TIMES			

We Dial...for Support

Instructions: Write on the four lines below family members, friends, or neighbors that your family calls on when they need support. When you have completed this sheet hand it to the family member who has volunteered to share your entire family's response to this task.

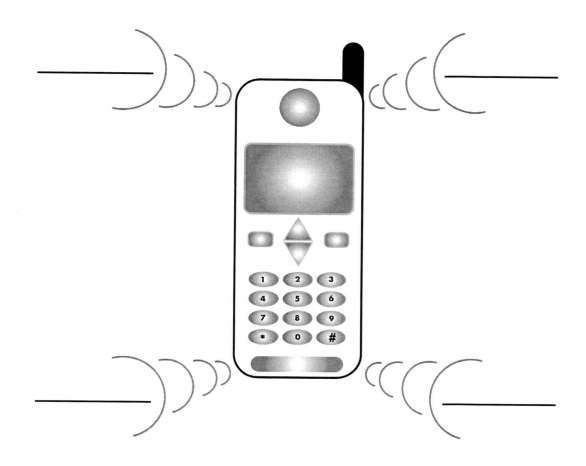

What's the Radio Playing at Your Home?

Instructions: Write the name of a real song or make up a song title that best summarizes your present life. When you are done hand this sheet to the family member who has volunteered to share your entire family's responses to this task with the group.

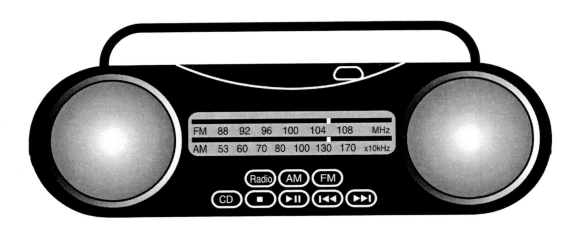

The title of the song playing on my radio is _____

_____

_____

_____

Strengths of Our Family

Instructions: As a family please list your familywide strengths on the incomplete picture below and then a volunteer from your family will share your responses with the group.

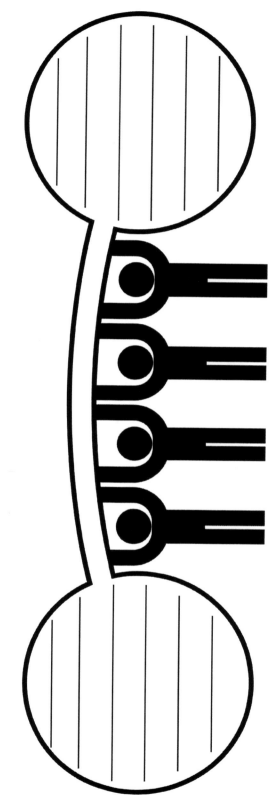

Tracking the Unique Me

Instructions: Please indicate the personality traits and talents you have received from each of the below sources. You will be asked to share this sheet with the group when you are done.

Unique Me Traits

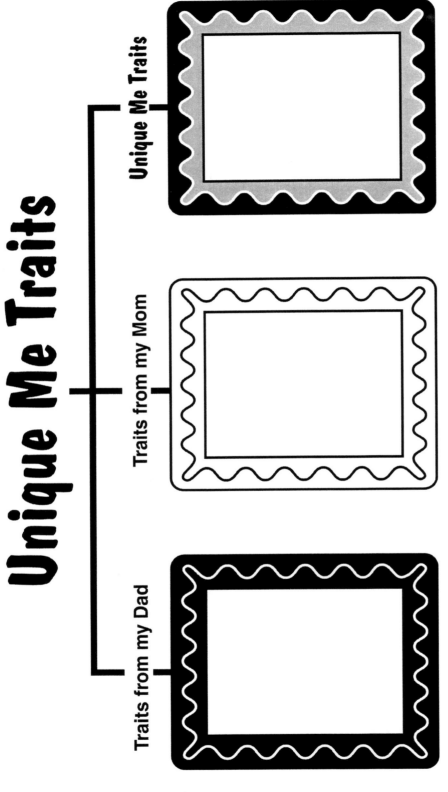

Unique Me Traits

Traits from my Mom

Traits from my Dad

Family Problem Checklist

Instructions: Please place a check in each box below that describes a problem your family is experiencing from your point of view. When you are done place your sheet face down on your family's pile. Your responses will be read anonymously to the entire group.

☐ Marital problems

☐ Discipline problems with teens and/or children

☐ Schedules too busy and stressful

☐ Lack of a support system

☐ School-related problems for teens and/or children

☐ Conflicts between family values and values of the environment

☐ Too many family hardships all at once

☐ Not enough loving and caring being conveyed in your family

☐ Trouble coping with current problems

☐ Very few family rituals or celebrations

☐ Not enough fun times together

☐ Financial problems

☐ Other _____

_____

_____

Good News/Bad News at Our Home this Past Week

Instructions: Complete the form below and then hand to the family member who has volunteered to share your entire family's responses to this task sheet with the group.

Weather
SUNNY
or
Cloudy

The Family Gazette

STOCKS
UP
Down

TODAY

GOOD NEWS / BAD NEWS

Fantasy Family

Instructions: Using the incomplete picture below draw a fantasy family for yourself. When you are done follow your facilitator's directions for the sharing of this picture.

What is Each Family Member's Mantra?

Instructions: Indicate your mantra by your position in your family and then hand this sheet to the family member who has volunteered to share the familywide pictures of everyone's mantra with the group.

Webster's New World Dictionary definition for mantra: "A hymn or portion of text...chanted or intoned as an incantation or prayer."

Rate Your Life

Instructions: Using the scale below rate each part of your life and feel free to add any parts of your life not listed. You will be asked to share your responses with the group when you are ready.

Rating scale to use for listed below

Not so Good   **Just Great**

1 --- 10

☐ School or work life

☐ Free time activities

☐ Friends and peer supports

☐ Immediate family life

☐ Extended family life

☐ Hobbies or sports

☐ Feelings and attitude toward self

☐ Other _____

_____

_____

If I Were the Parent/If I Were the Teen

Instructions: Please indicate by the picture below (select the one that shows you in a different role in your family) what you would do differently if you were either the parent or teen. When you are done you will be asked to share your responses to this task with the group.

If I were the teen I would _____   *If I were the parent I would* _____

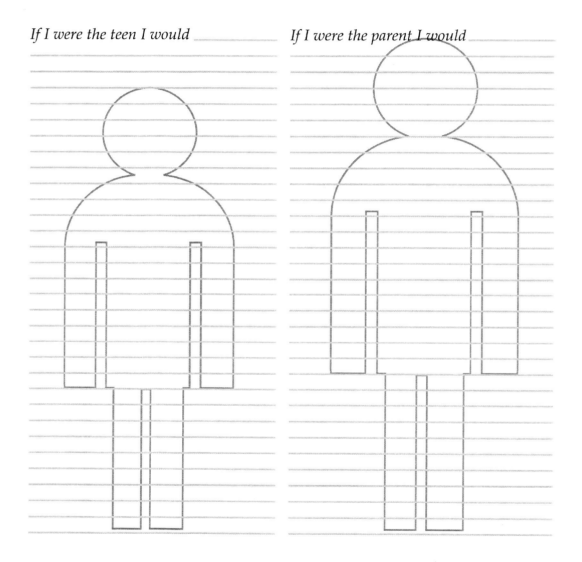

Take a Walk in my Shoes!

Instructions: Write or draw in the top shoe what you feel other people know about your life. Write or draw in the bottom shoe what you think many people around do not know or understand about your life. You will be asked to share your responses to this task when you are ready.

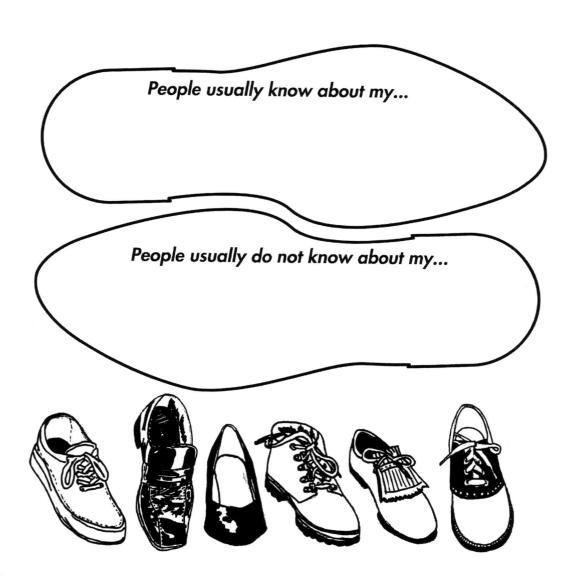

People usually know about my...

People usually do not know about my...

What is Becoming Extinct in Your Family?

Instructions: Complete the below picture by drawing or writing words that indicate both positive and negative parts of your family life that are becoming extinct. Please give your completed picture to the family member who has volunteered to share your entire family's responses to this task with the group.

Good-bye Group Letter Completion

Instructions: Complete the letter below by indicating what this group has meant to you and your family. Please give your letter when you are done to the family member who has volunteered to share your family's responses to this task with the group.

Dear Group,

When I first came to this group _____
_____

After I was here for a few sessions I _____
_____
_____

Now I realize that from this group I gained
_____
_____
_____

My family will miss this group because _____
_____
_____

Sincerely,

Family Poem Completion

Instructions: Please complete the parts of this poem that are related to your role in your family. When you are done hand in your poem to the family member who has volunteered to read the familywide poem to the group.

In the beginning of this group our family

_____

_____

_____

But as time went on we progressed with
The parents _____

_____

_____

The teens _____

_____

_____

The children _____

_____

_____

And now we are feeling_____

_____

_____

Thank you group from the

_____ family!

This Group Has Been Like...

Instructions: Please draw or write in the below picture something that best describes what this group has been like for you. When you are done please give your drawing to the family member who has volunteered to share your entire family's response to this task with the group.

Chapter 6

PSYCHOEDUCATIONAL INTERVENTIONS

In this chapter the reader will be provided an overview of the treatment goals for the initial phase of MFGT that are of secondary emphasis during the beginning group sessions. The rationale for these goals will be delineated such that clinicians will better understand the connection between the treatment goals of this phase and the suggested techniques outlined in this chapter. In addition, general instructions will be provided for conducting psychoeducational interventions with multiple family groups. Twenty-five interventions with related task sheets are then provided that compose the heart of this chapter. For each of these interventions the reader is given the following: title of the technique, purpose, specific instructions, related task sheet if relevant, and cautions with possible modifications. These directions should increase the consistent application of these techniques to a wide variety of multiple family group programs. Readers are strongly urged to carefully review this chapter when they begin their MFGT because psychoeducation has been reported by participants to be one of the major benefits of this unique treatment modality.

OVERVIEW OF TREATMENT GOALS FOR INITIAL PHASE

As the reader may recall from Chapter 3, the treatment goals are of secondary emphasis when following the Dennison Group Practice Model. Although these goals are not as important as the process goals (see Chapter 5), a group's attainment of these targeted areas will set the stage for a group to move into the middle phase. More specifically these goals include: 1) to delineate more specific treatment goals that are common to the membership and 2) to provide psychoeducation on targeted treatment areas of functioning. The interventions provided in this chapter are intended to simultaneously attain these two treatment goals. By conducting psychoeducational techniques, group facilitators should surface disclosure from individual family units that will assist in further specifying treatment goals to address in the middle phase that are common to the entire membership. Even though MFGT programs often focus on one targeted area of functioning, there will be differences among groups on which issues related to the problem area are of most relevance. For example, if a MFGT program is targeting adolescent substance abuse, there are many issues related to this problem that could potentially be difficulties for the involved families. Therefore, it is critical that facilitators utilize some of the psychoeducational interventions in this chapter such that the treatment goal focus for their groups in the middle phase can be more carefully delineated, and thus be more relevant to a particular group of family units.

The material in this book is intended to address the specific problems of at risk adolescents and their families. As a result, there are many potential problems that can be the focus of such a MFGT program. Targeted problem areas could include but are not limited to substance abuse, sexual promiscuity, aggressive acting out behavior, gang involvement, juvenile delinquency, school truancy, lack of motivation at school, lower than expected school performance, depression and/or suicide attempts, psychiatric problems, attention deficit disorder, and issues related to coping with a challenging situation (e.g., death of a loved one, disability, chronic medical illness, domestic violence, sexual abuse, or physical abuse). For this reason, the psychoeducational interventions in this chapter have been designed such that they could be used to address any one of these problem areas. In addition, some of the techniques focus on issues that are relevant to any at risk adolescent and their family. An example of this point would be the intervention that focuses on resilient attributes of at risk adolescents. This information could be relevant and helpful to families dealing with any number of difficulties involving teenagers. Moreover, by the time most at risk teens seek treatment they have often acquired a combination of problems, even though some of their difficulties may be of more importance to address initially. As a result, facilitators will find that some of the techniques in this chapter may surface additional problems that were not known at the time the teen and their family joined the group. Clinicians will need to use their assessment skills in determining if the new problems that surface should also be the focus of treatment along with the initial problems targeted by a group program. At the same time, facilitators will also have to be realistic about the number of problem areas that any one group can address. In some cases, the surfacing of new problems may be best addressed by the facilitator recommending that a particular teen and/or their family seek additional treatment services from another referral source.

The value of family education has long been recognized as one of the benefits of MFGT with its initial application on an inpatient ward with families dealing with psychiatric illness (Laqueur, 1976). More recent studies have found that psychoeducation in these groups has been helpful to a wide array of problems faced by families including marital conflict (Rabin, 1995), schizophrenia (Hyde & Goldman, 1993), obsessive-compulsive disorders (Black & Blum, 1992), attention deficit disorder (Greenfield & Senecal, 1995), anorexia nervosa (Marner & Westerberg, 1987), substance addiction recovery (Cwiakala & Mordock, 1997), adolescent chemical dependence (Polcin, 1992), medically ill children and teens (Wamboldt & Levin, 1995), and first time juvenile crime offenders (Quinn, Bell, & Ward, 1997). In addition, McFarlane, et al. (1996) more recently demonstrated the benefit of education with families seen in outpatient settings who have a member with a serious mental illness. It would appear that MFGT participants frequently report that learning more about a problem area helps in their coping skills and increases their sense of hopefulness. For this reason, psychoeducational interventions are an essential treatment method within the Dennison Group Practice Model and thus are provided in this chapter. Readers are strongly urged to individualize some of the techniques contained in this chapter such that the material presented via the suggested instructional strategy is more relevant and specific to each multiple family group.

Typically the interventions in this chapter would be utilized after an initial relationship is established among the membership. It is not necessary that a high level of trust be present in a group before these techniques are used. Therapeutic education often does not require that a group be cohesive, although higher levels of trust will usually increase the levels of disclosures shared during these interventions. In fact, facilitators will often find that particularly effective psychoeducational techniques may assist in building a group into a cohesive unit. These group techniques are usually nonthreatening and comfortable ways for families to initially disclose their particular problems or challenges to the group. As participants increasingly share during these interventions, the group naturally moves toward the middle phase when the membership can talk in more direct terms about their specific difficulties. Moreover, clinicians will find that any number of clients will benefit from combining therapeutic instruction with the more traditional therapeutic process. Many individuals require that didactic piece in order to more fully understand their own issues and concerns about a particular problem area.

GENERAL INSTRUCTIONS FOR USE OF PSYCHOEDUCATIONAL INTERVENTIONS

The interventions in this chapter are intended to be used as the main interventions (i.e., second part of the format presented in Chapter 4) for initial phase group sessions, after a beginning relationship is established among the membership. MFGT programs may, in fact, be ready for such techniques after the second or third session. Readers will want to review all the interventions in this chapter before determining the best choices for their particular groups. Beyond consideration of participants' needs, group leaders will want to also consider instructive techniques they are most comfortable in facilitating.

Specific instructions for each intervention include title of technique, purpose of task, directions on how to conduct the intervention, reference to task sheet at end of chapter if relevant, cautions in regard to the use of the task, and suggestions for modifying the technique. This information should assist facilitators' understanding of how to plan and utilize each of these interventions. Readers should feel free to duplicate the related task sheets, found at the end of this chapter, for use with their groups. (Duplication of these task sheets for other purposes (e.g., training) is prohibited and violates copyright.)

The interventions in this chapter should be introduced in a group session after a warm-up/relationship-building technique has been used with a group (see such techniques in Chapter 5). Usually a MFGT program will require about 20 minutes for such a warm-up task due to the larger size of these groups. The time required for a psychoeducational intervention will typically take longer since these techniques are intended to both provide instruction and elicit more sharing among the membership. The exact time required for each task in this chapter will vary depending on any number of variables including total length of group meeting time, size of group, and type of instructive intervention selected. Similar to recommendations for relationship-building techniques in Chapter 5, facilitators may want to share their own personal disclosures or examples of points as a way of modeling for the membership and enhancing their overall learning. Clinicians will want to carefully determine the type of sharing they do during these instructive interventions since disclosure of any current personal problems is not recommended.

If any lecture is part of a psychoeducational intervention, it is recommended that it be short and that the full range of cognitive and attention span levels in the group be considered. Facilitators will find that more effective therapeutic instruction will often take the form of discussions, brainstorming exercises, role-plays, problem-solving tasks, or sharing exercises. Typically it is not a good idea to only provide a lecture for this part of a group session. If a short presentation is provided, then the rest of the time should be spent eliciting group members' participation regarding the topic area. It is essential that participants be requested to be involved in this learning process otherwise the intervention loses its value as a therapeutic didactic task.

The reader will find that the majority of interventions provided in this chapter have related task sheets. The rationale for this planning is that the wide range of ages within a MFGT program requires such forms as a way of maintaining members' attention and enhancing their understanding of the material presented. In addition, the use of such task sheets provides an easy method for members to gather their thoughts on a particular subject and then more comfortably share with the group. In addition, some participants may take their task sheets home as a reminder of some of the things they learned in the group. Similar to the general instructions outlined in Chapter 5, it is best to have either individual members or family units (determined by the specific instructions for each technique) go around the circle in order and share their responses to the disclosure requested on the task sheet. This method of eliciting groupwide sharing helps to establish balanced participation in a beginning group. Also, some task sheets may be answered anonymously by members, as indicated in the specific instructions, and in these cases the facilitator will collect the sheets and share the groupwide responses in the session. It should be noted that this type of intervention can be effective with beginning groups since it is a nonthreatening way of introducing problem discussion. In addition, this method of sharing can help members start to feel they are not alone with their problems before they openly discuss their own difficulties in more direct terms.

It will be important that both during and at the completion of each intervention facilitators point out commonalities among the membership and reinforce participation. Such processing comments will contribute to the development of a cohesive and trusting group. Moreover, leaders may want to request the participants to process their response to the intervention after hearing all the membership's sharing. This request may surface some interesting and helpful feedback about the ongoing development of trust in a group.

Modification of some interventions will be necessary due to the age span among members of any one multiple family therapy group. This author has attempted to design techniques that are relevant and developmentally appropriate for a wide span of ages. However, it is impossible to create interventions that will be effective for all possible ages of group participants. Therefore, readers are strongly encouraged to modify or change interventions so they will be effective for their particular MFGT program. Also, facilitators should feel free to ask family members to assist younger members who might have difficulty with some tasks. Such assistance can serve some important therapeutic value as family members relate more positively to one another. Or, another example might be a teen who only relates well to a younger sibling and such assistance provides some positive reinforcement for this family member.

Readers are reminded to always remember that one of the unique strengths of MFGT is the mixing of at risk family members with healthier members. Sometimes the strengths from these latter individuals can be used to increase the effectiveness of a particular intervention. For example, if an at risk teen cannot articulate how to effectively share his or her anger with a teacher in school, a sibling might be able to point out some possible responses to his younger or older sibling. Facilitators of MFGT that focus on at risk adolescents and their families will find it immensely helpful to elicit feedback from other teens in the group. Adolescents are more likely to listen and respond to such teens who often have important skills and knowledge to share and model.

The remaining contents of this chapter will be a listing of psychoeducational interventions with related task sheets. Readers are encouraged to review this entire chapter before planning their multiple family groups. In addition, the planning guidelines provided in Chapter 4 will serve as additional guidelines for the timing and facilitation of these interventions.

TECHNIQUE 26

Title of Intervention: A Closer Look at a Family Problem
Purpose: To increase participants' awareness of the details surrounding their most concerning family problems.
Specific Instructions: Facilitators will want to prepare a short introductory presentation on the importance of specifying a family problem, particularly when considering the number of individuals often involved in the problem. Then the sheet titled *A Closer Look at a Family Problem* is passed out to each member. Participants are requested to anonymously complete this form with their ideas on how to breakdown a current problem of their family. Members should be cautioned to not indicate their name or the names of any family members when completing this task sheet. Once everyone is ready the task sheets are collected by the facilitator. At this point the group leader reviews the problems from each sheet and then tallies them by using a blackboard or newsprint pad. This method then provides the membership an overview of the problems reported. Once all the problems from all sheets have been indicated on the master list, the facilitator should pose some discussion questions that probe the participants' response to both the summary and breakdown of problems. Such discussion questions could include but are not limited to: What is your reaction to this master list of family problems? How do you feel now about your family problems after seeing this groupwide disclosure? What do you see as commonalities

among the members of this group from this exercise? What awareness or insight did you gain from breaking down your family problem in more detail? What do you see is the value of knowing more of the details regarding a family problem?

Related Task Sheet: A Closer Look at a Family Problem

Cautions and Possible Modifications: This is a nonthreatening and comfortable way to introduce the delineation of a family problem in a MFGT program. Often this technique allows members to become aware of one another's problems without the need to know who revealed what problems. In addition, this makes the group setting feel safe such that members see it as a place where they will be able to more directly talk about their difficulties in future sessions. This intervention is also a particularly good one for families where there are high levels of conflict, which is often the case when there are issues involving at risk adolescents. Facilitators are reminded that younger children in a MFGT program may require some assistance in completing the task sheet for this intervention. It is strongly advised that a co-facilitator, rather than a family member, assist the youngster so that the child can feel he or she can honestly reveal their view of the family's problems. Clinicians will often find that it is the youngest member of a family who has the most perspective about what is happening within their unit.

TECHNIQUE 27

Title of Intervention: Trash Your Problems

Purpose: To increase participants' disclosure of the most troubling problems in their current lives.

Specific Instructions: It is a good idea to start this session with a short presentation on the impact those very troubling problems have on our lives. Facilitators may want to conduct this part of the meeting by having the group membership brainstorm the type of impact (physical, emotional, work or school life, relationships, self-worth, etc.) very upsetting problems can have on their lives. It will be important to emphasize that everyone is different and so the ways such serious problems affect individuals can vary greatly. In addition, the same person can react very differently depending on the problem and other circumstances in their lives. The primary objective of this presentation and/or brainstorm discussion is to help the group understand the affect that a troubling issue can have on their lives. Next, the facilitator passes out a blank sheet of paper to all members and requests them to think of a very upsetting problem they are currently experiencing and would like to have solved. Then the membership is told that this exercise will provide them an opportunity to anonymously write down their problem, wad up their sheets into a ball, and then throw the wadded up ball into a trashcan in the center of the circle. It is important to ask members not to use their name or any other name so no one will know that a particular problem was one they wrote down. After everyone has written down their problem and wadded up their sheets, the facilitator starts by throwing their own ball into the trashcan and then has all members do the same by proceeding around the circle in order. After everyone has thrown their ball, the group leader picks up each ball and reads the problem that was written down. After all sheets have been read out loud, participants should be asked some processing questions. Such questions could be: How did it feel throwing away your problem? How did it feel having your problem read out loud to the group? What is your reaction to the combination of troubling problems that were read today? What did you enjoy about today's exercise? What have you learned from this sharing experience?

Related Task Sheet: Only blank sheets of paper for each participant.

Cautions and Possible Modifications: This is another nonthreatening way to introduce problem talk in a group. Often after a session where this intervention was utilized, members will spontaneously begin opening up about their problems in more direct terms. Similar to the family problem list exercise, this technique provides an opportunity for group members to see if they are not alone with their problems and to see how others react when their problem is shared anonymously in the group. If there are younger children present in a MFGT program, it may be necessary for a co-facilitator to offer assistance in helping the youngster to write out their problem. One way to modify this task and address this latter issue is to develop a troubling problem list that can just be checked off by members. Facilitators may find that this exercise does not take long to complete so this may be a session to have families continue to develop a trusting relationship by posing a number of disclosure questions that everyone answers.

TECHNIQUE 28

Title of Intervention: What Makes Children and Teens Resilient?

Purpose: To increase the parents' and teens' knowledge of what makes children or teens be resilient even during times of stress or serious difficulties.

Specific Instructions: Facilitators will want to review some of the reference material in Appendix E (References on Resiliency) to prepare and plan for this session. The material from these resources will be valuable in developing an outline of points to address when introducing the topic of resiliency to a MFGT program. The first part of this exercise can be a short but informative presentation on what is a resilient child or teen and why this is important for families to understand. After this presentation and possibly some discussion, facilitators will pass out the sheet titled *Picture of a Resilient Youth* to all participants. Members should then be requested to look over the information on this sheet that has been surfaced from many recent studies on resiliency among children and teens. Each child and teen in the group is then directed to circle the one attribute they either have or would like to develop. Then the parents are requested to do the same based on what they remember about themselves as teenagers. The facilitator completes this same sheet for purposes of modeling and begins the sharing by disclosing what he or she circled on the sheet. This same sharing continues around the circle in order. At the end of this disclosure, members should be asked to process their reaction to this exercise. Examples of questions to pose could include: What did you learn or find most helpful about this discussion on resiliency or what is sometimes termed protective factors for youth? How do you feel after hearing what everyone in the group shared about either their resilient attributes or what they would like to possess? What did you like or enjoy about this exercise?

Related Task Sheet: Picture of a Resilient Youth

Cautions and Possible Modifications: Teaching families about protective factors for children or teens can be very helpful. This knowledge can provide parents with more guidance in seeing what attributes will be most important in helping their youngsters deal with the trials and tribulations of life. In addition, by having the parents and facilitator share during this same task, the children and teens can learn how adults in the group were able to handle some of the difficulties they faced as adolescents. Facilitators are cautioned to only allow each group member to circle one resiliency attribute even if they feel they possess other ones. The rationale for limiting this disclosure for each group member is it avoids the possibility that some participants may possess many protective factors while others have few or none from the list. It can also be informative to point out to a membership that even if we do not have many protective factors from the task sheet, this information can provide some important insight into the types of skills one will want to develop in order to more effectively face and overcome adversities in life. Also, in the case of younger children, it may be necessary for a co-facilitator to provide some assistance with the reading of the task sheet and helping the child to decide which attribute to circle. In addition, group leaders may want to prepare an easy and simple-to-follow hand-out packet on this topic because many families will find it relevant and something they will want to refer back to at a later point.

TECHNIQUE 29

Title of Intervention: Bibliotherapy for Familywide Understanding
Purpose: To increase members' knowledge of important issues related to the problems of at risk adolescents. Also, to increase members' knowledge of healthy coping responses to the problems of youth.
Specific Instructions: Facilitators should select a book or article from the bibliotherapy references listed in Appendix F for this exercise. It will be important to select material on a problem topic that is relevant to most of the family units in any one group. Typically the targeted problem area being addressed by the group will provide guidance for this selection. For example, if the MFGT program is targeting adolescents and their families who are dealing with substance abuse issues, then a section of a book or article on this topic would be most appropriate. The material selected should be easy and simple to follow since a wide age group of members will be asked to read it. Leaders can either give out the reading material to the group members in the session before this one or can give it out in the same session and provide time for everyone to read it. Once all members have read the material facilitators should pose discussion questions that are individualized to

the material that was assigned. During this part of the session any number or combination of instructive strategies can be used such as short lectures, brainstorming discussions, question-and-answer periods, or sharing of real-life examples that relate to the reading material. At the end of this session it will be valuable to process members' response to this type of intervention and if they found it helpful to probe for specifics as to why it was helpful.

Related Task Sheet: No task sheet but instead refer to the bibliotherapy reference list found in Appendix F (Bibliotherapy References).

Cautions and Possible Modifications: Many group members will benefit from reading relevant material related to the problems they are currently facing. It will be important that the reading assigned is easy to follow particularly with the wide age range in the group. In addition, many at risk teens may have reading difficulties and so it is critical that the majority of participants can easily read and comprehend the material provided. In some cases, a book may be so valuable on a relevant problem topic that a facilitator suggest that families buy their own copy. The reading piece selected should address both the critical issues related to the targeted problem and some healthy coping responses. Facilitators should remember that several participants will be more likely to understand and remember reading material when it involves real-life stories.

TECHNIQUE 30

Title of Intervention: Self-rating on a Standardized Scale and Discuss
Purpose: To increase participants' awareness of various attitudes, feelings, or behaviors they are experiencing that can impact their problem coping skills.
Specific Instructions: Facilitators will have to determine a standardized scale that would be most relevant to the members of their MFGT program. There is a long list of possibilities but one suggested scale that is usually relevant to all group members is the *Life Change Index Scale* that was developed by Thomas Holmes and can be found in the book titled *The Mind Test* by Rita Aero and Elliot Weiner (1981, New York: William Morrow and Company). This same book contains a number of other scales that are intended to be self-administered and scored, which

may also be possible selections. There is also an adolescent form of a stress test (*Identifying Stress*) in the book titled *Building a Positive Self-Esteem: 113 Activities for Adolescents* by Marjorie Jacobs, Blossom Turk, and Elizabeth Horn (1988, Portland, Maine: Weston Walch, Publisher). The purpose of these two scales is to allow members to more objectively measure their stress level. The session begins with copies of the selected scale being passed out to all members. Then enough time is allowed so all participants can complete their scale and begin looking over their scoring results. Once everyone is ready the facilitator poses some discussion questions to probe members' responses to this awareness exercise. Rather than asking members to share the score they attained on the scale, it is best to have them process their reactions to that score and to completing the scale. After the group has completed their discussion on the scale results, the facilitator should shift the discussion in the group to ways members can address some of the concerns that surfaced around the scale results. This is an excellent opportunity to have group participants look at issues from the perspective of: What do I have control over? What do I not have control over? At the end of the session it is a good idea to process members' responses to this particular intervention.

Related Task Sheet: Copies of the standardized scale selected for this exercise.

Cautions and Possible Modifications: By having group members take a standardized scale and score their results facilitators can surface some increased awareness that may help participants in their overall functioning and coping. One of the challenges with this intervention is finding a standardized measure that can be administered to the wide range of ages often present in a MFGT program. Therefore, facilitators may need to take some time to carefully research and select a scale. Also, the *Life Change Test* could actually be answered by an entire family unit due to the nature of this instrument. Then each family unit would have one score and they can then share their reactions to the results. If a scale is selected that may be difficult for younger children, group leaders can either offer assistance to the involved youngsters or provide them an alternative task that is related to the topic area of the scale. For example, if the instrument is measuring stress levels, then the children can be asked to draw a picture of what stress looks like in their lives. One caution that facilitators should make to their members is that many standardized scales should only be administered by professionals who are trained in the scoring and interpretation of the results. For this reason, it is not a good idea to suggest to members any other sources that might contain scales. Rather, facilitators should select a scale and only bring copies of that instrument to a group to use for this exercise.

TECHNIQUE 31

Title of Intervention: Fun and Free Family Activities

Purpose: To increase families' awareness of activities they can enjoy as a family unit, particularly ones that would be acceptable to teenagers.

Specific Instructions: This is a brainstorming technique where the facilitator starts off the task by asking group members what they do or have done as a family to have fun together. It may very well be that there is limited discussion in response to this question. Some of the reason for this lack of response will often be related to the recent stress in family units that resulted in their attendance to the group. Next, the facilitator requests that the group members have a brainstorming session where they think of all the fun and free activities families with teenage members can have together. It will be helpful to write these suggestions on a blackboard or newsprint pad so all the group can view these ideas. At the end of this sharing, family units are asked to take some time and talk among themselves to determine which activity idea they would be willing to plan on a specific date. Once all families have completed this decision making, a representative from each family unit is asked to share with the entire group the activity they have planned. Hopefully, these activities will take place by the next multiple family group session so that there can be some follow-up discussion as to the family's response to the activity.

Related Task Sheet: No task sheet required, only a blackboard or newsprint pad to list ideas.

Cautions and Possible Modifications: This is an excellent activity for families to discuss the ways they can have fun as a family unit. Often families have to think more carefully and creatively when planning family time that involves their teenage members. As a result, the group members can be invaluable to one another in coming up with clever ideas of how families at this stage of their lives can still have fun as a unit. Moreover, this type of discussion can include the benefits of families having regular fun times together. For some groups, it may be helpful to type up the list of ideas brainstormed and then distribute copies at the next group meeting to all the family units.

TECHNIQUE 32

Title of Intervention: A Recipe for a Hardy Family

Purpose: To increase group members' awareness of what qualities help family units be resilient even in times of severe stress.

Specific Instructions: Facilitators start this technique by giving a brief overview of resiliency studies on families. A good reference for material on this presentation would be McCubbin, McCubbin, and Thompson's (1997) article titled *Families Under Stress: What Makes Them Resilient?* Often it will be necessary for facilitators to define resiliency for the participants when doing this presentation. Then the task sheet titled *A Recipe for a Hardy Family* is passed out to each participant. Members are asked to review this sheet and check off those recipe ingredients they feel their family possesses. One member from each family collects the sheets from all their relatives and then tallies up the responses. In cases where there are some conflicting perspectives, family members doing this tally of response should be directed to indicate this situation when they share their familywide response to this task sheet. After family units finish these sheets, one member from each family, going around the circle in order, reports on their family's responses to the sheet. It is important that facilitators point out commonalities among family units and reinforce the sharing. After all family units have shared their responses, facilitators can request the group to discuss ways families can acquire some of the protective factors that make families more resilient.

Related Task Sheet: A Recipe for a Hardy Family

Cautions and Possible Modifications: This intervention is an excellent nonthreatening way for families to learn how they can be more resilient even in the most difficult of times. In some cases, families may possess the qualities to be resilient but have not utilized those strengths in more recent times. For such families, it will be helpful to have a discussion on the advantages of having used some protective factors in the past and then utilizing them again on a more regular basis. This particular psychoeducation technique can increase knowledge that will be helpful to families for both current and future coping situations. Readers are again referred to Appendix E for references on resiliency among at risk youth and families.

TECHNIQUE 33

Title of Intervention: Typical Problems of Teenagers and Parents of Teenagers

Purpose: To increase members' awareness of typical problems among both parents of teenagers and teenagers.

Specific Instructions: The two check-off sheets titled *What Is a Normal Teenager Today?* and *What Is a Normal Parent of a Teenager?* are passed out to each member. Facilitators then instruct the group that these two sheets contain typical problems or qualities that parents of teenagers or teenagers themselves possess. Everyone is then requested to anonymously complete the check-off titled *What Is a Normal Parent of a Teenager?* based on either their view of themselves (i.e., the parents in the group) or their view of their parents (i.e., teens in the group). Then the facilitator collects two different piles of these sheets, ones completed by parents and ones completed by teens. Next, the contents of these check-off lists are read and tallied on the blackboard with one list from parents' perspective and one list from teen members' perspective. As this information is being surfaced it is important that facilitators acknowledge commonalities that surface in the group. Once both lists have been completed on the board, members are asked to discuss their reactions to the findings that were surfaced. Once this discussion has been completed this same method is used with the sheet titled *What Is a Normal Teenager Today?* Again facilitators will want to point out commonalities that surface and elicit a groupwide discussion in response to the two lists generated from parents and teens in the group.

Related Task Sheet: Two task sheets titled *What Is a Normal Parent of a Teenager?* and *What Is a Normal Teenager Today?*

Cautions and Possible Modifications: This is an excellent validating exercise for both parents and teens in a MFGT program. Just by the mere fact that the problems have been listed for parents and then teens provides some critical reinforcement that many problems that family units in the group struggle with on a daily basis are common to most families. By presenting this information in this format, group participants are often able to understand the common problems faced by families who have children going through their adolescent years. When surfacing this awareness, facilitators do not want to disregard the severity of some family units' problems. Rather the important message here should be that some of the issues faced by these families are common ones that many families experience in this stage of the family life cycle. At the same time, facilitators want to acknowledge that there are some issues or problems that families face that are beyond the usual ones that require services like counseling.

TECHNIQUE 34

Title of Intervention: How Families Can Always be Upset and in Conflict!

Purpose: To increase participants' awareness of common ways families find themselves constantly upset or in conflict with one another.

Specific Instructions: This is a fun and humorous way for participants to learn how families often end up being in a constant state of conflict with one another. Facilitators begin this intervention by asking the membership to discuss, without referring to their personal experiences or families, how families can be in lots of conflict. The ideas generated from this discussion should be listed on a blackboard or newsprint pad so the group can review the complete list. If it is difficult to get this type of discussion going then facilitators may want to provide stimulating material by indicating aspects of family functioning that can cause such states of stress like communication problems, lack of positive interchanges, disrespect for one another, and so on. Depending on the group, facilitators may want to ask members to then share which of the points listed would apply to times when their family has been in lots of conflict. During all these discussions it will be important that facilitators reinforce disclosure and commonalities that surface among the membership.

Related Task Sheet: None required, just a blackboard or newsprint pad.

Cautions and Possible Modifications: This can be a comfortable way for a group to begin discussing some of the causes or results of families being in a constant state of conflict. By directing this more light-hearted type of discussion, facilitators may find that participants can more comfortably share their ideas of what puts families into states of conflict and stress. As the ideas are suggested for this task, participants can be given some relevant instruction by the group leader which expands on these points and shows which parts of family conflict are within family members' control. Facilitators may choose to type up the responses to these discussion questions so copies can be distributed to the membership at the next meeting. In fact, such material could be presented as a checklist so families can refer to it when they find themselves in a state of lots of conflict and want to identify how they can stop it.

TECHNIQUE 35

Title of Intervention: 1–2–3–4 for Family Conflict Resolution!
Purpose: To increase participants' problem-solving skills.
Specific Instructions: The task sheet titled *1–2–3–4 for Family Conflict Resolution!* is passed out to each member. Then the facilitator provides a brief lecture on the steps to problem solving that help families identify and then resolve their conflicts. After providing this presentation with some examples, the group is asked if each family unit will take a few minutes to think of a very small problem they are having and then go through each of the four steps on the sheet to determine a resolution. Co-facilitators may want to go around to each family unit to see if they need any assistance in completing this part of the task. Once every family has completed a sheet on a small problem they all agreed on, a representative from each family is asked to share with the entire group the contents of their problem resolution sheet. This sharing continues around the circle in order until all families' task sheets have been shared. As families' problem resolution has been shared, facilitators can use the surfaced disclosure to further clarify or expanded on effective ways to resolve family conflict.
Related Task Sheet: 1–2–3–4 for Family Conflict Resolution!
Cautions and Possible Modifications: Many at risk adolescents and their families will appreciate knowing concrete steps to follow in resolv-

ing their conflicts. One of the challenges is that in some situations, what presents as a problem for a family may actually be a symptom for an underlying problem. For this reason, the problem addressed by each family unit should be a minor one since there will not be any helping professional involved initially in determining ways to resolve it. By having families work on a small agreed-upon problem, they begin to learn new skills in working together to resolve other more serious problems.

TECHNIQUE 36

Title of Intervention: Healthy Grieving for Families
Purpose: To increase participants' knowledge of the implications of unresolved grieving and resolved grieving on familywide functioning.
Specific Instructions: Facilitators begin this task by introducing the topic of grieving and its impact on family life. A short presentation can be given at this point in the group on the five stages of the grieving process using material from references like Kübler-Ross' book titled *On Death and Dying* (1969, New York, The Macmillan Company). This information can provide participants an overview of the healthy stages an individual goes through in resolving a significant loss. Then the facilitator moves the discussion to the implications of unresolved and resolved grieving on familywide functioning. The related task sheet titled *Healthy Grieving for Families* is passed out to assist in this part of the presentation. As the reader will note on this sheet the left column contains familywide impact when one or more family members does not reach a healthy resolution in the grieving process. Then in the right column are the familywide implications when all family members have attained a healthy resolution to the grieving process. The facilitator can go over the material on this instructional sheet to enhance the lecture/discussion for this session. In addition, members can be urged to keep the task sheet as something they can refer back to when issues around grieving are relevant for their family. If a participant is willing to share a personal grieving experience at any point during this task, this type of disclosure could assist in participants' understanding of the importance of healthy grieving for an entire family unit.
Related Task Sheet: Healthy Grieving for Families
Cautions and Possible Modifications: This particular task often sur-

faces some very relevant issues for group members since most families who have at risk adolescents have experienced some amount of grieving regarding dreams and hopes they had for those members. In some groups it may actually be a good idea to spend some time discussing what experiences could cause one to go through a grieving process. Many participants may only think of grieving in terms of the loss of a loved one to death. It is very important that members are assisted in understanding that grieving can involve any number of losses and what might be a loss for one family member may not be for another member. Facilitators are cautioned not to surface current unresolved grieving among any members since a group may not be ready to deal with such a situation. Instead, it may be better for the facilitator to share a personal resolved grieving experience or ask parents in the group to share times when their families of origin experienced grieving.

TECHNIQUE 37

Title of Intervention: Don't Worry–Act Out Your Worst Fear!
Purpose: To increase members' awareness of some of their worst fears in regard to any number of relevant issues.
Specific Instructions: It is best that facilitators provide a more limited focus to this intervention by determining a common concern among the membership that may be related to the targeted problem focus of the group. For example, if the group is addressing substance abuse issues of the at risk adolescents then the area of concern could be fears that participants have in regard to substance abuse by a family member. Once this focus has been given to the group, participants are informed that they will have an opportunity to role-play some of their worst fears regarding substance abuse by a family member or oneself (in the case of the at risk adolescent). Next, members are given a blank sheet of paper where they are requested to take a few moments and write out their worst fear in regard to the targeted problem area. Once everyone has completed this part of the intervention, the facilitator asks everyone to go around the circle and share this worst fear. After this disclosure is completed, the members should be asked if anyone is willing to role-play in the group this worst fear scene. Once someone has volunteered, the facilitator helps set up the role-play by having the member repeat

their worst fear, getting other group members to take parts in the role-play, and then having the actors act out the scene. At the end of the role-play (time length will vary depending on situation being posed) the facilitator should ask the member who shared his or her worst fear to process how they feel after having acted out this worst fear. It will also be important to elicit other members' response to both acting in the role-play and being observers. Facilitators will need to make sure they have fully processed role-plays since this part of the task will be more important than making sure everyone role-plays his or her worst fear. Many of the feelings surfaced by the volunteer member will be similar to what other members will also learn when they face their worst fears.

Related Task Sheet: No task sheet but blank paper for each member.

Cautions and Possible Modifications: This intervention can be an excellent method for helping group members surface some of their worst fears in regard to the particular problem area. It will also serve to help various family members understand how each member feels in regard to a troubling situation like substance abuse. Facilitators will want to reinforce disclosure by members and commonalities that surface during the sharing part of this task. There is much to be gained by members sharing their worst fears even if time does not allow for role-playing out each participant's scene. Many participants will feel better by just having shared what they often keep to themselves and/or experience obsessive thoughts regarding such fears. This task serves to surface some feelings that are often not shared in families and remain unknown. Fears are important to surface since they also provide insight into some of the other feelings family members are experiencing but not sharing with one another.

TECHNIQUE 38

Title of Intervention: Our Family Values versus the Jones' Family Values

Purpose: To increase family units' awareness of their own values and the ongoing struggles they have in maintaining those values.

Specific Instructions: The task sheet titled *Our Family Values versus the Jones' Family Values* is passed out to each member at the onset of this intervention. Members are informed that in the session the discussion will focus on the values of each family unit and how the greater society does not always support those values. The facilitator uses the material on this task sheet to conduct a brief presentation and discussion on the typical struggles families experience in trying to maintain their values. After this discussion members are requested to complete the bottom of this task sheet where they indicate their current family values and values they wish their family endorsed. Once everyone has completed this part of the task sheet, a member from each family unit volunteers to collect these sheets and share their familywide responses. It is important that when this sharing is done members are asked to not reveal any family names associated with the responses given. After each family unit has had their responses read, members should be asked what they found helpful or informative about this exercise.

Related Task Sheet: Our Family Values versus the Jones' Family Values

Cautions and Possible Modifications: This task is an excellent opportunity for families to consciously think about their value system. In families with at risk adolescents, this issue is particularly relevant since teens' mobility and developmental stage often cause them to experience even more conflicts between their family values and their peers' values. Facilitators may also find it helpful to point out to members that one's values directly influence how we each think and act. Therefore, it is essential that families talk in more direct terms about what each member views as their familywide value system. This type of disclosure may be quite informative to family units since in many instances they may never have talked about their values.

TECHNIQUE 39

Title of Intervention: Are You Hearing Me Now?

Purpose: To increase participants' knowledge of effective family communication skills.

Specific Instructions: At the onset of this technique, members are each given a copy of the task sheet titled *Are You Hearing Me Now?* Next, participants are asked to look over the instructions for this sheet that request that everyone circle those words that describe qualities they like from a person that they would define as a good listener. After everyone has completed this sheet, members are asked to go around the circle in order to share their responses to this sheet. It will be important to point out commonalities that surface during this sharing particularly those disclosures that are similar among members from the same family unit. At the end of this disclosure, participants should be asked to think of one communication skill they would like to improve when they talk and listen to others based on the earlier discussion. Then the group is asked to go around the circle while each participant shares in regard to this question. During all these sharing periods in the group, facilitators can provide instruction that further enhances the disclosure by members or points out some additional instructional material to members.

Related Task Sheet: *Are You Hearing Me Now?*

Cautions and Possible Modifications: Communication is a key to families working through their problems, regardless of the issues being addressed. Therefore, teaching entire family units good communication skills can be invaluable in helping families to learn more effective ways to resolve their problems. This is often a particularly challenging issue for families with teens since communication often becomes strained during these very difficult parenting years. Facilitators will find that both parents and teens will feel validated when their peers share some of the same perspectives on good communication qualities. Members should be encouraged to hang onto the task sheet since it can provide some reminders of what are effective listening and communication skills. In some groups, facilitators may find that spending more than one session on communication skills can be valuable to the involved participants.

TECHNIQUE 40

Title of Intervention: Whose Job Is It Anyways?

Purpose: To increase family members' awareness of the breakdown of who does which chores within their households.

Specific Instructions: The task sheet titled *Whose Job Is It Anyways?* is passed out to each participant. The facilitator uses this sheet as a springboard to introduce a discussion about the breakdown of who does which jobs within each family unit's household. Members are asked to take some time to indicate on this task sheet who in their family takes primary responsibility for doing each listed chore. Participants should be encouraged to add chores to this sheet that are not listed and also indicate who does those additional chores. Once everyone has finished their task sheet, family units should be given time together so they can compare and tally how each member viewed who completed each of their household chores. After this compiling of the results for each family is completed, one member from each unit is asked to volunteer and share the familywide view of who does which chores. Facilitators will want to reinforce this disclosure and commonalities that surface among the various family units. After each family's responses have been shared, participants should be asked to process their feelings in regard to this task. It will be particularly important to probe members and see if the exercise increased their knowledge of who does which chores and how balanced chore responsibilities are in their household.

Related Task Sheet: Whose Job Is It Anyways?

Cautions and Possible Modifications: Families benefit from this direct discussion about how the chores in their household are broken down. It is often an eye-opening experience for the family to realize that sometimes one family member is doing most of the chores. In addition, parents of at risk teens may tend to not expect as much from these adolescents due to the resulting difficulties in getting them to follow through with chores. Surfacing this material will serve as excellent discussion points since some families may begin to realize that teens need to be expected to also share in chore duty. In addition, mothers in some families will be seen as those individuals who take on the majority of household chores. It will be important to process both the mothers' and other family members' responses to this awareness. Facilitators may want to take some time during this exercise to point out some of the problems that result in families where the chore duty is not balanced across family members. Moreover, this task may also surface areas of conflict between spouses, particularly if one spouse is carrying the load of household chores. Facilitators are cautioned to provide assistance to families as they share and tally up their responses to this chore breakdown task sheet. This discussion within some family units may surface some conflicts that require outside assistance.

TECHNIQUE 41

Title of Intervention: Drawing Boundary Lines for Healthy Family Functioning

Purpose: To increase participants' awareness of healthy boundary lines within family units.

Specific Instructions: The facilitator begins this task by asking the membership what they think it means to have boundaries within a family. As members' respond to this question, material on family boundaries can be provided to the group. Lecture material for this part of the task can be found in Goldenberg and Goldenberg's book titled *Family Therapy: An Overview* (2000, 5th edition) where the subject of family boundaries is addressed in several chapters but particularly the one on the structural family therapy model. It will be helpful to use a blackboard or newsprint pad to draw out healthy family subsystem boundaries that could include marital couples, sibling units, and extended family units. Beyond the identification of these subsystems, it will be important to point out some of the practical implications of families maintaining healthy boundaries. It will also be useful to point out some common problems in families that do not maintain healthy boundaries.

Related Task Sheet: No task sheet but use of a blackboard or newsprint pad.

Cautions and Possible Modifications: Psychoeducational material and related discussion on healthy family boundaries can be very relevant and helpful to at risk adolescents and their families. Sometimes it will be apparent in a MFGT program that some family units have generational patterning problems in regard to family boundaries. In other words, parents in the group may have had some unhealthy modeling from their family of origin around this issue. Therefore, this exercise can be an eye-opening experience for both the parent and teen members of the family units represented in the group. It is extremely important that facilitators are able to point out some of the obvious results of families that have healthy boundaries and those that do not. In addition, this is another task where problems between the marital units may surface since frequently couples who are having marital stresses may turn to their children and involve them in roles that are not appropriate for them within the family unit.

TECHNIQUE 42

Title of Intervention: Brainstorm Ways to Build Family Members' Self-Esteem

Purpose: To increase participants' knowledge of ways families can help members develop more positive self-esteem.

Specific Instructions: This is a brainstorming intervention where participants are asked to think of ways that families can build their members' self-esteem. If a group has difficulty initially coming up with ideas in response to this request, it may be beneficial to have participants take some time to think of ways individuals can build this self-esteem. These contributions should be listed on a blackboard or large newsprint pad so members can continue to provide new ideas and view what points have already been made in the group. In cases where the discussion begins with ideas for building individuals' self-esteem, it will be necessary to have the group then connect how these suggestions can be implemented by family members or families as whole units. Facilitators may choose to provide some groups with a short presentation on ways to build self-esteem as a way to begin this brainstorming exercise. Material for such a lecture can be found in books like *Project Self-Esteem* by Peggy Beilen and Sandy McDaniel (1986) published by Pro-ed and *Self-Esteem Enhancement with Children and Adolescents* by Alice Pope (1988) published by Pergamon.

Related Task Sheet: No task sheet is required for this exercise but it will be helpful to have either a blackboard or large newsprint pad to write on for listing brainstorming ideas.

Cautions and Possible Modifications: This is an excellent intervention for eliciting participants' thoughts and ideas for building self-esteem among family members. Also, facilitators will find that this exercise provides an opportunity to discuss with a MFGT program the importance of everyone having a solid positive self-esteem. It may even be helpful to have a group discuss the impact that such self-esteem has both for the individual and for a family unit as a whole. If time permits, facilitators may want to add to this discussion by having each participant write his or her name on a 3 x 5 card and then passing it around the circle so others can provide feedback about that individual's strengths and positive personality qualities. Once all the cards have gone around the circle they are returned to the members and participants can then be asked to share their reaction to the feedback on these cards. This additional exercise will take some time in a MFGT but may be well worth the investment since such feedback is often not provided to individuals directly. Also, the feedback received on these cards will vary since some will be provided by folks who have just met one another in the group while other feedback provided on these cards will be from family members who will know one another more intimately.

TECHNIQUE 43

Title of Intervention: Living with Change, Challenges, and the Need for New Game Plans

Purpose: To increase participants' awareness that being open to change and having back-up plans will be very important to living a happy life.

Specific Instructions: The task sheet titled *Disappointments, Coping responses, and Opportunities for Growth* is passed out to each member. Participants are requested to take a few moments to fill out this form, indicating a past disappointment in their life, their coping response, and what they gained or learned from that experience. Members should be instructed that they will not have to share all their responses on this sheet with the group but rather only the parts they want to share. This will be a particularly important point since some members may not want to share a disappointment that they have had with other members of their family. Once everyone has completed their task sheets, members are asked to share the types of coping responses they have used in the past in regard to a disappointment in life or a challenge that interfered with their goals or plans. As these coping responses are shared, the facilitator may want to list them on a blackboard and also provide some additional points as a way of further enhancing this sharing around effective ways that we cope with disappointments in our life. After this discussion is completed, members are then asked to share what opportunity for growth or learning they gained from these disappointing experiences in life. This sharing proceeds in the same manner until the facilitator feels that the group has completely shared their ideas in regard to this request. Throughout this sharing by group members, leaders can provide helpful and relevant instruction on the importance of learning to be flexible and open to change so that one can instead learn and grow from such an experience.

Related Task Sheet: Disappointments, Coping Responses, and Opportunities for Growth

Cautions and Possible Modifications: This is an excellent intervention when working with at risk adolescents and their families. Raising teenagers often involves parents giving up on some of their goals for their kids because this is a time when it becomes increasingly clear that adolescents need to separate and individuate from their parents. In addition, many at risk teens have had to already deal with several disappointments in life, which can be very challenging and overwhelming. This exercise may surface some coping responses by adult members of the group or other siblings that will offer these teens some helpful ideas for developing more effective coping responses. It will be particularly important that participants walk away from this intervention realizing that everyone experiences some disappointments, losses, or other challenges in life that often result in changes to one's original goals or life plans. At the same time, it will be invaluable for members to also learn that some of the most upsetting disappointments in life often provide tremendous opportunities for growth.

TECHNIQUE 44

Title of Intervention: Try It Out and Report Back!

Purpose: To increase family units' skills in attempting new coping responses to a common problem that they face.

Specific Instructions: This intervention involves the development of an assignment for each family unit of a multiple family group. The session is started by asking each family to take a few minutes to discuss a problem that they have which impacts all members of their unit. During this discussion it may be helpful to have co-facilitators go around the group and provide assistance to families as they try to reach a consensus on what is a familywide problem they are currently experiencing. It will be particularly important that families are instructed not to determine a problem that they feel is only related to one family member. After all the family units have determined a shared problem that everyone feels they could help resolve, a volunteer from each family is asked to share their agreed-upon problem with the group. As these problems are shared, it will be important for the facilitator to reinforce the disclosure and point out commonalities that surface in the group. Next, the assignment sheet titled *Try It Out and Report Back!* is passed out to each participant. Members are then requested to indicate on their sheet what they are willing to do differently in an attempt to deal with the familywide problem. After everyone has completed this task sheet, one member of each family collects everyone's sheets. Then this same family member shares with the entire group what each member of their family is willing to do in response to resolving their problem. After each family unit's sheets have been read, the facilitator request other participants (not members of the family being presented) to indicate if they feel the familywide plan for responding to the problem seems realistic, equally shared by all members, and will be effective in resolving the difficulty they face. This same analysis by the group proceeds until each family unit's sheets have been read and responded to by the group. As the group makes suggestions or poses questions about familywide plans, it may be necessary to have family members modify their assignment. At the end of this part of the discussion, each participant should be requested to take their assignment sheet home (i.e., *Try It Out and Report Back!* sheet) so that before the next session they follow through with their commitment to a new coping response to their familywide problem. Then at the next session of the MFGT program all participants and family units are asked to report on the results of these assignments. In some groups this follow-up discussion may require most of the next session and so facilitators will want to plan accordingly.

Related Task Sheet: Try It Out and Report Back!

Cautions and Possible Modifications: This is an excellent technique for eliciting all members of a family to commit to a change behavior or new coping response regarding a familywide problem. It will be important that this exercise be planned after a MFGT program has met for few sessions because it may be too difficult for some family units to develop such a familywide response to a presenting problem. It may also be necessary to caution families to not select their most disturbing problem since there may be too much emotionality or stress present regarding such an issue. Rather families should be encouraged to consider something that is annoying or slightly upsetting to their family that could be worked on with little conflict being surfaced when discussing a familywide response to the problem. It is more important that a family learn to pull together such that each family member does their part to resolve a problem. The important learning goal is having each family unit experience the value of resolving a problem together, no matter how minor the problem may seem. By having families start with small issues, they will begin to build their skills and confidence that they can later tackle larger problems with the same familywide response. In addition, this intervention reinforces the importance of each member of a family doing his or her part to effectively cope with a presenting problem.

TECHNIQUE 45

Title of Intervention: Just Record and Watch
Purpose: To increase family units' awareness of their problems through utilization of a baseline assignment.
Specific Instructions: This technique starts with the task sheet titled *Just Record and Watch* being passed out to each participant. Members are then instructed to divide into subgroups with their family units to determine a problem they are experiencing that has been difficult to resolve. It may be necessary for co-facilitators to go around the group and offer assistance to families during this discussion. After the family units have completed this part of the task, one volunteer from each family is requested to share the problem that they feel has been very challenging. Next, the facilitator provides a brief presentation on the use of a baseline technique for more carefully observing and recording circumstances before, during, and after the identified problem occurs. Then members are asked to indicate on their task sheet the exact problem they will be observing (this should be the same for all members of the same family unit) over the next week. It will probably be necessary to again go around the circle to each family and clarify how they will be observing and recording a particular problem. At the end of this technique, each family member is asked to keep their own record over the next week (using the *Just Record and Watch* task sheet) of the problem identified. Members of each family are cautioned not to share the contents of their recording with one another during the week. Data from these **task** sheets are then brought back to the next session where facilitators will conduct a discussion on the results of this baseline technique,

with a particular emphasis on having individual family units compare their recordings and observations. The discussion at the next session on these observations may require the entire session and so facilitators will want to plan accordingly.

Related Task Sheet: Just Record and Watch

Cautions and Possible Modifications: The benefit of this assignment technique is that even the most troubling of family problems can be targeted for analysis since the baseline assignment requires no different responses from family members. Instead, this technique teaches families the value of watching and observing the circumstances around the occurrence of a particular problem that can often give them insight into possible solutions. This author found that about 75 percent of the families seen in parent skill training groups over a 5-year period resolved their parenting problems after a baseline assignment. Readers will be amazed how many families can resolve their own issues when they are instructed to more carefully observe and record events before, during, and after a particular problem surfaces. Hopefully, families can then utilize this same skill in resolving future problems that they encounter.

TECHNIQUE 46

Title of Intervention: Family Safety Issues

Purpose: To increase participants' awareness of safety issues that impact their families, including the value of a safe home and neighborhood.

Specific Instructions: This intervention begins with the task sheet titled *Family Safety Issues* being passed out to all members. Participants are then instructed to complete this sheet indicating places where they feel they have safety concerns for various family members or their entire family. At the bottom of this same sheet the reader will see that members should also be requested to finish the sentence completion that asks for ways they could better address some of their safety concerns for their family. After all members have completed their task sheets, one volunteer from each family collects the sheets and shares the familywide responses to this task sheet. Either at the beginning of this technique or after this sharing has been completed, facilitators may want to provide some instruction to the group on what the resiliency studies have found to be the value of a safe home and neighborhood for maintaining hardy families. Readers are referred to the McCubbin, McCubbin, and Thompson (1997) article fully referenced in Appendix E for material on this latter topic. At the end of this discussion, if time permits, participants can be asked to share some additional safety precautions they would like to add to their family life. During all discussions and sharing it will be important to reinforce disclosure and point out commonalities that surface.

Related Task Sheet: Family Safety Issues

Cautions and Possible Modifications: This is an important technique for helping families be more aware of safety concerns they have for their members. Parents of at risk adolescents often find that safety concerns for these youngsters weigh heavily on their minds on a daily basis. For this reason, probing parents' concerns around this issue may be validating and enlightening for all group members. It is also possible that during these discussions parents will recall safety concerns that they either had or did not have with their families of origin. Some of this disclosure may help families better understand the current importance they place on safety for their family. It is not uncommon that families in crisis may not monitor safety issues for their members as carefully. For this reason, it is extremely important for facilitators to emphasize the importance of maintaining safe environments for family members even during difficult times. Often times, leaders will be able to surface the importance of safe settings by probing for feelings from the youngest family members. If a group is able to discuss some safety plans they would like to add to their current family life, it would be helpful to spend some time having the group assist particular families in developing these plans.

TECHNIQUE 47

Title of Intervention: A...Each Week Keeps our Family Okay

Purpose: To increase participants' awareness of the activities or interactions that maintain their family as a happy functioning unit.

Specific Instructions: The task sheet titled *A...Each Week Keeps our Family Okay* is passed out to all participants who are given some time to complete their sheets. As the reader will see on these task sheets, members are asked to check off those activities or interactions that they have found make their family function more effectively each week when they are present. After everyone has completed this sheet, a volunteer from each family collects the sheets, tallies the results, and shares the family-wide responses to this task. As family members share this disclosure, facilitator will want to reinforce such sharing and point out commonalities that surface. It will also be important to address family members' responses to one another's check-off sheet. If time permits, a discussion regarding ways to maintain particular activities or interactions that surfaced will be helpful. Participants will benefit from learning ways to maintain critical activities and interactions in their lives. This type of discussion will be particularly helpful to families having an at risk adolescent member. As families go through various stages of family life (like raising teenagers) they often have to make modifications or changes in their lives. It will be critical to emphasize to parents that even though some family life changes are necessary, it is important to maintain some activities or interactions that help them function effectively on a daily and weekly basis.

Related Task Sheet: A…Each Week Keeps our Family Okay

Cautions and Possible Modifications: This is a good awareness exercise where all members of each family are able to contribute to what they perceive as essential activities or interactions that help their unit function smoothly. The wide range of ages among members of a MFGT program will be beneficial for this intervention. Family members in various positions will offer important insight into what they view as important to the healthy functioning of their family. It will be helpful at the end of this exercise to process members' response to this sharing and discussion.

TECHNIQUE 48

Title of Intervention: Family Relapse Prevention: Warning Signs and a Plan

Purpose: To increase participants' awareness of those warning signs that their family is regressing to a problematic level of functioning.

Specific Instructions: This intervention begins with the task sheet titled *Our Family Is in Trouble when…* is passed out to all participants.

Members are instructed to complete this sheet that requests that family members note the warning signs that their family is regressing to an unhealthy level of functioning. Participants should only complete the top half of this sheet that deals with warning signs. Once everyone has completed this first half of their sheet, members go around the circle in order and share their perceptions of these warning signs. After this sharing has been completed, members are asked to go back and complete the bottom half of the same task sheet that asks participants to think of ways to respond to these warning signs that will stop the regression in their familywide functioning. After everyone has completed the bottom half of this sheet, a volunteer from each family is asked to collect these sheets and share the various plans that are suggested by their family members. The group should be asked to pose questions and provide feedback to each family about these methods for responding to warnings signs after each familywide plan has been shared. At the end of this exercise it will be helpful to process group members' response to this technique.

Related Task Sheet: Our Family Is in Trouble When...

Cautions and Possible Modifications: This technique is a great awareness intervention that elicits family members to think about signs that indicate they are getting back into troubled times. Through this exercise families in a MFGT program can become more proactive in dealing with their problems by knowing the signs of regressive functioning and then having plans to stop that process. In addition, by having entire family units participate in this intervention, all members of each family unit can develop an agreed-upon approach for dealing with dysfunctional patterns that evolve in their families. This exercise and the related task sheet may require co-facilitator assistance with young children who may have difficulties reading or responding to the material on the sheet.

TECHNIQUE 49

Title of Intervention: Report Card on our Family
Purpose: To increase participants' awareness of the strengths of their families and the areas where they need to make some improvements.
Specific Instructions: The task sheet titled *Report Card on our Family* is

passed out to all members. Participants are asked to complete this report card on their current family functioning. Members should be requested to only note the grade they would give their family without mentioning why they indicated that grade. Once everyone has completed this task sheet, a volunteer from each family is asked to collect them, tally the grading results, and read the familywide report to the group. It will be important that the family member reading the grades given for each aspect of family life does not indicate who gave which grades. Facilitators will want to reinforce this sharing and note commonalities that surface during this disclosure. Next, participants should be asked to think of ways their families could improve their lower graded areas. As the membership seems ready, sharing in regard to this question should be conducted by going around the circle in order. At the end of this exercise members should be asked to process their reactions to this technique.

Related Task Sheet: Report Card on our Family

Cautions and Possible Modifications: It is usually best to utilize this technique after a group has met for several sessions. Facilitators want to be fairly sure that most family units will receive some good grades on this report card task sheet. At the same time, it is important that families' lower graded areas point out the parts of their functioning that need improvement. It is helpful to point out to the membership during this exercise that few family units would receive high grades on all areas of functioning. Also, this intervention will often surface different grade rating from family members on the same areas of functioning. In such cases, it may be helpful for the involved family units to process why these different grades were given for the same areas of functioning. This type of sharing can be very helpful in family members understanding one another's perceptions of their familywide functioning.

TECHNIQUE 50

Title of Intervention: Family Challenges in the 21st Century
Purpose: To increase participants' knowledge of the challenges that face most family units in the 21st century.
Specific Instructions: This is a brainstorming discussion where members are asked to think of challenges that face families in the 21st cen-

tury. It will be important to write the contributions made to this question on either a blackboard or large newsprint pad. Such a recording can help members see what points have already been made and also will provide a completed list at the end of this discussion. As members contribute to this sharing, facilitators can provide helpful instruction that further enhances the learning gained by the membership from this brainstorming exercise. After a list has been developed, the leader can ask the participants to process their reactions to all the challenges listed. Hopefully, members will note that they better understand why they feel some of the stress that they do on a daily basis. It will also be important that the facilitator shift some of this discussion to ways that families can effectively address these current challenges. This sharing can also be listed on the blackboard so members can see that there are ways to respond to these unique stresses of the 21st century.

Related Task Sheet: No task sheet required but use of a blackboard or large newsprint pad.

Cautions and Possible Modifications: This technique provides an opportunity for members to better understand some of the challenges that face families today. By surfacing awareness of these challenges, families can more effectively plan how they will address these stresses. In addition, this exercise often helps families see that some of their current difficulties are common to all families and have little to do with their particular family unit. Moreover, this intervention may reduce family members' tendencies to blame one another and instead, help them look at some of their challenges from a more objective perspective. It will be helpful to have groups process their reactions to this exercise at the end of the session.

SUMMARY

The reader was provided in this chapter an overview of the treatment goals for the initial phase of a MFGT program. The importance of attaining these initial phase treatment goals was emphasized since they set the stage for a group to move to the middle phase and begin addressing more specific and individualized treatment goals. In addition, the value of psychoeducation in multiple family group therapy programs was pointed out in this section of the book. Then 25 interventions were delineated for both the therapeutic instruction of group members and the determination of more specific family treatment goals that will be addressed in the middle phase. Specific directions for each intervention, along with related task sheets, were provided such that readers should be able to easily utilize the suggested techniques with their particular groups. The details provided for each technique listed in this chapter should also increase clinicians' ability to modify, change, and even create similar psychoeducational interventions.

A Closer Look at a Family Problem

Instructions: Think of a family problem you would like to see resolved and complete the requested details on that problem below.

How long has this problem existed?

☐ Less than 6 months
☐ About 1 year
☐ More than 1 year: specify_____

What are some important details regarding this problem?

_____
_____
_____
_____
_____
_____

How many family members view it as a problem?

☐ Everyone
☐ Just a few
☐ Only me

What are the chanced of your family resolving this problem?

☐ Not so good
☐ Guarded
☐ Fair
☐ Good

How will you feel if this problem is resolved? _____
_____
_____

Picture of a Resilient Youth

Instructions: Please look over the protective factors below that have been identified from studies of resilient youth. When directed by your group facilitator, circle one attribute that you either have or would like to have as a part of your personality. If you are a parent, circle the one attribute you had back when you were a teen.

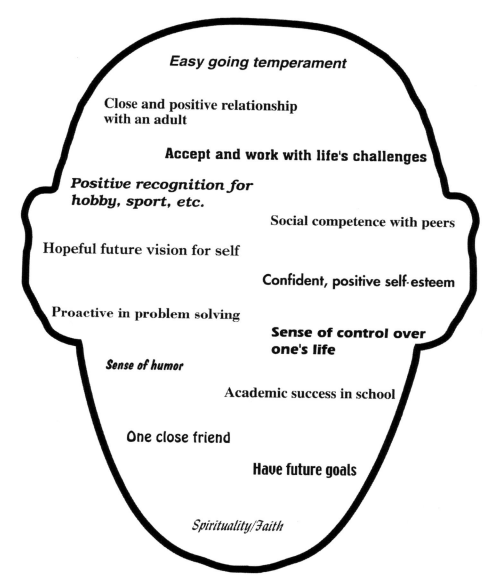

Easy going temperament

Close and positive relationship with an adult

Accept and work with life's challenges

Positive recognition for hobby, sport, etc.

Social competence with peers

Hopeful future vision for self

Confident, positive self-esteem

Proactive in problem solving

Sense of control over one's life

Sense of humor

Academic success in school

One close friend

Have future goals

Spirituality/Faith

*Please note that the above information is based on a combination of studies referenced in Appendix E.

A Recipe for a Hardy Family

Instructions: Please review the below checklist of those protective factors that studies have found help families stay hardy and resilient. Then check the ones that you feel your family currently possesses. You do not need to put your name on this sheet or indicate to anyone that these are your thoughts.

- ☐ Routines and consistency in family living (e.g., meals together, times for chores, attendance to a church or temple)

- ☐ One healthy, caring, and nurturing parent or other adult in the home

- ☐ Stable and safe home environment and neighborhood (both in terms of physical and emotional safety)

- ☐ Consistent discipline and supervision of children/teens from adults in home

- ☐ Faith affiliation or spirituality promoted in the family

- ☐ Availability and use of support system (including family, friends, coworkers, and neighbors)

- ☐ Family tradition, celebrations, and fun times together

- ☐ Effective family problem-solving skills

- ☐ Open communication among all members of the family

- ☐ Family hardiness: "We will survive as a unit and support one another."

Note: Above material is based on research by McCubbin, H., McCubbin, A. & Thompson, A. (1997). Families under stress: What makes them resilient? *Journal of Family and Consumer Sciences, 89*(3), 2–11.

What is a Normal Teenager Today?

Many researchers who have studied social/emotional development feel that adolescence today spans from as young as 10 years old to 20 years of age. Normal responses to this very turbulent time in development can include any or all of the following behavioral responses. Parents are reminded that extreme forms of the below behaviors may, however, be signs of more serious problems.

☐ Peers become all important in teens' lives.

☐ Control issues with adults are more frequent than at earlier ages.

☐ A search for identity may result in extreme forms of dress, tattoos, or body piercing.

☐ New and ever-changing interest in the opposite sex happens on almost a daily basis.

☐ Boys and girls can both become overly concerned about their appearance (taking long periods to shower and get dressed for the day).

☐ Sleeping in until late morning, particularly on nonschool days; daydreaming for long periods.

☐ May have frequent mood changes that appear unrelated to what is happening in their life.

☐ Shifts between childlike behavior and behavior that is almost at an adult level.

☐ Uncomfortable with body changes resulting in being shy, withdrawn from social situations, or have difficulty accepting compliments about one's appearance.

☐ May seem to enjoy arguments; much more curious about the reasons behind the various parts of our society.

☐ Starts to pull away from family-centered events; desire to be with peers instead.

☐ Struggles constantly for increased independence and has a need to try out new freedoms.

☐ May be more prone to take risks in various situations.

☐ Can be very talkative or go into periods of being very withdrawn.

*This list is by no means complete—many parents of normal teens will be able to easily add other observations.

What is a Normal Parent of a Teenager?

Parents also go through a number of changes as their children enter adolescence. Below is a list of some of their more common changes that can be quite challenging to their teens.

- ☐ Tend to be overprotective; they are learning how much freedom to give their teenager each year in this phase of development.

- ☐ They are eager to hear about their teen's daily activities and have trouble understanding the need for privacy.

- ☐ They worry, in some cases for good reasons, about the peers their son or daughter hangs around with at school or other places.

- ☐ They have trouble letting go during this age and so they may frequently get into control issues with their teenager.

- ☐ Sometimes their needs get confused with their teen's; at times they may want things for you that they did not have when they were a teen.

- ☐ They can go through a lost period when they start to realize their teenager would rather spend time with their peers than their family.

- ☐ They may not want the teen to grow up so quickly and may try to push childlike activities on them in an effort to slow down this process.

- ☐ They may start to feel their teen is no longer the same child; they may not realize that some of the phases teens go through will not last.

- ☐ Some parents may try to hang out with teens and their peers in an effort to still be involved in their teen's life.

- ☐ They may talk too much about all the changes a teen is going through; this may be their way of working through their responses to this new phase of development.

- ☐ Parents may become angry and withdrawn because of changes their teen is experiencing. They are working through the teen's need to separate and individuate.

- ☐ Parents may get into arguments about the rules at your home versus the rules at peers' homes. This is their way of saying they love you and want to make sure you are safe in other settings.

- ☐ They are almost constantly concerned about some of the more serious problems their teenager could confront like drug abuse, alcohol use, smoking, acquiring sexually related diseases, getting pregnant, or being places where there is violence.

1–2–3–4 for Family Conflict Resolution!

Instructions: Meet with the members of your family to determine a small problem everyone would like to resolve. Then follow the below steps to see if you can agree on a possible resolution.

1 State what the members of your family think is the problem. Avoid placing blame but rather focus on the details around the problem.

_____

_____

_____

_____

2 Think of all the possible ways to resolve this problem and list below.

_____

_____

_____

_____

3 Discuss the above suggested solutions to the problem with your family and write below the one everyone feels would be the best for attaining some resolution.

_____

_____

_____

_____

4 What is each family member willing to do in regard to this problem resolution plan?

_____

_____

_____

_____

Healthy Grieving for Families

Instructions: The contrasted impact on families of resolved grieving versus unresolved grieving is noted on the below table. This material will enhance the presentation on this topic by your facilitator.

Impact of Unresolved Grieving	Impact of Resolved Grieving
Family member or entire household feels depressed much of the time	Family still feels sadness about loss but most days is upbeat and back to normal affective state
Family members get into conflicts quickly and often do not resolve them	Family members have their differences but are able to resolve them as they arise
One or more family members are withdrawn from one another	Family members are fully engaged in their usual interactions with one another
Family has not engaged in their usual activities;social, church, work, etc.	Family is back involved in usual activities and maintains usual daily routines
Household and other task are difficult to complete on a regular basis	Family members can complete household tasks easily
Reluctance to celebrate usual holidays or former family traditions	Family continues to celebrate holidays and may make some modifications in family traditions due to the loss
Family finds it difficult finding joy or pleasure in usual life experiences	Family is able to enjoy experiences together and share in the pleasures of life
Family members lack energy for almost any activity or task	Family members are back to their usual energy levels
Family has difficulty talking about the loss or addressing their sadness	Family members can talk about the loss and continue to share their related sadness
Family members are fixated on the loss and continue to deny the reality that someone is gone or things have changed	Family members have their memories of times before the loss but are able to move on in their lives

Our Family Values versus the Jones' Family Values

Instructions: Below is the list of Common struggles families go through today in trying to maintain their values versus some of the values promoted in our society. This material will enhance the presentation provided by your facilitator in group.

Your Values	Families	Jones' Values
Enjoy process of life	Families	Enjoy products only
Healthy Dependence	Families	Excessive self-reliance
A season for everything	Families	Everything must be attained now
Be light-hearted about life, laugh and dream	Families	Always be based in reality
Success is personal happiness	Families	Money is success
Be happy with what you have	Families	Always seek more to be happy
Quiet heroism is fine	Families	You must be recognized for your successes
Being at peace comes from within	Families	Being at peace comes from outside oneself
The most important possession in life is caring and supportive family and friends	Families	The most important possessions are money, success, and recognition

Are You Hearing Me Now?

Instructions: Please circle the words or phrases below that best describes a person that you feel is a good listener.

Eye contact with you

Pays attention to what you are saying

Request clarification of some points

Validates your feelings

Shows interest by body language

Takes time to listen to you

Probes for more of your feelings or other details around the disclosure

Does not interrupt your sharing

Gives you their full attention

Questions you when unclear

Points out things you may have missed

Shows sensitivity to your feelings around the disclosure

Listens!

Does not judge you

Reinforces your strengths regarding disclosure

Provides a hug or smile when needed

Gives you time to fully share

Whose Job Is It Anyways?

Instructions: Please list in the right-hand column of the table below who in your household generally does the indicated chore.

Household Chore	Who usually does this chore?
Laundry	
Dishes	
House cleaning	
Takes out the trash	
Walks the dog or other pet duty	
Keeps bedroom clean	
Mows and maintains the grass/garden	
Maintains cars and other vehicles	
Pays the household bills	
Cooks the meals	
Provides transportation to children and teens to their activities	

What are other chores that need to be done at your household that are not listed above? Indicate who does each additional chore listed below.

_____

_____

_____

_____

Disappointments, Coping Responses, and Opportunities for Growth

Instructions: Indicate below a past disappointment you have had in your life, then write down the coping responses you used to deal with that disappointment (both healthy and unhealthy ones), and then indicate what you realize now is some positive growth you gained from having experienced that disappointment. You will be asked by your facilitator to share the parts of this task sheet that you feel comfortable sharing.

Think of a past disappointment in your life that you experienced and indicate it below.

_____

_____

_____

_____

What were the coping responses you used to deal with this disappointment?

Healthy Coping Responses	Unhealthy Coping Responses

What was a coping response you wished now you had used instead?

_____

_____

What positive growth did you gain from having to deal with this disappointment in life?

_____

_____

_____

_____

Try It Out and Report Back!

Instructions: Indicate the familywide problem below that your entire family is willing to work toward resolution this next week. Then think and write down what you are willing this week to do to make sure this problem gets resolved for your family.

Indicate below the familywide problem your family has agreed to work on this week.

_____

_____

_____

_____

Think about what you can do to contribute toward the resolution of this problem.

What attitude change will you try to have in regard to this problem?

_____

_____

_____

_____

What behavioral change will you make to help resolve this problem?

_____

_____

_____

_____

How will you feel if your family resolves this problem or issue?

☐ Extremely good
☐ Good
☐ OK
☐ Other _____

Just Record and Watch!

Instructions: Complete the below information so you will know what specific problem you are to observe over the next week at your home. Be sure to keep this record without showing your observations to anyone in your family during this observation week assignment. Bring this recording sheet back to your next group session so the results can be discussed and compared among the members of your family.

Indicate below the problem you and your family have agreed to observe this week so more details regarding it can be obtained.

_____

_____

_____

_____

Use the below log to record any time this problem occurs with your family during the next week. Be sure to write what you observed just before the problem surfaces, what is happening during the problem, and what happens afterwards.

Date	Observations before the problem occurs	Observations during the problem	Observations after the problem occurs

Family Safety Issues

Instructions: Indicate below the family members and/or places where you have had safety concerns during the past year.

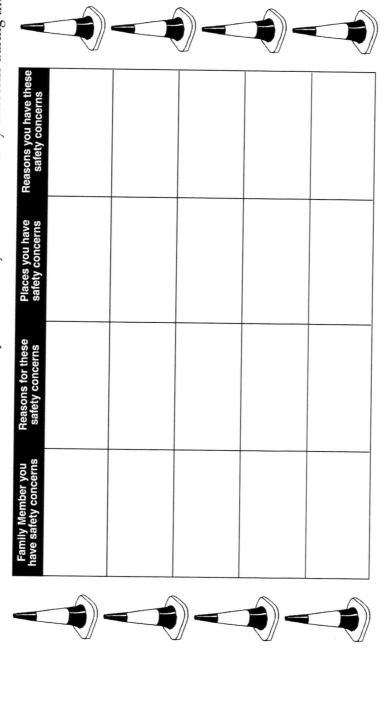

Family Member you have safety concerns	Reasons for these safety concerns	Places you have safety concerns	Reasons you have these safety concerns

Some ways I could better help address these safety concerns are _____

_____

_____

A...Each Week Keeps our Family Okay

Instructions: Indicate with a check which of the below things listed are important to keeping your family functioning on a healthy and happy level. Be sure to add things that are not listed.

☐ At least some family meal time together.

☐ Everyone does their part of the household chores.

☐ Open communication between all family members.

☐ If both parents in home, they have one night out together.

☐ At least one fun family event.

☐ Children and teen family members have an event to look forward to each week.

☐ A particularly favorite meal for the entire family is prepared.

☐ Dad and/or mom have time to just talk and catch up with their kids.

☐ Dad and mom have time to talk and catch up with one another.

☐ Family attends church or temple and related activities.

☐ Children and teen family members get all their school work completed.

☐ No calls from anyone that family members have been in trouble.

☐ Other _____

_____

☐ Other _____

_____

☐ Other _____

_____

☐ Other _____

_____

Our Family Is in Trouble When...

Instructions: Complete only the first half of this sheet that requests that you indicate what you have noticed are warning signs that your family is regressing in its functioning. Then when directed to do so by your facilitator, complete the bottom half of this sheet, which requests that you think of ways you could help stop your family's regressive functioning when it first begins.

I know our family is headed for trouble when I notice...

When I notice these warning signs I could...to help our family get back to a healthy level of functioning.

Report Card on our Family

Instructions: Please indicate what grades you would give your family in regard to the areas indicated on the below report card by using the grading system provided.

Grading system to use with below report card:

A = Our family is doing an outstanding job with this area of functioning.

B = Our family is doing a good job with this area of functioning.

C = Our family is doing an okay job with this area of functioning.

D = Our family needs to work on improving this area of functioning.

AREA OF FUNCTIONING	GRADE
Open communication among members	
Division and completion of household chores	
Good work performance of members outside the home (like work and school)	
Routines and celebrations in family life	
Ongoing support system for all family members	
Consistent rules and discipline for children and teen family members	
Regular family fun time together with laughter and joking	
Effective problem-solving skills	

Please comment on the area you would be most interested in seeing your family improve their functioning.

_____

_____

_____

_____

Chapter 7

PROBLEM-SOLVING INTERVENTIONS

In this chapter the reader will be provided an overview of the middle phase of a multiple family group therapy program. The process and treatment goals of this phase will be reviewed so that clinicians can better understand the connection between these goals and the suggested techniques. In addition, general instructions for conducting the problem-solving interventions will be outlined so facilitators can easily duplicate these therapeutic tasks with their own groups. Twenty interventions with related task sheets are then delineated that compose the heart of this chapter. For each of these interventions the reader is provided the following: title of technique, purpose, specific instructions, related task sheet if relevant, cautions, and possible modifications. These latter directions should increase the consistent application of these techniques to various multiple family group therapy programs. Readers are strongly urged to carefully review this chapter as their MFGT program moves into this middle group phase.

OVERVIEW OF MIDDLE PHASE OF MFGT

As the reader may recall from Chapter 3, the treatment goals are of primary emphasis in the middle phase when following the Dennison Group Practice Model. These are the goals that are directed at helping members resolve some of the problems that resulted in their participation in this group program. More specifically these goals include increasing members' awareness of their specific problems, increasing awareness of alternative solutions to problems, and assisting members in selecting alternative responses to their problems that can then be integrated into their repertoire. The interventions provided in this chapter are intended to address these three treatment goals. As indicated in Chapter 3, a trusting and cohesive group relationship must be established in a MFGT program before these interventions should be utilized. For this reason, many readers may find that their multiple family groups never enter this phase of treatment because the total length of treatment time is not sufficient for the members to develop a high level of trust and cohesiveness as a group. In following the Dennison Group Practice Model, even though groups may not enter into this middle phase they can still be successful treatment interventions. Consistent with many group studies, MFGT participants often report that the most valuable benefits of this group approach include they no longer feel alone, they have an increased level of hopefulness, and they have learned to share some of their most troubling concerns. These latter changes can and will usually be attained among group members after they have successfully completed the initial phase of MFGT. As a result, many group participants may report that their MFGT program, which was in the initial phase and then terminated, effectively helped them with their presenting problems.

Readers are reminded, as noted in Chapter 3, that the process goals (i.e., to continue building an attractive group setting, to maintain balanced participation, and to continue developing a trusting and cohesive group unit) are of secondary emphasis in this phase. Facilitators should continue to utilize the warm-up questions outlined in Chapter 5 as the initial task for each middle group session. By requesting increasing disclosure of the membership via these warm-up questions, clinicians will be able to continue to address the process goals of this phase. Typically, facilitators should find that groups in this phase require less assistance in maintaining these process goals. In fact, many groups by this point in treatment will be able to attain higher levels of these same goals since they have already established a significant level of trust and cohesiveness as a group in the initial phase. Readers should also remember that positive processing questions (e.g., What was helpful about today's session? What was the most meaningful thing you learned in group today?) at the end of each group session can also contribute toward the process goal attainment for this phase. These closure comments can also provide invaluable feedback to facilitators in terms of what is going well with their group programs.

When a MFGT program is ready for this phase there is an even higher probability that family units will be able to change long-term chronic problematic behaviors. Once a group of family units have bonded, members are much more open to opening up and helping one another in the problem-solving process. In addition, one of the unique benefits of MFGT programs is that the teens have an opportunity to teach or be heard by the parents of other teens. And, a similar cross-family learning process occurs with the parent members of these groups. Moreover, these groups may also include family members (e.g., siblings of the at risk teens) who may be healthier in their problem-solving skills. As a result, facilitators will be able to utilize these members' strengths such that they can assist in teaching problem-solving skills to other members of the group.

Facilitators will also want to keep in mind that the parent members of MFGT programs can share some important problem-solving skills by recalling how they coped with their own adolescent years. Since there are usually more boys in MFGT that target at risk teens and their families, it will be invaluable to have members who are fathers share some of their problem coping experiences from adolescence. In fact, facilitators may find that a particular at risk teen has a father who never had the same challenges in his teenage years. With this awareness in mind, the clinician could shift to another father in the group who had some similar challenges in his adolescence. This father can then share with the at risk teen how he coped and responded to similar difficult situations. Same gender feedback is critical during these teenage years and so facilitators will want to utilize these unique strengths of multiple family groups.

Multiple family groups have the unique opportunity to elicit family-wide changes among all of its members. Unlike more traditional approaches to treatment, this modality involves changing entire family systems by providing opportunities for families to assist one another in this process. Regardless of the problem being targeted in any one middle group session, this author has found multidimensional levels of learning are occurring in these groups. Facilitators will note the impact of modeling that regularly happens between the members. Most family units will enter these groups with their own strengths that can then be shared and taught to other group members and their families. This modeling between members is an important shift that should occur by this point in the treatment process. Readers are reminded that at this phase the facilitator no longer shares for modeling purposes. At this time the leader must be careful to stay out of the problem sharing discussions so that he or she can retain a therapeutic role within the group. For this reason, it is important that facilitators actively work on creating opportunities for members to provide this modeling in this middle phase. Group participants will walk away from these groups particularly remembering specific knowledge and skills they learned from one another. In addition, this problem/coping response sharing may increase the chances that group participants will become ongoing supports for one another even after their MFGT program ends.

GENERAL INSTRUCTIONS FOR USE OF RELATIONSHIP-BUILDING INTERVENTIONS

The interventions in this chapter are intended to be used for the main part of each middle group session. There are a number of problem-solving interventions provided so facilitators can choose ones that are most relevant to their group's needs. When conducting MFGT, leaders must be sensitive to the importance of creating a safe, nonthreatening, and comfortable environment where participants will spontaneously begin opening up about their presenting problems. Even though a level of trust and cohesiveness will have been established in the initial phase, facilitators should be aware that the members are now being asked to share in more direct terms about their problems. In addition, such sharing has the potential of surfacing more conflict within family units that will have to be monitored and addressed as the need arises.

Specific instructions for each intervention in this chapter include title of technique, purpose of the task, directions on how to conduct the technique, reference to task sheet at end of chapter if relevant, cautions in regard to the use of this intervention, and suggestions for modifying the technique. This latter information should assist facilitators' understanding of how to plan and facilitate each of these interventions. Readers should feel free to duplicate the related task sheets, found at the end of the chapter, for use with their groups. (Duplication of these task sheets for other purposes (e.g., training) is prohibited and violates copyright.)

Unless otherwise indicated, facilitators should conduct these interventions in the same consistent manner at each middle phase group meeting. First, the intervention is introduced to participants and, if relevant, task sheets are passed out to each member. The group should be given some time to gather their thoughts or write down their responses on a task sheet before being requested to share with the group. At this point in the group the facilitator no longer discloses in regard to the problem-solving task. The only exception to this is in cases where the facilitator has fully resolved a problem from his or her past and feels that such sharing would be therapeutically beneficial to the group. With this change in the group, it will be important in these middle group sessions to ask for a volunteer to be the first to disclose. It is particularly critical that members or family units determine if they want to be the first to disclose since these tasks will require much more open sharing about one's specific problems.

After a volunteer member or family unit has shared in regard to the problem-solving task, members are requested to go around the circle and share in a similar way. For some interventions, such sharing may be done by the family as a unit rather than by each individual family member. Leaders will need to decide how families determine who will do such sharing for the entire unit. In some groups the family member can be selected freely by the family whereas in other groups facilitators may want to have a set order as to who does the sharing for the family unit. Practitioners will need to use their clinical skills and individual preferences in deciding which method they choose to use for this familywide sharing. The rationale for having some interventions that require a familywide response is that such tasks will necessitate family members share first with one another, which can serve as a corrective relationship building experience. In addition, this method of sharing requires less time in the session, which can be very helpful in these much larger groups.

It will be important that both during and at the completion of each intervention facilitators point out commonalities among the membership and reinforce participation. Such processing comments will contribute to the ongoing development of a cohesive and trusting group. In

179

addition, these reinforcing comments by the facilitator will be important as a group is asked to open up in more direct terms about their problems. Moreover, leaders may want to request the participants to process their response to the intervention after hearing all the membership's sharing. This request may surface some interesting and helpful feedback about the increasing problem disclosure in a group.

The amount of time any particular intervention will require varies between groups. Such timing will depend on the size of the group, age span of participants, and amount of sharing that surfaces. Facilitators are cautioned to monitor both the amount and level of disclosure among participants. It is important that balanced participation be maintained throughout the life of a group. Otherwise, clinicians will find themselves conducting individual or family therapy with an audience.

Modification of some interventions will be necessary due to the age span among members of any one multiple family therapy group. This author has attempted to design techniques that are relevant and developmentally appropriate for a wide span of ages. However, it is impossible to create interventions that will be effective for all possible ages of group participants. Therefore, readers are strongly encouraged to modify or change interventions so they will be effective for their particular MFGT program. Also, facilitators should feel free to ask family members to assist younger members who might have difficulty with some tasks. Such assistance can serve some important therapeutic value as family members relate more positively to one another. Another example might be a teen who only relates well to a younger sibling and such assistance provides some positive reinforcement for this family member.

Readers are reminded to always remember that one of the unique strengths of MFGT is the mixing of at risk family members with healthier members. Sometimes the strengths from these latter individuals can be used to increase the effectiveness of a particular intervention. For example, when an at risk teen cannot articulate her strengths within the family, a sibling might be able to point out some strengths in his younger or older sibling. Facilitators of MFGT that focus on at risk adolescents and their families will find it immensely helpful to elicit feedback from other healthier teen members in the group. Adolescents are more likely to listen and respond to such teens that often have important strengths to share and model.

The remaining contents of this chapter will now be a listing of problem-solving interventions with related task sheets. Readers are encouraged to review this entire chapter before their MFGT program enters this middle group phase.

TECHNIQUE 51

Title of Intervention: What Do You Visualize?

Purpose: To increase participants' awareness of what changes they would like for their family.

Specific Instructions: Facilitators begin this intervention by explaining to the membership that sometimes it is helpful to imagine what your family would be like if they were functioning at a healthier and happier level. Then participants are instructed to get into a relaxed position, close their eyes, and visualize what their family life looks like when they are doing better as a unit. Next, members are provided the task sheet titled *What Do You Visualize?* Everyone is asked to finish this incomplete drawing of the image they visualized while they were relaxed and reflecting on this question. Once everyone has finished their drawing, each person is requested to share their drawing with the group, going around the circle in order. It is recommended that commonalities that surface from drawings of members from the same family unit be noted by the facilitator. Commonalities that surface between family units should be reinforced and pointed out. At the end of this sharing, participants can be asked to share what they learned both from their own drawing and seeing the drawings of their other family members.

Related Task Sheet: What Do You Visualize? Facilitators may want to have crayons available for participants to use with this task sheet, particularly when younger family members are involved in the group.

Cautions and Possible Modifications: This intervention can be an excellent way for members to begin thinking about what changes they would like in their family unit. By having participants imagine their family at a better place, members will use their fantasizing skills to visualize changes in their family. Sometimes it is a good idea to have group members think initially about such changes from a fantasy perspective rather than a reality perspective. By having participants share their vision of a better family life, family units may become more aware of what needs to change so all members of their household will be happier. One of the benefits of this task is it can be easily done by a wide range of group members. Younger participants may even provide some of the most insightful views of changes that need to happen with their families.

TECHNIQUE 52

Title of Intervention: First Steps to Your Problem Resolution Journey
Purpose: To increase participants' awareness of the ways they can begin working on some of the changes they want for themselves and their families.
Specific Instructions: This is a task that will require a group to do a series of discussions on effective ways to start the change process. The intervention is introduced by the facilitator presenting a short lecture on some of the challenges people face when they first think about making changing in their usual behavior patterns or responses. This presentation is best when some amount of groupwide discussion is stimulated among the participants. Next, the members are asked to think about the typical first steps they require when they decide to make a change in their behavior. Facilitators will want to write these ideas on a blackboard or large newsprint pad so members will remember what has been shared in regard to this part of the discussion. Then participants are requested to get together with their family units and determine an aspect of their family functioning they would all like to change. Members should be encouraged to consider issues that are not major ones and also ones that could be more easily resolved. Family units should also be instructed during this discussion to determine what beginning steps they could take to work toward resolution of the agreed-upon issue. Once all families have finished this discussion, the group is asked to have a volunteer from each family unit share the issue they would like to address and some of the beginning steps toward resolution. After each member shares this information, the group is requested to ask questions and provide feedback about the potential of the planned first steps working. At the end of the session members should be asked to share what they found most helpful about this task.
Related Task Sheet: No task sheet is required for this technique but

use of a blackboard or large newsprint pad is suggested.

Cautions and Possible Modifications: This is a nonthreatening way for members to begin thinking about making changes in their family-wide functioning. By having the family units consider making changes in regard to less challenging issues, facilitators are able to begin building their confidence in their problem solving as a unit. Some group leaders may decide to have family units commit to trying out the first steps they delineated as an assignment for the next week. Then the results of this assignment can be discussed at the next group meeting. This exercise also has the potential of providing some important instruction to group members. Sometimes at risk family members do not know how to go about starting a change process or resolving a problem. The didactic part of this intervention can provide some invaluable educational material in regard to these latter skills.

TECHNIQUE 53

Title of Intervention: Believing is Seeing!

Purpose: To increase members' awareness of the important of motivation in their behavior change process.

Specific Instructions: This intervention begins with members being given a copy of the task sheet titled *Rate your Believing!* Participants are asked to take a few moments to complete this task sheet. Once everyone is done, members are requested to use their responses on this sheet as a reference point during the next part of the group discussion. Then the group members are asked how important they feel motivation is for someone to begin making some changes in their behavior. After the group seems to have completed their sharing in regard to this question, members are asked to look over their task sheet answers and share what they learned about their own motivation levels for making changes in problem behaviors. Participants should go around the circle in order and share their response to this question. Facilitators should point out commonalities as they surface and reinforce members' disclosure. At the end of the session participants should be asked to reflect on the impact of this exercise on their own motivation to make changes in their behavior.

Related Task Sheet: Rate your Believing!

Cautions and Possible Modifications: The purpose of this task is to help group members understand how important motivation is to the change process. This intervention can provide valuable insight for each participant and also to entire family units. Sometimes the primary reason some family members will not change is because of this motivation factor. By having the membership address this issue in a more direct way, participants can begin to see how this part of the problem needs to be resolved before any change can occur. In addition, facilitators may find that if a member indicates he or she has very low motivation levels to make any changes, the group can then help that individual figure out the reasons behind that issue. By eliciting the group to assist such a member, important points related to this lack of motivation can be identified and then be addressed. In groups dealing with at risk teens, facilitators may find that some of their motivation is affected by control issues that are common in this age group. It may be helpful to a multiple family group to point out this variable when it surfaces and then have a group discuss ways to address control issues as they impact family members' motivation to make changes.

TECHNIQUE 54

Title of Intervention: Dissecting Your Family Problems
Purpose: To increase members' skills in being able to breakdown the important parts of a family problem in order to more effectively resolve it.
Specific Instructions: This technique begins with the task sheet titled *Dissecting Your Family Problems* being passed out to each member. Then the participants are asked to meet with their family units to determine a troubling familywide problem they have been experiencing. These discussions may require some assistance from co-facilitators depending on the amount of conflict that arises during such discussions. Once each family unit has agreed on a problem they would like to dissect or delineate into smaller parts, each participant is requested to indicate that problem on the top of their task sheet where requested. Next, members are asked to work individually on their task sheets that request a breakdown, from their perspective, of the important parts of the targeted family problem. Once everyone has completed his or her task sheet, a

volunteer from each family is asked to collect these sheets and compare the results. As these volunteer family members are ready, they state the familywide problem they agreed to delineate and then summarize the responses from these task sheets. It will be important during this sharing that facilitators point out commonalities that surface among family members and also note areas of disagreements. Once every family unit has been involved in this part of the sharing, group leaders may have time to process families' reactions to the information that surfaced from this problem dissecting exercise. It may also be beneficial to see if family units would be willing to start to work on some parts of their problem over the next week as an assignment. If a facilitator does choose to give such assignments, it will be important that these tasks are clarified such that all members of a family know exactly what they are committed to working on in regard to the targeted problem area.

Related Task Sheet: Dissecting Your Family Problems

Cautions and Possible Modifications: This can be an excellent technique for helping family members learn the importance of breaking down critical parts of a chronic problem. It also can help provide insight among family members so they better understand a problem from each of their perspectives. The skills that families learn in participating in this exercise can then be easily generalized to other problems they face. At the end of this session, it can be helpful to ask members to process what they learned from this task.

TECHNIQUE 55

Title of Intervention: Cut Your Losses and Move On!

Purpose: To increase members' awareness of those family issues that are troubling them but might be best addressed at a later point in time or not at all.

Specific Instructions: This technique is started by the facilitator introducing the topic of knowing when to not address a family concern. The group leader then goes on to provide a short lecture on this topic, while at the same time utilizing some group discussions on this subject. It may help participants to provide some simple examples of times when a particular family concern is best not addressed until some later date or not at all. After this presentation/discussion has been completed, members are each given a copy of the task sheet titled *Cut Your Losses and Move On!* Participants should be asked to complete this sheet following the instructions on it. Once everyone has completed this part of the exercise, members are asked to go around the circle in order and share the family concerns they have that need to go in the "later" or "not at all" basket. As members share in regard to this disclosure, facilitators should reinforce commonalities that surface, particularly those common to the members of the same family unit. At the end of this session members should be asked to process what they found to be the most beneficial part of this intervention.

Related Task Sheet: Cut Your Losses and Move On!

Cautions and Possible Modifications: This particular task provides members an opportunity to think carefully about which battles they choose to fight and which they do not. This point is of particular relevance to families with adolescent members. Typically these teenage years surface many potential battles between parents and their adolescent children. Therefore, it is essential that both parents and teens understand that some careful thought needs to go into deciding which issues have to be addressed and which can wait or not be addressed ever. Families in crisis often have trouble seeing this point clearly. As a result, they often find themselves fighting every battle that surfaces, using little rational thinking as to the value of these battles in the big picture. This exercise will often also surface some of the control issues that are common among teens and their parents. There is great benefit in bringing these control issues out in the open so family members can discuss them directly. At the same time, some family members may actually experience some grieving in response to issues that need to be put on the back burner. In these situations, facilitators will have to validate, support, and assist such members in their process of coming to terms with the most important issues even though this awareness may mean letting go of some hopes and dreams they have had for their children.

TECHNIQUE 56

Title of Intervention: Expectations and Changing Behavior
Purpose: To increase members' expectations of themselves and the

effect of those expectations on their ultimate behavioral changes.

Specific Instructions: This intervention begins with the facilitator informing the group that the session will be focusing on the effect one's expectations have on the degree to which one attempts to change problem behavior. Then the task sheet titled *Expectation Checkup* is passed to each member. Participants are requested to take a few minutes to indicate their usual expectations of themselves on this check-off form. Once everyone has completed this task, members are asked to go around the circle in order and share what expectation patterns they see in themselves, based on the items they checked off on the task sheet. It will be important for facilitators to point out commonalities that surface and reinforce disclosure. Next, the membership should be asked to share how this expectation awareness exercise may impact their behavior change process. The more specific members can be in their disclosure of this information, facilitators will find that such details can greatly help members determine additional ways to address problem behavior. At the end of this session members should be asked to process the value of this exercise to their problem-solving efforts.

Related Task Sheet: Expectations Checkup

Cautions and Possible Modifications: Facilitators will find that this technique often helps participants become more aware of the significant role one's expectations have on ultimate behavior changes. At the same time, this task may surface the issue of expectations between family members. If time permits, it can be quite beneficial to have members discuss the effect other family members' expectations have on one's behavior. Facilitators may find it helpful to have parents in a MFGT program share the impact their own parents had on their ultimate behaviors and performance. When dealing with at risk adolescents and their families, a task like this one can be very helpful in determining barriers to behavior change. Sometimes the challenge for parents of at risk teens is to modify their expectations so they have more realistic goals. By attaining this awareness, the teens will feel less like failures and be more likely to attempt to make some behavioral changes or perform at a higher level.

TECHNIQUE 57

Title of Intervention: Weather Report on my Family Life
Purpose: To increase members' awareness of the current state of their family life from each family member's perspective.
Specific Instructions: This technique begins with the task sheet titled *Weather Report on my Family Life* being passed out to each member. Participants are given a few minutes to complete this sheet. Facilitators should remember that due to the symbolic nature of this task members may need a longer period to determine their responses to the questions on the sheet. Next, members are asked to go around the circle in order and share their responses to this symbolic task. Some facilitators may choose to modify this part of the intervention by having a volunteer from each family unit collect all the task sheets and share their family-wide responses. Regardless of the way this information is shared, facilitators should reinforce commonalities that surface, particularly those common among the members of the same family unit. At the end of this exercise, participants can be asked to share how this experience affected their view of their family life.
Related Task Sheet: Weather Report on my Family Life
Cautions and Possible Modifications: Symbolic tasks like this one are great interventions for surfacing gut level feelings among the members of a group. Often these techniques take longer for participants to respond to but their responses are often the underlying issues that may not be usually addressed directly within a family unit. The task sheet for this exercise provides an opportunity for members to share their greatest concerns about their families along with their strengths. At the same time, part of this task sheet elicits some disclosure at a preventive level as members are asked "what stormy weather could be ahead." This can be a difficult task for some members but often the challenge will be worth the benefits. Also, younger family members may need assistance with this task since some of the abstract thinking that is required may not be appropriate for their developmental level. Facilitators can either provide assistance to these younger children, in terms of filling out the task sheet, or ask them to share their responses verbally.

TECHNIQUE 58

Title of Intervention: Spring Cleaning for Family Attitude Adjustment

Purpose: To increase family members' awareness of attitude changes among family members that will positively impact their family life.

Specific Instructions: The task sheet titled *Spring Cleaning for Family Attitude Adjustment* is passed out to each member. Participants are requested to anonymously complete this form and place it face down on a pile in front of their family unit. Once everyone has completed this task sheet, a volunteer from each family is asked to collect the sheets and tally the results. Then these volunteers go around the circle in order sharing their familywide response to this attitude adjustment questionnaire. Facilitators should point out commonalities that surface during this sharing, both between families and within family units. Since some sensitive disclosure could be surfaced from this exercise, it is essential that facilitators allow enough time for family members to process their reactions to this task sheet. Group leaders may want to process at the end of the session members' reactions to the benefits of this particular exercise.

Related Task Sheet: Spring Cleaning for Family Attitude Adjustment

Cautions and Possible Modifications: This technique should not be attempted until a MFGT program has attained a fairly high level of trust and cohesiveness. Even when groups are at this level of development individual members of family units may find the disclosure surfaced to be uncomfortable and upsetting. Therefore, it is critical that enough time is allowed in the session to process all participants' responses to this technique. One of the unique benefits of this intervention is it surfaces "attitude" issues that are often not as obvious but clearly impact a family's daily functioning. Disclosure elicited from this exercise can provide much needed awareness and insight for specific family members.

TECHNIQUE 59

Title of Intervention: Concerns and Areas of Control

Purpose: To increase members' awareness of the areas of control and areas of no control they have in regard to their major family concerns.

Specific Instructions: This technique begins with the task sheet titled *Concerns and Areas of Control* being passed out to each member. Participants are given some time to complete this form. In particular, members should be instructed to think of one major family concern they have and then determine what parts of that concern are within their control and what parts are out of their control. Once everyone has completed this task sheet, the members go around the circle in order sharing their responses to this exercise. It will be important that facilitators reinforce disclosure and point out commonalities that surface. Either during the sharing part of this task or at the end, it will be beneficial for the membership to discuss the value of knowing which areas you actually have control over in terms of family concerns.

Related Task Sheet: Concerns and Areas of Control

Cautions and Possible Modifications: This intervention is particularly helpful and relevant to families with at risk adolescents. Many times parents' concerns become more upsetting because they assume they have more control than they actually do with some issues. At the same time, it is beneficial for teens to hear about the worries their parents experience as they make various behavior choices. As always, it is a good idea to have a group process their reactions to this exercise at the end of the session. It will be helpful if participants can make the connection to other family concerns and see how the same process can be used to identify areas to focus their efforts.

TECHNIQUE 60

Title of Intervention: You Should Chill Out When...

Purpose: To increase members' awareness of times when they need to stop, think, and either response or not react.

Specific Instructions: This task addresses the issue that some situations require that folks think before they react or even decide to not react. Facilitators introduce this intervention by presenting a brief lecture on the importance of knowing if, to what degree, and when to react to a particularly upsetting situation. This presentation should focus on examples of issues that are common to family members, particularly when certain family members do not typically handle some situations effectively. After this presentation/discussion, members are requested to complete the task sheet titled *You Should Chill Out When...* This particular form requests participants to indicate times in their families that they should learn to chill out, meaning think before they react or not react at all. After everyone has completed this task sheet, members are asked to go around the circle in order and share their responses to this task sheet. Again, facilitators will want to reinforce disclosure and point out commonalities as they surface. At the end of the session, members should be asked to process what they learned from this exercise.

Related Task Sheet: You Should Chill Out When...

Cautions and Possible Modifications: For any number of reasons, some family members are like water and oil when they are together. This situation may be a temporary state that is related to the family life stage (i.e., raising a teenager) or it may be that some family members will always have difficulties in any number of situations. This same point could also be relevant to specific situations that arise in families (e.g., a teen asking to use the family car) where there have been consistent difficulties around such events. This exercise provides members an opportunity to stop and analyze which situations they should avoid, not react to, or think carefully about before they respond. The use of humor in this exercise can help some participants feel less threatened when addressing this issue directly. This task also targets self-talk skills that many at risk teens may need to acquire in order to more effectively respond to potentially difficult family situations. In addition, some family members who have had long histories of conflict may have to work on these same skills since their emotions are often heightened in specific situations.

TECHNIQUE 61

Title of Intervention: Dear Family Consultant

Purpose: To increase members' family problem-solving skills.

Specific Instructions: This task begins by the facilitator requesting that family members gather into a small circle and work together to determine a familywide problem they could use some assistance with resolving. Then the sheet titled *Dear Family Consultant* is passed out, one to each family unit. One volunteer from each family agrees to write the responses on the top half of this sheet. Also, if the family wishes to remain anonymous, a code can be put on the back of this task sheet to later identify the family. Each family is asked to delineate in detail a problem they are currently facing that they could use some assistance in resolving. After each family has completed this sheet, the facilitator collects all the sheets. Then the contents of each task sheet are read out loud to the group. If a family was comfortable with sharing their name on this sheet then this information can also be shared. All the participants are asked to serve as a family consultant and provide some alternative coping responses to each family problem that is described. It will be important that a co-facilitator complete the bottom half of the task sheet with the suggestions provided by the group discussion. Each family problem should be completely discussed before the next one is addressed. If a family provided their name on the task sheet, the facilitator may want to ask the involved family their response to the suggestions that were made by the group. At the end of the session, a volunteer from each family is asked to pick up their task sheet so they will have some notes reminding them of the suggestions made by the group. Participants should be asked, if time permits, to share the benefits of this exercise for themselves or their family units.

Related Task Sheet: Dear Family Consultant

Cautions and Possible Modifications: This is a nonthreatening way for family units to share a particularly upsetting problem that they have been unable to resolve. At the same time, all participants can benefit from hearing the various suggestions for handling a particular family-wide problem. This author has found that families are more likely, in the future, to remember those ideas when faced with a similar difficulty. Also, this technique can be modified such that after the family units determine the problem to be analyzed, the task sheets are exchanged between family units. Then time is allowed for each family unit to develop suggestions for addressing the problem of another family. These suggestions are shared with the whole group so again the learning can benefit all members of a MFGT program.

Title of Intervention: Alternative Coping Responses for 21st Century Families

Purpose: To increase members' awareness of effective coping responses for families in current times.

Specific Instructions: This is a brainstorming exercise where participants first are requested to think about all the unique challenges facing families in current times. These points should be written on a blackboard or large newsprint pad so members are able to remember what has been shared. Then members are asked to look over the list created by the group discussion and then brainstorm effective coping responses for some of those challenges. Participants should be encouraged to provide examples from their own family lives. These coping responses should also be noted on a board or newsprint pad to provide an overview of these coping ideas. After both of these lists have been developed, facilitators should ask members to reflect on their responses to these discussions, particularly when thinking about how they might use some of the suggested coping responses. At the end of this session, members should be requested to process what they found most instructive about this exercise.

Related Task Sheet: No task sheet is required but use of a blackboard or large newsprint pad is helpful.

Cautions and Possible Modifications: These brainstorming tasks serve several important benefits for a MFGT program. First, such discussions are validating and help families understand better the stresses they face. Second, the strengths of the group can be surfaced by having the participants share in developing coping responses for some of these current challenges. Third, this task could spontaneously surface some of the parents' feelings of not having learned such coping responses from their families of origin. This latter point is an important one because it identifies the need for many families to be instructed in these new coping responses. Such instructional material may be particularly relevant to families with at risk adolescents. In addition, raising teens often surfaces some of the toughest challenges facing families today because of their mobility and access to various sources of material (e.g., computer programs, Web sites, etc.).

TECHNIQUE 63

Title of Intervention: How to See the Glass as Half Full!

Purpose: To increase members' skills in reframing some of their presenting problems.

Specific Instructions: This is a type of strength-based technique since the task begins with members being instructed on the benefits of seeing the progress in their problem-solving efforts (i.e., glass as half full) as opposed to the issues that still need to be addressed (i.e., glass as half empty). After a brief presentation is provided by the facilitator, members are requested to get into a small group with their family and determine a problem they have been working on that is only partially resolved. Once all families have decided on a problem, a volunteer from each family is asked to go around the circle in order and share the details regarding that problem. This sharing should include the parts of the problem that have been resolved and those parts that still are unresolved. After each volunteer from a family unit discloses, members should be asked to suggest ways to look at the family's problem solving from a strength perspective. In other words, identify what the family has done successfully in addressing the problem and then articulate the remaining challenge from a more positive perspective. After all family units' problems have been discussed accordingly, members can be asked to process what they found helpful about this exercise.

Related Task Sheet: No task sheet but use of a blackboard or large newsprint pad is helpful.

Cautions and Possible Modifications: This is an excellent opportunity for group members to help one another retain both some objectivity about their problem-solving attempts and a positive viewpoint of their successes. The discussions from this exercise can be very validating for family units and even surface strengths they had not realized. This is a particularly helpful intervention for those most challenging problems that families will need patience and commitment to fully resolve. Typically this exercise is best timed after a group has been in the middle phase for several sessions.

Title of Intervention: Pass the Basket for Problems!

Purpose: To provide a nonthreatening way for family members to share problems they would like to resolve.

Specific Instructions: The multiple family group is informed that in this session they will have an opportunity to anonymously share problems they would like to resolve in their lives. Then a blank sheet of paper is passed out to each member with the instructions that they are to write down a problem they would like to no longer have without using any identifying information. Once everyone has completed this problem disclosure sheet they are asked to fold it up and drop it in a basket that is passed around the circle. After all sheets have been collected the basket is then passed around the circle again for each member to pick one that they will share with the group. Usually it is a good idea to have members immediately share the problem that they selected before passing on the basket to the next member. This latter step safeguards that members do not have to share their own problem in case they initially pick their own sheet. When a member picks their own problem sheet they should be instructed to place it back in the basket and pick another one. After all members have selected and shared a problem from the basket, the group is asked to process their reactions to this exercise.

Related Task Sheet: None required but provide blank sheets for each member.

Cautions and Possible Modifications: This is an excellent technique for initially eliciting members' sharing of their problems. Due to the anonymous way this disclosure is surfaced, participants will be more likely to disclose particularly troubling problems. Facilitators should feel free to participate in this intervention since it does not require that they directly share their problem. Such participation serves as good modeling for the group and further includes the facilitator in the development of group trust. Groups will often feel more comfortable sharing their problems in future group sessions after this intervention. It is amazing how the surfacing of groupwide problems serves to validate members' feelings that they are not alone with their difficulties. As a result of this intervention, this author has found members appear more trusting of one another and more open about sharing their problems or concerns.

Title of Intervention: Computer Files to Delete, Add, and Modify

Purpose: To increase members' cognitive restructuring skills as related to their problem solving.

Specific Instructions: This is a type of cognitive behavioral technique since members are being asked to delineate their thoughts and self-talk before a problem situation, during, and afterwards. By using the symbolic representation of self-talk in the form of computer files, participants may be able to more easily identify the connection between self-talk and behavioral responses. Facilitators begin this technique by passing out the task sheet titled *Computer Files to Delete, Add, and Modify* to each member. Participants are asked to take about 10 minutes to complete this sheet on a situation in which they usually have problems. Members should be told that they will not have to reveal this problem to the group. Rather, they will be asked to identify their self-talk that has been beneficial (computer files to save), harmful (computer files to delete), or that needs some changes for better coping responses (computer files to modify). Once everyone has finished this sheet, members go around the circle in order sharing what they have learned via the task sheet about their self-talk and its connection to their behavioral responses. At the end of this session, participants should be requested to process what they found most beneficial about this intervention.

Related Task Sheet: Computer Files to Delete, Add, and Modify

Cautions and Possible Modifications: For many children who have been raised on computers, this is an excellent symbolic task that shows how self-talk is related to responses. Some younger members of families may need assistance with this task sheet that co-facilitators will need to provide. If time permits, increased self-awareness surfaced from this exercise could provide excellent material for developing a self-talk log assignment. Members would be asked to baseline their thoughts before, during, and after a problem situation. This record would be maintained over the week and the results discussed at the next group meeting. This author has found that self-talk can be a major contribution to some group members' problems. In the case of Attention Deficit Disorder (ADD) teens, this point is particularly relevant since they often need to learn to think before they react to a situation.

Title of Intervention: Scenes from Your Family Life to Cut

Purpose: To summarize for members problem situations that they need to avoid in terms of their family life.

Specific Instructions: This particular technique should be utilized toward the end of the middle phase and just before a MFGT program is about to end. The primary purpose of this intervention is to help members recall and, thus remember, those family situations (scenes) that need to be either avoided or responded to differently in the future. Facilitators begin the session by passing out the task sheet titled *Scenes from Your Family Life to Cut* to each member. Participants are then instructed to take a few minutes to complete this form by indicating the family situations that have typically caused problems in the past for them. After they list these situations, members should then be asked to indicate whether they have learned to avoid such situations or respond to them differently. After everyone has completed this task sheet, members go around the circle in order and summarize their responses on the task sheet. Facilitators should reinforce disclosure during this sharing and point out commonalities that surface, particularly those identified by the members of the same family unit. At the end of this session participants should be asked to share what they found most helpful about this summarizing exercise.

Related Task Sheet: Scenes from Your Family Life to Cut

Cautions and Possible Modifications: This is an excellent task for helping members remember which family situations need to be avoided or responded to differently in the future. Participants should be encouraged to keep their completed task sheets from this exercise because it can serve as a future reminder of some potential problematic situations for them. Due to the nature of this task, younger members of some families may require co-facilitator assistance in understanding and completing the task sheet. This intervention can also provide valuable validation and clarification to members about all that they have learned regarding improving their family life functioning, particularly how they can contribute to such changes.

TECHNIQUE 67

Title of Intervention: When the Rubber Hits the Road!

Purpose: To increase group members' skills in maintaining ongoing problem solving.

Specific Instructions: This is a type of preventive instruction/group discussion task where facilitators introduce the topic of relapse prevention. It is explained that this topic is being addressed in the group so members will be ready for some of the more common challenges they will face as they continue to work on their problems after treatment ends. Due to the nature of this intervention, this task should be scheduled just as a group is about to terminate. Facilitators will present a brief presentation on relapse prevention guidelines by using the material provided on the task sheet titled *When the Rubber Hits the Road!* For this reason, the sheet should be handed out to all members so they can refer to the relapse prevention guidelines as this presentation is being made. It is ideal to elicit ideas and discussion from the group as this material is being presented. Also, the group will gain even more from this discussion if members are asked to point out particular guidelines that will be most relevant to them. At the end of the session participants should be encouraged to take this task sheet home so they will be able to remember some of the relapse prevention guidelines. Moreover, it is a good idea to have the group process what they gained from this task.

Related Task Sheet: When the Rubber Hits the Road!

Cautions and Possible Modifications: It is very important that at risk adolescents and their families realize that relapsing back into some dysfunctional patterns can and probably will occur, but the critical point is to know how to stop that regression before it is too late. This exercise also helps participants think about their own personal signs that they are relapsing to some unhealthy behavioral responses. The other critical message to get across to the group is some relapsing is normal and it is important to not throw out all of one's progress just because of an isolated situation. In addition, family units should be given the message that they need to not give up on one another when some temporary relapse happens. Rather, this intervention should provide families with some healthier ways to respond to such regression so they do not push a family member further into their old patterns of responding.

TECHNIQUE 68

Title of Intervention: Things You Could Do to Help Your Family

Purpose: To increase each participant's knowledge and commitment to what they can do to contribute to the more positive functioning of their family unit.

Specific Instructions: This session begins with the task sheet titled *My Commitment to my Family* being passed out to each member. Then the facilitator gives a brief presentation on how important it is that everyone in the family system contributes to the ongoing healthy and positive functioning of their unit. Next, participants are instructed to read over their task sheet and think about one thing that they have learned in the group that will be an important contribution to their family's ongoing positive functioning. Then members are asked to write down that idea in the form of a commitment to their family. Once everyone is done participants go around the circle in order sharing with their families what behavioral response they are committing to in an effort to help their family maintain a healthy level of functioning. At the end of the session, all members are asked to share what they found helpful about this exercise.

Related Task Sheet: My Commitment to my Family

Cautions and Possible Modifications: This task needs to be planned just before a MFGT program is about to end. Members should be requested to write down a commitment based on something they learned from their group participation. In the case of younger children, co-facilitators may have to provide assistance when they are completing their task sheets. The important message to get across to the membership from this intervention is all family members must be committed to work toward establishing and maintaining a positive level of functioning for the family unit.

TECHNIQUE 69

Title of Intervention: Coming Home and Feeling Good!

Purpose: To increase family members' awareness of one another's view of what it means to have a happy and healthy functioning unit.

Specific Instructions: This task begins with the sheet titled *Coming*

Home and Feeling Good! being passed out to each member. Facilitators may also want to provide crayons for younger group members since this task sheet could also be drawn on or colored. Then members are asked to discuss for a few minutes what it means to each of them to come home to an environment where things just feel good. After a discussion on this topic, members are instructed to complete their task sheets with words or pictures that provide their view of a home setting where it feels good being there for them. Once everyone has completed their sheets, members go around the circle in order sharing their response from this sheet. At the end of the session, family units should be asked to share what they found particularly informative about this exercise.

Related Task Sheet: Coming Home and Feeling Good!

Cautions and Possible Modifications: This is a wonderful intervention to summarize what members have learned from one another, particularly in regard to what they each see as a happy home life. By providing this opportunity during a later middle phase group session, family members are able to understand their differences and similarities in terms of what makes for good feelings within the family. For this reason, it is important for facilitators to point out commonalities that surface, particularly those among members of the same family unit. Also, if time permits, it could be beneficial to address differences that surface so families can think about how these varying viewpoints can be effectively handled by their family unit. This is also a great task for the younger members of families since the drawing and coloring will be at their developmental level. In addition, it may be that some of the children's drawings on this topic will be the most insightful. It is not unusual for youngsters to be the most perceptive members of some families.

TECHNIQUE 70

Title of Intervention: Your Bag of Tricks!

Purpose: To summarize for members what they have learned are the most effective coping responses for them as individuals and with their families.

Specific Instructions: Depending on the total length of a MFGT program, participants may have gained lots of different knowledge and skill regarding more effective coping responses. This task provides members with an opportunity to pull all those ideas together so they are validated in what they have learned. In addition, by having members discuss and write down these coping responses, they are going to be more likely to remember and utilize them in future situations. The session begins with the task sheet titled *Your Bag of Tricks!* being passed out to each member. Participants are asked to think about what they have learned in the group are more effective and healthy coping responses for them either as individuals or as members of their families. Facilitators provide the group with several minutes to complete this sheet and then go around the circle in order and have each member share their responses to this sheet. At the end of the group all participants should be asked to share what they found most helpful about this exercise.

Related Task Sheet: Your Bag of Tricks!

Cautions and Possible Modifications: This intervention is ideally scheduled just before a group is to enter the termination phase. Validation of progress and summarization of learning are two of the key benefits of this particular task. Younger members of families should be allowed to draw on their task sheets so this intervention can be administered more at their developmental level. At the same time, youngsters may still need some co-facilitator assistance in completing this task sheet due to their memory skills. Participants should be encouraged to bring home and keep their sheets as reminders of coping responses that will assist them in maintaining healthy levels of functioning.

SUMMARY

The reader was provided in this chapter an overview of the treatment and process goals for the middle phase of a MFGT program. The importance of attaining these middle phase goals was emphasized because they address the presenting problems that resulted in families joining a MFGT program. In addition, the need to shift discussions to more direct problem disclosure and resolution was pointed out in this section of the book. Then 20 interventions were delineated in this chapter for the more specific identification of members' problems and possible alternative solutions to resolving them. Specific directions for each intervention, along with related task sheets, were provided such that readers should be able to easily utilize the suggested techniques with their particular groups. The details provided for each technique listed in this chapter should also increase clinicians' ability to modify, change, and even create similar problem-solving interventions.

What Do You Visualize?

Instructions: Complete the below picture with a drawing of what your family will look like when it is functioning better as a unit.

Rate your Believing!

Instructions: Using the below rating scale indicate to what degree you believe that you can and will make changes in each of the areas listed. If a problem area is listed below that does not apply to you just mark the rating score as NA.

Rating Scale
5 = I have a high degree of belief that I will make the needed changes.
4 = I believe I will make the needed changes.
3 = I have a fair amount of belief in my willingness to make the needed changes.
2 = I have so-so belief in my willingness to make the needed changes.
1 = I have little belief in my willingness to make the needed changes.
0 = I have no belief in my willingness to make the needed changes.

1. Personal problems that are the most troubling to you at this time.   Rating:_____

2. Difficulties related to a conflicted relationship with one family member.   Rating:_____

3. Problems related to familywide functioning difficulties.   Rating:_____

4. Problems you are experiencing either at work or school.   Rating:_____

5. Problems you are having in your peer relationships.   Rating:_____

6. Difficulties related to your level of self-confidence.   Rating:_____

7. Problems related to your expression of feelings.   Rating:_____

8. Problems you have had for a long time in your life.   Rating:_____

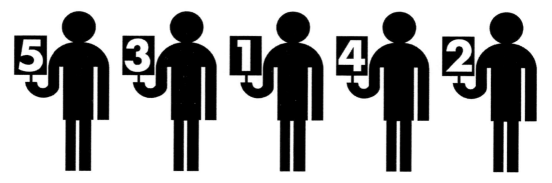

Dissecting Your Family Problems

Instructions: From your perspective break down the important parts of the family problem that your family has agreed to work on for this task.

Family Problem: _____

_____

1. List what you view are the most difficult parts of this problem to resolve.

_____

_____

_____

2. What could you do to help your family resolve this problem?

_____

_____

_____

3. What are some ways your family has resolved similar problems in the past?

_____

_____

_____

4. What strengths of your family could be used in resolving this problem?

_____

_____

_____

5. What would be the first step toward resolving this problem?

_____

_____

Cut Your Losses and Move On!

Instructions: Indicate below some of your current family conflicts or problems that need to be addressed at a later time or not at all.

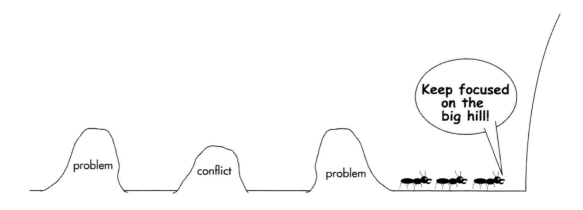

Expectation Checkup

Instructions: Please read over the list of behaviors below and place a check by each one that applies to your usual expectations of self and others.

☐ I expect perfection in most things that I attempt to do.

☐ I am not easily discouraged by a lack of success in some of my endeavors.

☐ I have difficulty having patience in resolving problems that take time.

☐ I have realistic expectations of myself in most things I attempt.

☐ I have high expectations of myself in most areas of my life.

☐ I expect others to do things to the best of their ability.

☐ I usually try to encourage others even after they seem discouraged with their performance of a particular skill.

☐ I judge others' performance by my own standards.

☐ I have fair expectations of others in most areas of their functioning.

☐ I am often critical of others' performance.

☐ I have high expectations of others in all areas of life.

☐ I am often critical of my own performance.

Weather Report on my Family Life

Instructions: Make believe that you are doing a weather report on your family. Complete the weather reports on your current family functioning.

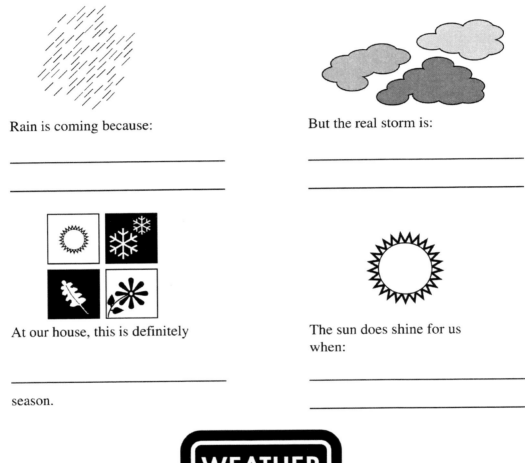

Rain is coming because:

_____

_____

But the real storm is:

_____

_____

At our house, this is definitely

_____

season.

The sun does shine for us when:

_____

_____

The weather forecast for my family over the next year is:

_____

_____

Spring Cleaning for Family Attitude Adjustment

Instructions: Complete this check list without using your name so you will feel that you can be as honest as possible. Indicate with a check those attitude adjustments that need to be made by members of your family. Disregard those items that are not relevant to your family unit.

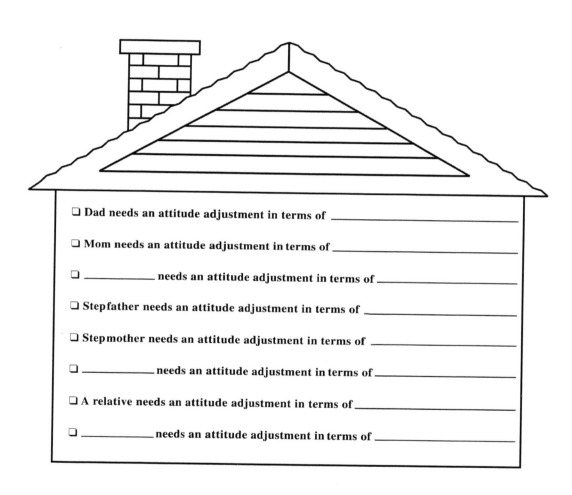

❑ Dad needs an attitude adjustment in terms of _____

❑ Mom needs an attitude adjustment in terms of _____

❑ _____ needs an attitude adjustment in terms of _____

❑ Stepfather needs an attitude adjustment in terms of _____

❑ Stepmother needs an attitude adjustment in terms of _____

❑ _____ needs an attitude adjustment in terms of _____

❑ A relative needs an attitude adjustment in terms of _____

❑ _____ needs an attitude adjustment in terms of _____

Concerns and Areas of Control

Instructions: Indicate below major concerns you have had lately and then determine which parts of those concerns you have control over.

Area of Concern: _____

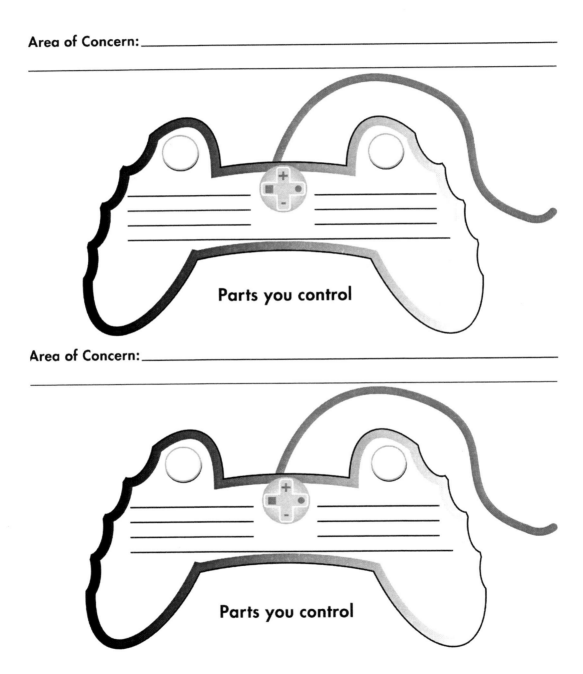

Parts you control

Area of Concern: _____

Parts you control

You Should Chill Out When...

Instructions: Indicate by the pictures below times when a family member, yourself, or the entire family should chill out rather than react.

_____ **should chill out when**

_____

_____

I should chill out when

_____

_____

My entire family should chill out when

_____

_____

_____

_____

_____

Dear Family Consultant

Instructions: When directed to do so by your group facilitator, complete with your family the below letter to a family consultant. Families do not have to indicate their name on these letters.

Dear Family Consultant,

We all agree that we are having the following family problem: _____

_____

_____.

This problem has existed for _____.

We have had trouble resolving this difficulty because_____

_____

_____.

We have already tried the following in an attempt to solve this problem: ___

_____

_____.

Dear Family,

Here are some suggestions for resolving this problem:

_____

_____

_____

_____

_____

_____

Sincerely,
Your group family consultant

Computer Files to Delete, Add, and Modify

Instructions: Indicate below a problem situation in which you often have difficulties. Then think about your self-talk or thoughts in this situation as if they were computer files. Write in the spaces below self-talk you would like to stop having (files to delete), self-talk that needs to be changed slightly (files to modify), and self-talk that you want to keep (files to save). You will only be asked to share your learning in regard to your self-talk awareness. It will not be necessary to actually share the problem situation you have analyzed for this task.

Problem situation: _____

_____

_____

Computer files to save

Computer files to delete

Computer files that need to be modified

213

Scenes from Your Family Life to Cut

Instructions: Complete the below film scene strips with situations that you and your family need to remember to either avoid or handle differently in the future.

Scenes that my family needs to cut _____

Scenes that my family needs to cut _____

Scenes that my family needs to cut _____

When the Rubber Hits the Road!

Following are some guidelines for helping families maintain their positive changes and prevent relapse. This information will be reviewed with your facilitator as your group discusses these points for this task.

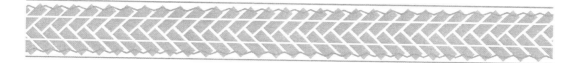

Each family member must be committed to doing his or her part in maintaining changes.

Know and talk openly about the signs that indicate that your family is about to regress to earlier times of unhealthy functioning.

As soon as some regressive functioning is noticed stop and process with the family unit as a whole.

Develop a problem prevention plan with your family while functioning at a more positive time.

Accept some regressive functioning and do not let it discourage you—we are all human and there are many stressful times ahead for families.

Pick and choose your future battles carefully—remember sometimes you need to cut your losses and move on as a family.

Never forget the big picture—focus on what will really matter in the long run for your family.

Keep seeing your glass as half full—work on positive self-talk and reframing of your family problems.

Remember to use coping responses that have worked for your family in the past.

Every family needs to have fun and relaxing times together—you cannot work on your problems all the time.

My Commitment to my Family

Instructions: Complete the below contract as your commitment to your family in terms of doing your part to help your family maintain positive changes.

Contract to my Family

I _____ do hereby make the following commitment to my family as part in helping us maintain the positive changes we have made:

_____

_____

_____

_____

_____

_____

If I start to slip up on this commitment I would ask my family to _____

_____

_____

_____

_____

Signature: _____

Date: _____

Coming Home and Feeling Good!

Instructions: Complete the drawing with pictures or words that describe what your home is like when it feels really good to you.

Me at Home and
Feeling Really Good!

Your Bag of Tricks!

Instructions: Write or draw in the bag below the things you have learned from this group that will help you more effectively cope with future problems.

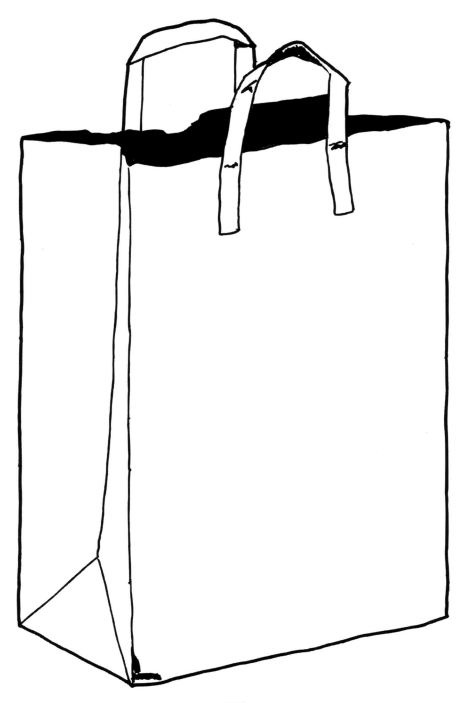

Chapter 8

GROUP TERMINATION
AND CLOSURE INTERVENTIONS

In this chapter the reader will be provided an overview of the process and treatment goals for the termination phase of MFGT that are targeted during the ending group sessions. The rationale for these goals will be delineated such that clinicians will better understand the connection between the process and treatment goals of this phase and the suggested techniques outlined in this chapter. In addition, general instructions will be provided for conducting psychoeducational interventions with multiple family groups. Ten interventions with related task sheets are then provided that compose the heart of this chapter. For each of these interventions the reader is given the following: title of the technique, purpose, specific instructions, related task sheet if relevant, and cautions with possible modifications. These latter directions should increase the consistent application of these techniques to a wide variety of multiple family group programs. Readers are strongly urged to carefully review this chapter as they prepare for the termination of their MFGT because positive and corrective termination experiences can be of tremendous value to at risk adolescents and their families.

OVERVIEW OF TERMINATION PHASE OF MFGT

As the reader may recall from Chapter 3, the process goals are of primary emphasis in the termination phase when following the Dennison Group Practice Model. These are the goals that are directed at helping members validate the progress they have made in the group and explore other ways they will be able to maintain their positive changes. More specifically these goals include having members acknowledge the value of the group and grieve its ending, having members acknowledge their progress as individuals and family units, and having members identify sources outside the group that will help them maintain their changes. The interventions in this chapter are primarily intended to address these three process goals. It is essential that facilitators plan specific sessions for a MFGT program that shifts the focus from new problem discussion to acknowledgment of members' progress. Group participants will benefit greatly from this opportunity to reinforce themselves and one another regarding the progress they have made in this treatment modality. This focus on a positive group closure will also serve as important modeling for participants in regard to healthy termination experiences.

Readers are reminded, as noted in Chapter 3, that the treatment goals (i.e., to have members acknowledge their attainment of treatment goals and to have members develop a relapse prevention plan for maintaining their positive changes) are of secondary emphasis in this phase. Even in these ending sessions, facilitators should continue to utilize the warm-up questions outlined specifically for this phase in Chapter 5. These questions are intended to also help in addressing both the process and treatment goals for this phase. Typically, facilitators will find that groups in this phase, with little assistance, will simultaneously attain the treatment goals as they work on the process goals. Readers will note that these two sets of goals are quite similar due to the nature and purpose of the termination phase. In addition, facilitators should continue to utilize positive processing questions (e.g., What was helpful about today's session? What was the most meaningful thing you learned from this discussion of your progress in group?) at the end of each termination group session since they will also contribute toward the attainment of both the process and treatment goals of this phase. These closure comments can also provide invaluable feedback about members' areas of growth from their experience in MFGT.

MFGT programs enter this group stage either because they are ready due to members' goal attainment or as a result of time limits on this treatment modality. In this age of managed care, many of these groups will end more for the latter rather than the former reason.

Subsequently, it is important that facilitators plan time in these ending sessions to address relapse prevention and exploration of other sources outside the group for maintaining positive changes. Since treatment is focusing on all members of several family units, it is realistic to expect that not all the changes needed in these at risk families will be attained by MFGT. Hopefully, this intervention modality will have helped families start the change process and identify areas that will still need to be addressed as they work toward a healthier level of functioning. In addition, family units that have at risk members need to be realistic, at this ending point of a group, so they can expect that there will be new challenges ahead. Facilitators will want to reinforce the coping skills that family units have acquired and point out that many of these skills can now be used to effectively address future issues that they will face.

One unique aspect of this phase of a MFGT program is that even in the most successful groups members will often resist dealing with termination. There are often several possible reasons for this response including participants found the group to be so helpful they do not want it to end, members are concerned that they and their families are not yet ready to continue and maintain their changes without the group's support, and participants may lack the skills to address termination and the related feelings it surfaces for them. As a result, facilitators will usually have to take on a more directive role in this phase such that members will shift their focus to issues specifically related to the process and treatment goals of this phase. In fact, clinicians may even find that they will have to stop discussions of new problem areas by group members that are often one way participants resist dealing with the ending of a group. It is possible that new issues that surface will need to be addressed in further treatment. However, in these cases the facilitator should meet with the individual or family unit outside the group and process how such treatment can be attained via another resource. Facilitators will find that such situations require walking a fine line between conveying sensitivity to challenges that still face a family and yet consistently acknowledging that the MFGT is ending and cannot provide further treatment or support. When these new problems do surface in an ending group, it will be important to note to the entire membership that an individual or family unit will be seen outside the MFGT in order to develop a plan for further treatment services. This latter intervention will convey the message that the facilitator cares about members' current concerns and the group is then relieved of their responsibility in addressing such issues. It is extremely important that clinicians consistently emphasize the group's focus in this stage on validation of progress and exploration of outside supports rather than the surfacing of still unresolved problems or concerns.

Termination of multiple family groups, even the most successful ones, will sometimes surface members' feelings from earlier experiences of terminations or loss in their lives. For this reason, facilitators will need to be prepared to deal with strong emotional reactions or avoidance responses from members. It is not unusual for participants who have had unresolved endings in their lives to lack the skills to address group termination in a healthy manner. However, as a result, the ending of a MFGT program can provide such individuals with a corrective experience so they are able to acquire new skills for dealing with termination experiences that all participants will face at some point in their lives. Facilitators modeling of healthy termination responses will add to members' learning experience regarding these skills. For this reason, clinicians should share their honest reactions during these ending sessions, sharing tears or feeling of pride around members' success.

Although there are typically fewer sessions in this termination phase of a MFGT program, this stage is an essential ingredient to providing an effective group intervention. It is important that members have an opportunity to acknowledge their progress both as individuals and as family units. This validation experience will serve to reinforce the positive changes among participants and point out their strengths and skills for addressing future issues. In addition, this phase of a group allows members to explore other ways they will be able to maintain some of the changes they have made in this group modality. This focus will also help members naturally develop a relapse prevention plan that will assist in reducing the occurrence of regressive patterns among family units. Positive closure of this unique treatment approach will solidify changes among the membership and validate the contributions made by the total group.

GENERAL INSTRUCTIONS FOR USE OF
RELATIONSHIP-BUILDING INTERVENTIONS

The interventions in this chapter are intended to be used for the main part of each termination group session. There are a number of closure interventions provided so facilitators can choose ones that are most relevant to their group's needs. When conducting MFGT leaders must be sensitive to the importance of maintaining a safe, nonthreatening, and comfortable environment where participants will spontaneously begin sharing their feelings and reactions about the group's termination. Even though a level of trust and cohesiveness will have been already established in the group, facilitators should be aware that the members are now being asked to validate their progress and deal with their feelings about no longer having the support of the group. For this reason, members may struggle initially with sharing such feelings and addressing some of their emotional reactions to the group experience. This response will further validate members' progress and the value of this treatment modality.

Specific instructions for each intervention in this chapter include: title of technique, purpose of the task, directions on how to conduct the technique, reference to task sheet at end of chapter if relevant, cautions in regard to the use of this intervention, and suggestions for modifying the technique. This latter information should assist facilitators' understanding of how to plan and facilitate each of these interventions. Readers should feel free to duplicate the related task sheets, found at the end of the chapter, for use with their groups. (Duplication of these task sheets for other purposes (e.g., training) is prohibited and violates copyright.)

Unless otherwise indicated, facilitators should conduct these interventions in the same consistent manner at each termination phase group meeting. First, the intervention is introduced to participants and, if relevant, task sheets are passed out to each member. The group should be given some time to gather their thoughts or write down their responses on a task sheet before being requested to share with the group. At this point in the group the facilitator shifts back to disclosing, as a modeling intervention, in regard to these termination exercises. Therefore, clinicians should feel free to be the first to disclose during these tasks as a way of more easily eliciting similar disclosure from the membership. Such sharing from the group leader will assist in shifting the group's focus to termination-related discussions.

After the facilitator or a member and/or family unit has volunteered to share in regard to the closure task, members are requested to go around the circle and share in a similar way. For some interventions, such sharing may be done by the family as a unit rather than by each individual family member. Leaders will need to decide how families determine who will do such sharing for the entire unit. In some groups the family member can be selected freely by the family, whereas in other groups facilitators may want to have a set order as to who does the sharing for the family unit. Practitioners will need to use their clinical skills and individual preferences in deciding which method they choose to use for this familywide sharing. The rationale for having some interventions that require a familywide response is such tasks will necessitate that family members share first with one another, which can further validate their positive changes as a unit. In addition, this method of sharing requires less time in the session, which can be important due to the number of members in a MFGT program. It will be important that both during and at the completion of each intervention facilitators point out commonalities among the membership and reinforce participation. Such processing comments will contribute to the group's positive closure experience. In addition, these reinforcing comments by the facilitator will be important as a group is asked to open up in more direct terms about their reactions to the group's ending. Moreover, leaders may want to request the participants to process their responses to the intervention after hearing all the membership's sharing. This request may surface some important feedback about unresolved feelings among the participants regarding the termination of a group.

The amount of time any particular intervention will require varies between groups. Such timing will depend on the size of the group, age span of participants, and amount of sharing that surfaces. Facilitators are cautioned to monitor both the amount and type of disclosure among participants. It is important, even in this ending phase, that balanced participation is maintained throughout the life of a group. Otherwise, clinicians will find themselves conducting individual or family therapy with an audience.

Modification of some interventions will be necessary due to the age span among members of any one multiple family therapy group. This author has attempted to design techniques that are relevant and developmentally appropriate for a wide span of ages. However, it is impossible to create interventions that will be effective for all possible ages of group participants. Therefore, readers are strongly encouraged to modify or change interventions so they will be effective for their particular MFGT program. Also, facilitators should feel free to ask family members to assist younger members who might have difficulty with some tasks. Such assistance can serve some important therapeutic value as family members relate more positively to one another.

The remaining contents of this chapter will now be a listing of termination interventions with related task sheets. Readers are encouraged to review this entire chapter before their MFGT program enters this ending group phase.

TECHNIQUE 71

Title of Intervention: A Profile of a New You and a New Family
Purpose: To increase members' awareness of the positive changes in themselves and their family units as a result of the group experience.
Specific Instructions: This technique begins with the task sheet titled *A Profile of a New You and a New Family* being passed out to each member. Participants are given a few minutes to complete this sheet. Facilitators should remember that due to the reflective nature of this task members may need a longer period to determine their responses to this task sheet. Next, members are asked to go around the circle in order and share their responses to this intervention. Some facilitators may choose to modify this part of the intervention by having a volunteer from each family unit collect all the task sheets and share their familywide responses. Regardless of the way this information is shared, facilitators should reinforce commonalities that surface, particularly those common among the members of the same family unit. At the end of this exercise, participants can be asked to share how this task affected their view of their progress in the group.
Related Task Sheet: A Profile of a New You and a New Family
Cautions and Possible Modifications: This is an excellent exercise to help participants validate both the changes they have made as individuals and those made by their family units. It may take members longer

to complete the related task sheet and, in some cases, the group can be asked to add to the things that each member has indicated as positive changes they have made. As a result, this intervention also can provide members the opportunity to reinforce one another's progress and point out changes that may not be as obvious to individual participants. This particular task has been developed such that it can be easily completed by even the youngest group members. In some ways, this intervention is a type of free association since the task sheet requests members to draw or write major changes they have seen in themselves and their family units as a result of this treatment intervention. Also, facilitators may want to encourage members to save this task sheet as a reminder, after the group ends, of the changes they have made from this therapeutic experience.

TECHNIQUE 72

Title of Intervention: A Work in Progress
Purpose: To increase groups members' awareness of both their positive changes and areas they need to continue to work on after the group ends.
Specific Instructions: This technique is intended to emphasize the message to members that everyone has continued growth they want to make in their life. Subsequently, it is important to be satisfied with one's progress and be confident other changes will follow in due time. In many ways this task should help convey the idea that we can eventually reach our goals of self-change but not all at once. These points should be made via a brief presentation to the group before they begin working on the related task sheet. Then the facilitator passes around the sheet titled *A Work in Progress* and requests that everyone take time to complete this form. Once everyone is ready, participants proceed around the circle sharing the contents of their task sheet. After each person discloses, it will be important to ask the group if that individual forgot to mention some changes he or she has made in the group. It will also be helpful to reinforce commonalities that surface and reinforce participants' disclosure. At the end of this task, members should be requested to process the benefits of doing this particular exercise.
Related Task Sheet: A Work in Progress

Cautions and Possible Modifications: This is a wonderful intervention for conveying the message that it is important to take time to celebrate one's accomplishments and then be confident future changes will happen. Many times group members will be so encouraged by their progress that they, unfortunately, proceed to set unrealistic expectations regarding future changes. This same response can occur between families and their individual members, particularly in regard to at risk adolescents or children. Facilitators may find it helpful to also conduct a discussion on the possible consequences of setting expectations too high for future changes after the group ends. Hopefully, this latter intervention will instruct participants on the increase possibilities of relapsing back to old unhealthy patterns of behavior. In addition, members should be encouraged to take their task sheets home and save them for future reference when they are dealing with expected changes either for themselves or other members of their family.

TECHNIQUE 73

Title of Intervention: Before and After Group Pictures!
Purpose: To validate members' positive changes from the MFGT experience.
Specific Instructions: This is a type of free association technique or what may also be termed an incomplete picture task. Members are asked to initially get into a relaxed position, close their eyes, and visualize two different pictures. First, ask them to think about what they were like when they first entered the group. Then, participants should be requested to visualize a picture of what they are like today after having been in the MFGT program. Once this part of the task has been completed, the task sheet titled *Before and After Group Pictures!* is passed out to each member. Participants are requested to take a few minutes to either draw or write on the two contrasting pictures. Once everyone has completed his or her sheet, members go around the circle in order sharing the contents of their two pictures. Facilitators should request, after each person shares, if the membership would add any prior unhealthy behavior patterns or positive changes that the participant had not indicated. Members should be reinforced for sharing and commonalities that surface can be pointed out. At the end of the session, participants

227

should be asked to process what they found most beneficial about this exercise.

Related Task Sheet: Before and After Group Pictures!

Cautions and Possible Modifications: This particular task provides both parents and children the opportunity to easily articulate or draw changes they have seen in themselves as a result of the group. Facilitators can modify this technique and instead have participants draw before and after group pictures of their family life. This latter modification can also provide invaluable validation to family units in terms of their progress as a whole. Here again facilitators may want to encourage members to hang onto their task sheets as a reference point for later work on their problem areas.

TECHNIQUE 74

Title of Intervention: Validation of Members' Progress and Strengths

Purpose: To provide members' feedback on their progress and strengths from the group.

Specific Instructions: This technique begins with 4 x 6 lined cards being passed out to each group member with the instruction that they write their name on the top of one side. Then the membership is informed that they will have the opportunity in this session to provide one another with feedback regarding both progress and strengths they have seen in one another. Next, the group is requested to start passing the cards around the circle such that each person can decide if he or she wants to indicate any feedback on cards as they are received. Participants should be encouraged not to duplicate the same feedback already on a card but rather indicate that they too agree with that point (this can be done with a checkmark for purposes of space concerns). Also, members should be given the choice if they want to indicate their name or not by the feedback they provide to an individual. After the cards have gone around the entire circle, members are asked to read over their own cards and think about their reactions to the feedback. Then participants are requested to share their responses to these compliment cards. It will be important that facilitators also have a card for themselves included in this exercise so they too can be given feedback about their strengths. At the end of this sharing, members should be asked to process their reactions to this task.

Related Task Sheet: No task sheet required but 4 x 6 cards for validation comments for each member.

Cautions and Possible Modifications: Even though members may be initially uncomfortable with providing and receiving this feedback, very quickly they will begin to enjoy this opportunity for compliment sharing. Younger members of some families may require assistance with this task since it requires a level of writing skills. In the case of very young children, a co-facilitator may work the entire task with the child to write down the ideas that he or she shares regarding the person on the card. Interestingly, facilitators will find that participants enjoy this opportunity to provide feedback and appreciation to them for all their efforts in running an effective group program. Members should be encouraged to put these cards somewhere such that they can refer to them when they are feeling depressed or somewhat down after the group ends. The author has been amazed at the number of at risk children and teens that have kept such cards for many years after a particularly therapeutic group experience.

TECHNIQUE 75

Title of Intervention: Group Good-bye Card
Purpose: To increase members' awareness of the value and benefits of their MFGT experience.
Specific Instructions: This task provides members with an opportunity to gather and share their thoughts on the value of the group in terms of their own progress. The session begins with the task sheet titled *Group Good-bye Card* being passed out to each member. Then participants are requested to complete this letter that summarizes the contributions the group has made to their positive changes. After everyone has completed this sheet, members are asked to go around the circle in order and read their letter to the group. Facilitators should reinforce such disclosure and point out commonalities that surface during this part of the task. At the end of the session, members should be asked to share what was helpful about participating in this intervention.
Related Task Sheet: Group Good-bye Card
Cautions and Possible Modifications: This incomplete letter to the

group serves as a nonthreatening means for members to share the important role that the group has served in their change process. By completing this letter, participants will be able to more specifically identify how the group has helped them to make progress. While members are sharing their letters with the group, facilitators will want to take the opportunity to point out aspects of the group that members may want to look for in future supports. This connection will be an important one to help participants make so they also realize that they have experienced the benefits of having a healthy support group. Through this realization, some members should be more knowledgeable about the types of support they will need in the future. In addition, facilitators will obtain important feedback about the most beneficial parts of this therapeutic experience. This feedback will provide invaluable guidance in planning future MFGT programs.

TECHNIQUE 76

Title of Intervention: A Vision of Your Family 5 Years in the Future!
Purpose: To increase members' hopes and goals for their family life in future years.
Specific Instructions: This task begins with the facilitator doing a brief presentation on the value of family members knowing what they want from their family in the future. In a way, this task will provide members with the opportunity to share their fantasy of their family life in 5 years. Next, members are each given the task sheet titled *A Vision of Your Family 5 Years in the Future!* and asked to complete it. Once everyone has finished their task sheet, members go around the circle in order sharing their future vision. It will be important for the facilitator to check on members' (of the same family unit) reactions to the future visions shared. At the end of this session, members should be asked to share what they gained from participating in this visualization task.
Related Task Sheet: A Vision of your Family 5 Years in the Future!
Cautions and Possible Modifications: This particular intervention provides family units an opportunity for all their members to share their hopes and dreams for their future as a family. Surfacing such disclosure can help maintain families' motivation to continue making positive changes so that they are at a different place in 5 years. Also, this

task may elicit some new awareness in individual members that they had not shared with their families. By completing this future vision at the end of a MFGT program, members are more likely to be optimistic about future changes that their families are capable of making. Facilitators may want to encourage families to take these pictures home and save them as points of reference in the future.

TECHNIQUE 77

Title of Intervention: Your Personal Motto for Happiness

Purpose: To increase members' awareness of one major way they have learned can help ensure their happiness.

Specific Instructions: This task begins with a group being instructed that they will have a chance in the session to think very carefully about the one thing they know they need to continue in their lives if their progress is to be maintained. It may be helpful to request members to have a brief discussion on some of the critical changes they have made that seem to have had the most impact on their progress in the group. After this sharing, members are each given a copy of the task sheet titled *Your Personal Motto for Happiness* and asked to complete it. Once everyone has completed this sheet, members are requested to share their motto by going around the circle in order. As each member shares, it will be important to reinforce the disclosure, point out commonalities that surface, and ask the membership for their reactions to the participant's motto. At the end of the session, members should be asked to share what they learned and found helpful about this exercise.

Related Task Sheet: Your Personal Motto for Happiness

Cautions and Possible Modifications: Typically this task will take longer for members to respond to because they will have to determine one behavior, thought pattern, or attitude that will be most critical to maintaining their positive changes. This exercise will be invaluable because it will help participants focus on one particularly important change that will be essential for their future happiness. Facilitators should strongly encourage members to take home and save these task sheets for future reference, particularly when they are going through some difficult times or new challenges.

TECHNIQUE 78

Title of Intervention: Mapping Out Your Keys to Success
Purpose: To increase members' knowledge of specific ways they can continue to work toward success in their lives.
Specific Instructions: This is a brainstorming task where the membership is asked to summarize the important knowledge and skills they have gained from their MFGT experience. The session begins with members being informed that today's technique will provide everyone with an opportunity to review what they have learned are the most important ways to maintain positive changes and make future changes. It may be helpful to have the members do two different brainstorming exercises; one on ways individuals can maintain their progress and a second one on ways families can maintain the positive changes they have made. The facilitator should indicate the contributions made for each of the lists on either a blackboard or large newsprint pad. By writing these points down, members will be more likely to both remember and appreciate the value of all the suggestions. At the end of this task, members should be asked to process what they found beneficial about this brainstorming exercise.
Related Task Sheet: No task sheet required for this intervention but use of a blackboard or large newsprint pad would be helpful for this brainstorming discussion.
Cautions and Possible Modifications: This is an extremely helpful intervention for one of the ending sessions of a multiple family group. Members will benefit from this review exercise and will often be amazed at how much they have learned from this group experience. Facilitators may want to type up the responses shared during this brainstorming task so a summary of the ideas can be handed out in written form to all members at the next session.

TECHNIQUE 79

Title of Intervention: A Family Insurance Plan
Purpose: To assist family units in developing a relapse prevention plan for maintaining their positive changes after the group ends.
Specific Instructions: Members are informed at the onset of this task

that they will be asked to develop an insurance plan in today's session that will serve as a type of relapse prevention. Then families are requested to form smaller circles such that all their members are together. Next, the task sheet titled *A Family Insurance Plan* is passed out to all members with one member of each family being designated to complete this form based on their discussion as a family unit. All family units are given enough time to both discuss and complete their task sheets. After everyone is ready, a volunteer from each family unit shares the contents of their family insurance plan. After each of these participants shares, other members should be requested to indicate any reactions they have to the plan that was developed by the family unit. Facilitators should reinforce disclosure during this sharing and point out commonalities that surface between family units. At the end of the sessions, participants should be asked to share what they think will be helpful about having developed a family insurance plan.

Related Task Sheet: A Family Insurance Plan

Cautions and Possible Modifications: This exercise affords families an important opportunity to openly discuss ways that they as a unit will be able to maintain their progress. In addition, this sharing will provide important relapse prevention guidelines that have been individualized for each family and will serve as essential guidelines after the group ends. Facilitators should strongly encourage family units to place these insurance plans in a visible location of their home so all members will be regularly reminded of what is needed for their family to maintain a healthy level of functioning.

TECHNIQUE 80

Title of Intervention: A Meditation for You and Your Family

Purpose: To increase members' awareness of ways they can help maintain the positive changes in their families.

Specific Instructions: This task provides members another intervention to share what they feel will be an important guideline for maintaining their positive changes. Participants are requested to indicate on the task sheet titled *A Meditation for You and Your Family* a type of prayer that will help guide them in their future efforts to both maintain their progress and deal with new challenges. Once everyone has completed their meditation, all participants are asked to go around the circle in order and share their responses on this task sheet. Facilitators will want to reinforce disclosure and point out commonalities, particularly those among members of the same family units, during this part of the task. At the end of the session, members should be asked to process how this meditation will be helpful in future times for both them as individuals and their families.

Related Task Sheet: A Meditation for You and Your Family

Cautions and Possible Modifications: This task affords another opportunity for family members to develop a relapse prevention plan that is individualized to their needs and issues. Here again facilitators may want to encourage members to take home and save their meditation as a future reference point as they deal with new problems that arise. This particular task may require that a co-facilitator provide assistance to younger family members so that they too can fully participate in this exercise. Clinicians are cautioned to be sensitive and respectful of members' religious beliefs when conducting this intervention. For this reason, terms like "prayer" may not be a term to use with some groups.

SUMMARY

The reader was provided in this chapter an overview of the treatment and process goals for the termination phase of a MFGT program. The importance of attaining these ending phase goals was emphasized since they address the need for members to validate their progress and explore other sources for maintaining their changes. In addition, the importance of shifting discussions to the attainment of members' positive changes rather than surfacing new problem areas was pointed out. Then ten interventions were delineated in this chapter for addressing the process and treatment goals of this phase. Specific directions for each intervention, along with related task sheets, were provided such that readers should be able to easily utilize the suggested techniques with their particular groups. The details provided for each technique listed in this chapter should also increase clinicians' ability to modify, change, and even create similar group closure interventions.

A Profile of a New You and a New Family

Instructions: Complete the below profiles by first indicating the changes you have made as an individual and then the changes you have observed in your family as a result of this group treatment experience.

A NEW You

My thoughts are _____
_____
_____

Most of the time I feel _____
_____
_____

My general attitude is _____
_____
_____

I have changed my
behaviors of _____
_____
_____

A NEW Family

Family interactions are usually
_____
_____

Everyone seems to get along
better in terms of _____
_____

I have particularly liked seeing changes
in my family's _____
_____
_____

I really like being with my
family these days when _____
_____
_____

I hope in the future that my family
continues to make changes in regard to
_____
_____
_____

A Work in Progress

Instructions: List in the table below those changes you have made, those you are currently working on, and areas of change you would like to work on in the future.

POSITIVE CHANGES YOU HAVE MADE	POSITIVE CHANGES YOU ARE WORKING ON	AREAS OF CHANGE YOU WOULD LIKE TO WORK ON IN THE FUTURE

* Go back when you have finished the above table and circle the changes you have made that mean the most to you.

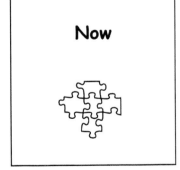

Now

5 years from now

10 years from now

Before and After Group Pictures!

Instructions: Draw or write in the two pictures below what you and your family looked like when you came into this group and then how you look today as you are about to finish this group experience.

A BEFORE GROUP PICTURE

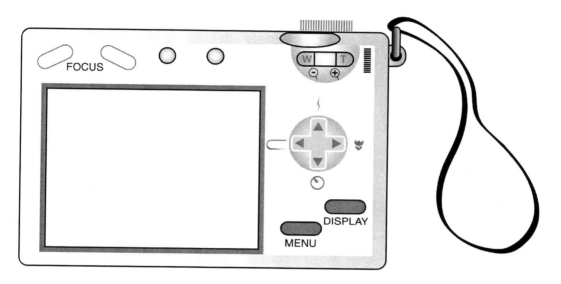

AN AFTER GROUP PICTURE

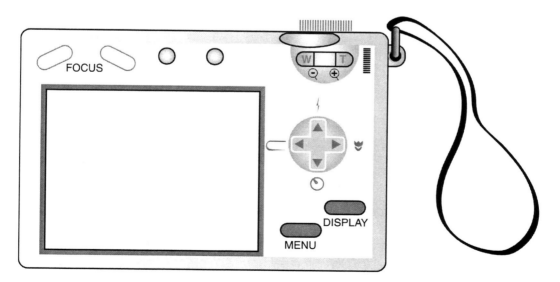

Group Good-bye Card

Instructions: Complete this card to your multiple family group as a way of indicating what this group has meant to you.

Dear Group, _____

_____

When I first came to this group I felt _____

_____

_____

_____

_____

As I attended each session in this group I began to feel __

_____

_____

_____

_____

I particularly found the group helpful for _____

_____

_____

_____

What I will most miss about this group is _____

_____

_____

_____

_____

Sincerely, _____

_____

_____

A Vision of Your Family 5 Years in the Future!

Instructions: Inside the crystal ball write or draw a picture of what you hope your family is like in 5 years.

Your Personal Motto for Happiness

Instructions: Take some time and think about a motto that you have found will be the key to your future happiness. Make sure this motto involves something you have total control over so you can ensure it will be a part of your daily living.

A Family Insurance Plan

Instructions: Make believe that you are creating an insurance policy that will ensure that your family functioning in the future is happy, healthy, and satisfying to all members.

Insurance Policy

I_____ do hereby insure my family of a long life of happiness, healthy functioning, and a satisfying existence for all members if the following are adhered to by all our members.

In regard to daily chores we must _____

_____

In regard to communication we must_____

_____

In regard to having fun as a family we must_____

_____

In regard to coping with problems we must_____

_____

I personally guarantee that this policy will provide insurance for my family's happiness, healthy functioning, and satisfaction for all members if the above policy requirements are adhered to by myself and all other family members.

Date of Policy:_____

Seal of Approval

A Meditation for You and Your Family

Instructions: Complete the meditation below for you and your family, keeping in mind the things you have learned from this group experience.

A Meditation for me & my Family

May I come to accept

_____

May I learn to appreciate

_____

May I start reaching out

_____

Let me now begin

_____

Let all my family

_____

With this meditation I hope for inner peace

for myself and my family.

Signature_____

Date _____

Chapter 9

PARALLEL/CONJOINT MFGT

In this chapter the reader will be provided a modified form of MFGT that is the parallel/conjoint group approach. Major findings regarding the use of this treatment modality will first be summarized along with practice implications. Then the rationale for selecting this group approach rather than the traditional form of MFGT will be outlined with the unique benefits of this treatment format highlighted. Next, the reader will be given specific guidelines for setting up, planning, and facilitating this approach to group work with at risk adolescents and their families. A sample plan for a 12-session parallel/conjoint MFGT program will then be delineated utilizing interventions provided in Chapters 5, 6, 7, and 8. Experienced group workers should find that this chapter, along with the first eight chapters of this book, will provide the essential treatment guidelines for effectively setting up, planning, and conducting parallel/conjoint MFGT programs with at risk adolescents and their families.

MAJOR FINDINGS FROM RELATED LITERATURE

The use of parallel/conjoint groups within the MFGT approach has been reported in the literature from as early as the 1970s. For example, the Community Guidance Center, a training center at the University of Texas, has provided parallel groups to children, adolescents, and their parents since 1971 and then added the MFGT component in 1979 (Matthews & Cunningham, 1983). A wide variety of problems have

243

been successfully treated over the past four decades using this modified form of MFGT. Parmenter, Smith, and Cecic (1987) applied this treatment method with families who had young children with emotional and behavioral problems. About the same time, Marner and Westerberg (1987) effectively addressed the problems families face when their adolescent is diagnosed with anorexia nervosa. Greenfield and Senecal (1995) applied this method to their work with families having children diagnosed with attention deficit with hyperactivity disorder. Dennison (1995) introduced an application of this form of MFGT for families and their adolescents who are experiencing family life changes (i.e., divorce, remarriage, etc.). Behr (1996) treated socially isolated families with long-standing dysfunctional interactions while Goldstein (1996) focused on families dealing with psychotic disorders. Mandell and Birenzweig (1990) applied this form of MFGT to stepfamilies with concurrent group sessions conducted for parent/stepparents and for their children. In addition, Fristad, Gavazzi, and Soldano (1998) effectively addressed mood disorders in children by utilizing this unique MFGT approach. Wamboldt and Levin (1995) utilized this form of MFGT with medically ill children/adolescents and their families. Even though this modified treatment form has not been applied to as many population groups as traditional MFGT, it has been found to be successful with some of the most challenging issues that families face. Moreover, several authors have noted that the parallel/conjoint form of MFGT appears to be particularly effective with chronic family problems (Parmenter, Smith, & Cecic, 1987; Mandell & Birenzweig, 1990).

The studies on the use of this treatment method have also surfaced some of the areas of functioning that seem to be the most positively impacted. For example, several researchers have found this approach improves family communication, provides much needed support for family units and individual members, and decreases attention on "identified patients" (Pasnau, et al., 1976; Cunningham & Matthews, 1982). In addition, Greenfield and Senecal (1995) reported improved parenting skills, decreased isolation, and increased sensitivity to children's strengths. Behr (1996) also found that this approach engaged more fathers in the problem-solving process with their families. This particular MFGT method appears to combine the benefits found with traditional multiple family groups and peer groups. Although further studies on this approach are needed, clinicians are reporting that this group format more effectively attracts both parents and adolescents, along with providing simultaneous support for peers and family units (Dennison, 1995).

Two different formats of parallel/conjoint MFGT are reported to date in the literature. The first approach utilizes the use of parent groups and children/adolescent groups that meet separately for a specific number of sessions and then, at designated sessions, participate in a multiple family group (Marner & Westerberg, 1987; Dennison, 1995; Behr, 1996). The second approach combines parent groups, children/adolescent groups, and multiple family groups within the same meeting sessions (Parmenter, Smith, & Cecic 1987; Greenfield & Senecal, 1995; Fristad, Gavazzi, & Soldane, 1998). Further study of these two formats is needed so the benefits of each can be more clearly identified such that practitioners can utilize the format that will most effectively treat their particular targeted population.

RATIONALE FOR THIS APPROACH BEING THE TREATMENT OF CHOICE

This form of MFGT has been included in this text primarily due to its focus on at risk adolescents and their families. The nature of adolescence is such that most teens find themselves in states of crisis on a regular basis throughout this period of development. As a result, many researchers have found that a combination of treatment approaches offered simultaneously to adolescents and their parents usually is the most effective. In addition, there are a number of additional reasons why a clinician may find that parallel/conjoint MFGT is the treatment of choice when working with teens and their parents. Readers should carefully review the following list before planning their MFGT program because this particular format might be more effective in both engaging and effectively treating some of the problems of this at risk population. Practitioners will find the following treatment issues are by no means the only reasons why this MFGT format might be the treatment of choice. Rather, this information is intended to provide guidelines to group workers as they plan their MFGT program. In addition, readers will have to use their clinical expertise in ultimately determining which format will work best with their client population, realizing that there are many factors that must be considered before developing the final design of a multiple family group treatment approach.

Following are some of the treatment issues that could make parallel/conjoint MFGT the treatment of choice:

1. Family units where members are having strong emotional feelings and interactions, particularly between parents and their adolescent children.
2. Families that are difficult to engage in treatment because all the group meetings require all family members in attendance.
3. Family units where boundary issues need to be addressed in the treatment process.
4. The composition of families for a particular multiple family group involve a wide age range among the members.
5. Families that are experiencing serious and long-term communication problems.
6. Families that have experienced chronic and severe problems.
7. Family units where individual members have low self-esteem that could benefit from peer support, validation, and feedback.
8. Family units where it will be challenging to schedule multiple family group sessions regularly due to the varying schedules of potential members.

Practitioners may find that they have one or a combination of these issues relevant to their treatment efforts with a targeted group of families. Here again, readers must use their group knowledge and skills to determine if the parallel/conjoint form of MFGT is the treatment of choice for their client group. In addition, clinicians will have to consider the resources that will be needed to provide this treatment approach. Resources will include both space for separate group meetings and additional staff time to facilitate separate groups, particularly if they meet at the same time. Moreover, readers will have to carefully consider if there are group workers available to run the groups that possess the needed expertise. For example, clinicians may feel qualified to conduct MFGT but may not have the training to facilitate parent groups and/or adolescent groups. Also, if groups meet at different times, places, or days of the week, then facilitators may have to address transportation issues or childcare problems. The decision to utilize this MFGT approach obviously must consider both treatment and logistical issues.

SETTING UP PARALLEL/CONJOINT MFGT

Readers are referred to Chapter 4 for general guidelines for setting up MFGT. The information in the Chapter 4 should be utilized along with some of the more specific guidelines provided in this chapter. Most of the suggestions provided thus far in this text for effectively establishing MFGT programs will apply to this modified format. Some additional points that readers will need to consider when utilizing this approach include the following:

1. It is ideal to interview family members separately for these groups so that the motivation level of each member can be determined and the various types of group involvement marketed to them. During these same pregroup interviews it will be critical to obtain a signed contract from each member that outlines their commitment to attendance at the various group sessions and adherence to basic group rules.

2. The schedule for adolescent groups, parent groups, and multiple family groups should be clearly delineated at the onset of a treatment program such that all involved group members will know when they should attend various group meetings.

3. Facilitators will need to make sure that arrangements can be made for additional group workers if the parallel groups meet on the same day and time. Also, it will be important to select facilitators who are trained and experienced in the groups they will be conducting. At the same time, some groups may require co-facilitators so this same arrangement must be planned before treatment is initiated.

4. Clinicians will have to decide what types of parallel groups they will be conducting with a targeted client population. For example, if there is a fairly wide age span among the children/adolescents of the identified family units, then it may be ideal to conduct both a teen group and a children's group. Here again, readers will have to plan for additional staff resources if such groups are needed within this MFGT format.

5. Because this approach involves a combination of groups, facilitators will have to plan age-appropriate therapeutic activities that are developmentally appropriate and effective with each type of group (i.e., parent groups, children groups, teen groups, and

MFGT). In the case of children's groups, more careful planning and preparation of materials may be necessary due to the interests and attention span of these youngsters.

6. Readers are strongly encouraged to utilize material from relevant age group treatment programs for their parallel groups. The material in this book is primarily intended to be used with multiple family groups. When facilitators are conducting children, teen, or parent groups it is best to complement this material with literature that has been specifically developed for these age groups. For example, this author has written a book for setting up and facilitating children's groups (Dennison, 1997) and another one for conducting adolescent groups (Dennison, 1999). There is extensive literature on the market today that provides guidelines for both facilitating and planning these specific groups. Readers will find that their parallel groups will be more effective when they incorporate material from such references.

7. When this MFGT format is utilized, facilitators may have to address several logistic issues such as transportation of young children or teens to group meetings or childcare arrangements when parents are attending their group sessions. It will be important to request ideas and feedback from the targeted client group when planning ways to address these issues. For example, what might appear to be a need for childcare among members of a parent group could be addressed by having older siblings care for younger ones. Facilitators should always ask parents to indicate if they anticipate any problems or challenges in having their family members attend all the required group sessions.

8. Due to the use of parallel and conjoint groups when following this approach, it will be critical to address the issue of confidentiality. This issue will be particularly important to teens that place a high value on their privacy during this developmental period. Facilitators will have to address, both in pregroup sessions and beginning group sessions, the requirement that all members are expected to not disclose material surfaced in a particular group outside that group. In addition, facilitators will have to clearly indicate their commitment to confidentiality and the limits of it. Adolescents and children need to know that if they share a disclosure that indicates potential danger to self or others, then facilitators are required by the law to report such disclosure to their

parents and possibly other appropriate authorities. It is strongly suggested that the requirements around confidentiality be included in the group contract signed by all members. Readers are reminded that one of the challenges of this approach to MFGT is that both facilitators and members will sometimes have a hard time remembering where certain disclosure surfaced in terms of which group treatment setting (i.e., parent group, teen group, MFGT). For this reason, it may be a good idea to suggest that members and facilitators, as a rule, check with the involved person first to see if he or she is comfortable with sharing a disclosure that he or she had made in an earlier session.

9. Facilitators will have to delineate their goals for each parallel and conjoint group such that the overall purpose and thrust of treatment in each modality is clear and will provide guidance for the actual planning of each session. It is a good idea to also note these goals on the contract that each family member signs before they begin treatment in a parallel/conjoint MFGT program. Readers are referred to Appendix A for a sample of a Multiple Family Group Therapy Contract. This form may need to be modified or expanded when readers are using this particular treatment approach. Also, the clear specification of treatment goals will make the evaluation of this form of MFGT easier to conduct.

10. Facilitators should design an evaluation of this form of MFGT such that the treatment outcomes of each group approach can be individually determined. In addition, readers may chose to conduct a process outcome study on their treatment program so they can determine which parts of the group process contributed to the positive or negative outcomes of the intervention. Due to the multiple groups being utilized in this particular approach, the evaluation design for this treatment format will typically be more involved and challenging. Facilitators may consider using a research consultant when planning this part of their parallel/conjoint MFGT program. Also, readers are referred to Chapter 10 for more specifics on evaluation designs for MFGT.

It is hoped that these guidelines will provide readers additional issues to consider when they are setting up parallel/conjoint MFGT programs.

Table 9.1

Session Plans for a Parallel/Conjoint MFGT Program

Session Number	Type of Parallel/Conjoint Group	Technique Number/Title
1	Teen/Child Group	#2: Give Us the Family Rap! #3: What's in Style for Your Family (or You)?
1	Parent Group	#4: Your Family's Coat of Values #5: Family Rituals at Your House
2	Teen/Child Group	#7: Our Family Cartoon #9: It's On my Mind these Days!
2	Parent Group	#10: We Dial...for Support #9: It's On my Mind these Days!
3	Teen/Child Group	#11: What's the Radio Playing at Your Home? #30: Self-rating on a Standardized Scale and Discuss
3	Parent Group	#6: Words that Describe Your Family #28: What Makes Children and Teens Resilient?
4	Teen/Child Group	#13: Tracking the Unique Me #33: Typical Problems of Teenagers and Parents of Teenagers
4	Parent Group	#12: Strengths of our Family! #33: Typical Problems of Teenagers and Parents of Teenagers
5	Multiple Family Group	#6: Words that Describe Your Family #27: Trash your Problems
6	Teen/Child Group	#8: Good Times and Difficult Times in our Family History #40: Whose Job Is It Anyways?
6	Parent Group	#8: Good Times and Difficult Times in our Family History #41: Drawing Boundary Lines for Healthy Family Functioning

7	Teen/Child Group	#16:	Fantasy Family
		#39:	Can you Hear me Now?
7	Parent Group	#16:	Fantasy Family
		#39:	Are You Hearing Me Now?
8	Teen/Child Group	#20:	Take a Walk in my Shoes
		#45:	Just Record and Watch
8	Parent Group	#21:	What is becoming Extinct in our Family?
		#45:	Just Record and Watch
9	Multiple Family Group	#17:	What is each Family Member's Mantra?
		#42:	Brainstorm Ways to Build Family Members' Self-esteem
10	Teen/Child Group	#19:	If I Were the Parent/If I Were the Teen
		#34:	How Families can Always be Upset and in Conflict!
10	Parent Group	#19:	If I Were the Parent/If I Were the Teen
		#34:	How Families can Always be Upset and in Conflict!
11	Teen/Child Group	#18:	Rate your Life
		#47:	A…each Week Keeps our Family Okay
11	Parent Group	#18:	Rate your Life
		#47:	A…each Week Keeps our Family Okay
12	Multiple Family Group	#25:	Our Family Leaves this Group Feeling…
		#48:	Family Relapse Prevention: Warning Signs and a Plan

251

PLANNING PARALLEL/CONJOINT MFGT

When utilizing this approach to multiple family group therapy, facilitators should expect that the planning of parallel and conjoint groups will be more involved and time-consuming. For this reason, readers will want to consider having additional facilitators for this approach since the groups will typically require different plans and related materials. Clinicians will find that the wider age span of these groups necessitates that session plans are carefully determined such that they are age-appropriate and based on the treatment goals of each group. As a result, there is not one correct plan to follow for every parallel/conjoint MFGT program. The reader is referred to the planning section of Chapter 4 in this text that contains some overall suggestions for planning group sessions and the importance of using a set format. This information is also relevant to this form of MFGT and, in fact, younger age groups will respond positively to a more planned approach that follows a consistent routine in each session.

The reader will find on Table 9.1 a sample parallel/conjoint MFGT program for 12 sessions. This planning sample utilizes techniques from Chapters 5, 6, 7, and 8 so that readers are given actual interventions they can utilize when conducting this type of MFGT. In addition, the sample plan has been delineated for teen groups, parent groups, and multiple family groups so that it is the most relevant to the focus of this text. Facilitators who determine that they need to also conduct a younger children's group will have to determine session plans that are developmentally appropriate. As indicated earlier in this book, interventions in the four technique chapters (i.e., Chapter 5, 6, 7, and 8) have been developed such that they can be easily modified to address different age groups and interest levels of potential members.

The sample parallel/conjoint MFGT plan follows the simultaneous but separate group session format where parent group sessions and teen group sessions are held in different locations and then at set dates are joined together for multiple family group sessions. Readers are reminded that some researchers have promoted the use of parallel/conjoint groups within the same meeting time of a MFGT program. If a facilitator chooses to use this approach it will be important to consider this modification when planning this form of MFGT. Planning of this approach will require careful consideration of the time required for interventions for the separate groups and the MFGT. Many of the interventions in this text can still be used for this MFGT format.

When conducting a parallel/conjoint approach readers will find that the parent groups and teen groups will typically progress further in their group development as compared to the MFGT. The reason for this difference is primarily related to the number of meeting times. The parallel groups (i.e., parent groups and teen groups) will have met nine times during the 12-session treatment program while the MFGT will have met only three times. It is absolutely essential that facilitators keep in mind the number of meetings of each group (i.e., parent group, teen group, or MFGT) within their total treatment time. Differences in the number of meetings will usually result in groups being in different phases of the group (i.e., initial phase, middle phase, or termination phase). This latter point is very important when planning groups since the phase of the group will determine which plans will be most appropriate. For example, if the reader follows the sample plan, it would be expected that the teen groups and parent groups will be either in the middle phase or close to entering it at the end of the 12 sessions whereas the MFGT will probably only be in the initial phase since it would have only met for a total of three times during the 12 sessions. Readers should be aware that this is why some researchers promote the simultaneous parallel groups within the same MFGT session. This latter MFGT format would have a higher probability of having all groups at the same group phase when treatment ends. However, facilitators still have to remember that total time in treatment is not the only variable that determines the group phase; there are many other factors involved in the progression of group treatment. Readers are referred to Chapters 3 and 4 for more specifics on other variables to consider when determining the treatment phase of a group. However, it is still important to remember that the total meeting times of groups within the parallel/conjoint MFGT model will have to be considered when determining appropriate interventions for each group session.

Readers will see on Table 9.2 that the goals for each of the parallel and conjoint groups have been delineated so the connection can be seen between these treatment goals and the interventions planned for each group's sessions. The specification of these goals is essential for providing a clear thrust for treatment throughout the combination of group sessions. In addition, this goal delineation is needed in order to

Table 9.2

Process and Treatment Goals for a Parallel/Conjoint MFGT Program

Group Phase	Process Goals	Treatment Goals for Adolescent/Child Group	Treatment Goals for Parent Group	Treatment Goals For Multiple Family Group
Initial	1. To create an attractive group setting. 2. To initiate balanced participation among members. 3. To build a trusting relationship among members.	1. To delineate treatment goals specific to the teens. 2. To provide psychoeducation on substance abuse and its impact on self and family.	1. To delineate treatment goals specific to the parents. 2. To provide psychoeducation on substance abuse and its impact on a family.	1. To surface knowledge gained from peer groups. 2. To provide psychoeducation on familywide responses to substance abuse issues.
Middle	1. To continue building an attractive group setting. 2. To increase member-to-member participation and maintain balanced participation. 3. To continue developing member trust and group cohesiveness.	1. To increase teens' awareness of their substance abuse. 2. To increase alternative healthy responses. 3. To integrate healthier behavior into members' repertoire.	1. To increase parents' awareness of their responses to teen's substance abuse. 2. To increase alternative healthy responses. 3. To integrate healthier behavior into members' repertoire.	1. To increase awareness of familywide responses to substance abuse. 2. To increase awareness of alternative healthy responses. 3. To integrate healthier familywide responses into members' repertoire.
Termination	1. To have members acknowledge the value of the group and grieve its ending. 2. To have members acknowledge their progress. 3. To have members identify other sources that will support their changes.	1. To have teens acknowledge attainment of treatment goals. 2. To have teens develop a relapse prevention plan for maintaining positive treatment gains.	1. To have parents acknowledge attainment of treatment goals. 2. To have parents develop a relapse prevention plan for maintaining positive treatment gains.	1. To have families acknowledge attainment of treatment goals. 2. To have families develop a relapse prevention plan for maintaining positive treatment gains.

design an evaluation of such programs that will accurately measure treatment outcome.

Facilitators should keep in mind that planning parallel/conjoint MFGT is more challenging and time-consuming than traditional MFGT. It is absolutely critical that clinicians be prepared and ready for this aspect of the parallel/conjoint approach. In order for the separate and joint groups to be effective, they must be planned at the developmental level of the participants, address the goals of the group, and easily attract and engage the members in the treatment process. For this reason, facilitators must be trained and experienced in conducting a wide range of age groups or utilize additional group workers who have the needed expertise to effectively facilitate some of these groups. Readers should feel free to use the planning sheet provided in Appendix B (MFGT Planning Sheet) for planning both their separate and joint group sessions. Parallel/conjoint MFGT will require more pregroup planning in order that this modality can provide maximum treatment benefits to all the participants.

FACILITATING PARALLEL/CONJOINT MFGT

Many of the points addressed in the previous section for the planning of this group approach are relevant to the facilitation of parallel/conjoint MFGT. Readers will want to review Chapter 4 of this text for facilitation guidelines that will be most relevant to the joint group sessions (i.e., MFGT) when utilizing this treatment modality. One major difference in the joint group sessions will be that these groups will typically not progress as quickly through the group phases, particularly when the separate parallel/conjoint format is used. However, if facilitators choose to follow the parallel/conjoint groups within each session model then the joint groups could potentially progress through the group phases in a pattern similar to traditional MFGT. This latter point is critical to the facilitation of these groups since the reader will note from Chapter 4 (Table 4.1 Guidelines for Facilitation of Groups in Each Phase) that the conducting of any group changes as the group moves into different phases. It is advised that readers refer to Table 4.1 in Chapter 4 when facilitating both their parallel and conjoint groups. This writer specifically developed these guidelines such that they address the treatment issues that are relevant to a wide range of group members.

One important variable that will have to be determined before starting a parallel/conjoint MFGT program is who will facilitate each group. There are many ways to handle this issue ranging from having separate therapists facilitate each of the parallel and conjoint groups to having the same clinician run all the groups. The decision as to how this part of the treatment is planned will depend on several variables. However, probably the most important one from a cost perspective, will be the availability of staff resources or budget. This variable will then determine if additional therapists can be utilized in running the various groups. As a result of many cutbacks in social services today, some readers may find they have no choice but to facilitate all parallel and conjoint groups. At the very least it would be helpful if a co-facilitating team could be available so that two group workers could be involved in all groups but particularly in the conjoint group sessions. Clinicians, as was addressed in Chapter 4, will find that the mere size of multiple family groups makes facilitation by one group worker very challenging and difficult.

If two facilitators are available to conduct the conjoint groups then they will have to also determine if they want to co-facilitate the parallel groups or each conduct one of these groups. There are advantages to each of these two facilitation formats. For example, the co-facilitation approach provides the benefits of two facilitators being able to monitor the process of group sessions, one facilitator is available to remove a member if necessary without the group being completely disrupted, facilitators can use one another as role models for the benefit of the members, more assistance can be provided to participants that may need help with various therapeutic tasks, and there are more places to seat members who have a tough time staying on task (e.g., two facilitators could provide seating for up to four members with one on each side of them). Readers can see from this list that many of these benefits are particularly relevant to adolescent groups or children's groups. These age groups would be more likely to have members who have trouble staying on task or need assistance with some of the tasks. On the other hand, if the two facilitators decide to run the parallel groups by themselves (i.e., each facilitates one group) then one major advantage is there is less of a chance for the facilitator to forget in which group disclosures were made by members. This point is a particularly important one since this is one of the challenges when the same facilitator(s) is involved in all the parallel and conjoint groups. Readers will find that both adolescents and parents will want to be assured that any disclosure they make in their respective peer group is only shared in the conjoint group if they choose to do so. When facilitators are involved in all the groups it will be obviously more challenging to monitor and make sure they maintain this confidentiality between the parallel and conjoint groups.

It will be essential that facilitators of the parallel and conjoint groups are trained and experienced in running each type of group. Readers will find that the various groups within this format will be challenging in different ways based on several variables including the age group of members, interests of members, personality types involved in the group composition, levels and types of presenting problems of the membership, and members' motivation to be involved in their group. For this reason, when one or two facilitators have to run all the parallel and conjoint groups it will be important that they process between group sessions regularly. In the case of a single facilitator, he or she should regularly process the groups with an experienced group worker who is a colleague or supervisor. Such processing is particularly important when following the parallel/conjoint format because each group will have its own unique issues that surface. In addition, when the same facilitator is not involved in all the groups, it will be critical that facilitators process and keep one another posted about the progress/problems of each respective group.

The guidelines and techniques provided in the first eight chapters of this text should provide very relevant material for the facilitation of parallel/conjoint MFGT, particularly with the conjoint groups (i.e., multiple family groups). At the same time readers will have to modify some of the guidelines or interventions such that they are developmentally appropriate and address the treatment needs/goals of each parallel group. Facilitators should again complement the material in this book with group facilitation manuals that target specifically the facilitation of parent groups, adolescent groups, and children's groups. Such resources will provide valuable additional guidance so the facilitation of these parallel groups will be the most effective.

SUMMARY

In this chapter the reader was introduced to the parallel/conjoint form of MFGT. Relevant findings from the related literature were provided with specific implications for treatment groups. This review of studies also highlighted some of the rationale for selecting this approach to MFGT. In addition, many of the unique benefits of this treatment modality were outlined so facilitators would understand when this form of MFGT would be the treatment of choice for a targeted client population. Then the reader was provided additional guidelines for planning and facilitating this MFGT format. Moreover, a sample 12-session plan of a parallel/conjoint MFGT program was provided where interventions from Chapters 5, 6, 7, and 8 were utilized. Also, treatment goals for each of the parallel and conjoint groups were delineated so the reader could better understand the connection between these goals and the resulting intervention plans. Facilitators should find that the material in this chapter, combined with the first eight chapters, should provide clear guidelines for effectively setting up, planning, and facilitating parallel/conjoint MFGT.

Chapter 10

EVALUATION AND
FUTURE DIRECTIONS FOR MFGTS

Although this text is intended to primarily serve as an intervention manual for conducting MFGT, it is critical that readers understand the importance of program evaluation when they are setting up and planning their multiple family groups. Therefore, this final chapter provides the reader with specifics on designing and conducting an evaluation of their MFGT programs. Facilitators will find that this chapter provides many examples of research designs with related evaluation methods (i.e., standardized scales and qualitative methods) that should greatly assist in the planning this part of a MFGT program.

In this chapter the reader is provided an overview of the current status of research on MFGT. Particular voids in both treatment and process outcome studies are identified with suggestions for more ideal program evaluation designs. Readers are then provided an outline of the steps involved in developing an evaluation of a MFGT program. In order to further assist facilitators in determining the most ideal program evaluation of their multiple family groups, several research designs are delineated. Next, examples of both quantitative and qualitative measurement procedures are provided with complete reference material such that facilitators can easily obtained further information on such assessment interventions. In the section on quantitative methods, standardized measures for evaluating these group programs are listed with references to related studies when instruments noted have been reported in past research. Under the section on qualitative sources of data, the reader is also given a listing of several examples of program evaluation using these research methods. Facilitators should find that material in these latter sections is user-friendly and provides a full array of methods for effectively evaluating a MFGT program. The last part of this chapter addresses some of the future research and program development needs for MFGT such that this unique approach to treatment continues to be refined, making it more effective for an ever-growing group of clients.

CURRENT STATUS OF RESEARCH ON MFGT

Numerous articles have been written over the past five decades on the clinical application of MFGT involving an increasing number of client groups and treatment settings. However, the majority of these publications have consisted of program descriptions and studies based primarily on clinical impressions (Edwards, 2001). Both comprehensive reviews of MFGT identified that there have been limited empirical studies on this approach with further research required to determine its efficacy (Strelnick, 1977; O'Shea & Phelps, 1985). There is clearly a need for more controlled and rigorous studies particularly where MFGT is not an additive to other therapies (Carlson, 1998). In fact, O'Shea and Phelps' (1985) review found that only two studies focused solely on MFGT with neither being an outcome study of the intervention.

What types of research studies are needed to provide more empirical support for MFGT? Strelnick's (1978) early review of this literature concluded that more studies that utilize randomized pre/posttest control group designs were needed. However, O'Shea and Phelps' (1985) later review indicated that even though more rigorous studies are needed, other evaluations could be conducted that utilize data typically available in clinical reports. Although the majority of studies to date have relied on clinical reports, it is interesting that much of this research has surfaced very similar positive findings (McFarlane, 2001).

In more recent years, there has been more appreciation and understanding of the complexity of this treatment modality since it incorporates family therapy with group therapy. Rose (1998) validated this perspective when he summarized the impact that this issue has on subsequent group research in general.

Group therapy is a highly complex endeavor. As a target of research, one must consider a variety of factors. These include the population being served, the targets of intervention, the type of interventions, the intensity of treatment, the composition of the group, the characteristics of the group therapist, the patterns of group interaction, the demands of the sponsoring agency, the material and psychological resources of the members, the concerns of significant others of the group members, and the type of outcomes one can expect from group therapy. (p. 47)

As a result, researchers in the past decade have identified several aspects of MFGT that require further study. For example, Meezan, O'Keefe, and Zariani (1997) have stressed the need for more follow-up studies to see if the positive changes at the end of treatment are maintained. Cassano (1989) advocated for more process outcome studies where the interactional patterns in these groups could be more carefully studied. McKay, Gonzalez, Stone et al., (1995) urged for more research that examines the usefulness of this treatment modality when compared with other more traditional methods. Garrett and Rice (1998) suggested that future studies focus on race and ethnicity of members, training and credentials of facilitators, cost efficiency for various client populations, and optimal ratio of families to therapist. Due to the complexity of this approach to treatment, there are many other variables that have not been studied that need to be the focus of future MFGT research (e.g., those variables listed in quote from Rose, 1998).

So how does a facilitator determine the most ideal research design for their particular MFGT program? And how do clinicians conduct their evaluation so that it will build on our current knowledge base? These are understandable questions since the literature review identifies many aspects of multiple family groups that require further study. In addition, readers must carefully consider the goals of their MFGT program and the resources available for conducting research. Facilitators must be confident that the research design they develop can, in fact, be accomplished within their treatment setting. As a result, the following section will outline the steps involved in successfully designing a MFGT program evaluation, with particular emphasis on the resources and support required within a treatment setting. Readers should be aware that this chapter is not intended to provide all the material needed to set up and conduct program evaluation. Instead, the purpose is to outline in general terms the usual procedure for planning a program evaluation, various types of research designs, and measurement procedures (both qualitative and quantitative) that might be utilized in evaluating a MFGT program. It is important that readers complement the material in this chapter by referring to research textbooks and/or conferring with a research consultant.

STEPS TO FOLLOW IN PLANNING MFGT PROGRAM EVALUATION

Many readers may find themselves in settings where they do not have a research consultant on staff or access to such a professional when they are designing a program evaluation of their multiple family group therapy. For this reason, facilitators are provided the following steps to follow in order to effectively and ethically plan a program evaluation of their multiple family groups.

1. **Determine the research protocol required in the agency setting.** It is critical that facilitators identify the research protocol they are required to follow when planning a program evaluation of this treatment service. Typically agencies require the completion of specific forms and outline steps that need to be completed before any proposed research is initiated. The program evaluation proposal forms will usually require information on the following parts of the study: background to the study indicating the rationale for conducting it, study design (i.e., type of study, sampling method, procedures and timing for collecting data, and data analysis plan), evaluation methodology being utilized with samples of standardized measures when relevant, informed consent forms that all participants will complete before beginning study, safeguards for keeping subject data confidential, procedure for destroying of study data once research is completed, and any risks that subjects could experience by being involved in such a study. Due to the nature of MFGT, facilitators should make sure that they obtain consent forms from all group participants. Also, all parents must sign a consent for any youngster under the age of 18. This parental consent form is in addition to the consent form that the youngster should also be asked to sign. If agencies do not provide guidelines for the contents of such consent forms, readers are urged to contact a local university to obtain such guidelines and even samples of consent forms. Usually the research proposal will have to be submitted and

reviewed by a committee designated by the agency. This research review committee will have to provide written approval of the study before any research is initiated. For this reason, facilitators will want to allow enough time for this research approval protocol before they begin a MFGT program.

2. **Complete an online course on the use of human subject training.** Before beginning a program evaluation, facilitators should consider completing a "use of human subjects for a research study" online training that is often available through local universities. Such training will provide invaluable information on the rights and protection expected of clients involved in research studies. This training can also provide more guidelines in the development of subject participation informed consent forms. In addition, facilitators will be provided a clear understanding of what constitutes ethical research. Usually it is a good idea for all professionals involved with a study to complete such training.

3. **Formulate clear and measurable goals for the MFGT program.** It is essential that groupwide goals be formulated such that they can be measured and are based on the intervention plan for the MFGT. Facilitators must remember that it is critical that their session plans connect directly to the goals formulated for a particular group. These group goals will determine the treatment outcomes that are expected from participants of a MFGT program. Moreover, the goals delineated will provide guidance in determining relevant and appropriate measures for evaluating the treatment outcome of a MFGT program.

4. **Design the study.** A research design (examples outlined in next section) must be selected after facilitators determine what type of study they would like to conduct (e.g., treatment outcome study, process outcome study, or both). This research design will also involve planning the following parts of the program evaluation: identifying data that will be collected on all participants, measures that will be used (see examples listed in two later sections of this chapter), timing and collection of data, data analysis plan, and any other issues related to conducting the study.

5. **Collect data.** At specific planned points in the treatment process (e.g., pregroup, postgroup, or follow-up), the facilitator(s) will be

responsible for the collection of data. These data collection times will be determined by the research design utilized in a program evaluation. It will be helpful if a written schedule can be maintained with the logging of subject data to ensure data are collected from all clients who are to be involved in the research. Readers must remember that any study should allow for voluntary consent and the opportunity for withdrawal at any point during the study. Therefore, it is possible that some members of a MFGT program may have elected not to be involved in a study or may choose to withdraw after a study begins. It will be important that such information is kept in mind as data are collected from all those group members who have agreed to be involved in the research.

6. **Process data.** Depending on the type of data collected in a study, the processing of such data may be more time-consuming. For example, if a facilitator elects to use a case-analysis design (see next section for a definition) then the preparation of such data will involve more time and often consultation with a researcher. It is important that facilitators consider very carefully their resources and level of agency support for a study before deciding on a design. Some research designs are going to require more time and research expertise to successfully carry them out. In addition, qualitative research will usually require the use of trained professionals who are not involved in the facilitation or planning of the MFGT program. Such individuals would be needed to conduct structured interviews with individual group members or facilitate focus group sessions.

7. **Data analysis.** Most forms of data collected in program evaluation will have to be coded and entered into a computer data analysis program. Therefore, it is important that a facilitator check to see if such a program is available in their agency or could be purchased. The type of data analysis program needed will depend on several factors and it is usually best to consult with a researcher before making this decision. In addition, facilitators will have to determine who will code and enter the data along with running the analyses. It is essential that such a professional is trained in these research tasks and understands their responsibilities in maintaining confidentiality regarding the data.

8. **Interpretation and reporting of findings.** After the data have been analyzed, the facilitator along with others involved in the research will have to interpret, summarize, and prepare a written report on the findings that were surfaced. It is extremely important that this last step be completed because this is the primary way that the research will inform future practice of MFGT. In addition, it is important to have such written summaries of program evaluations so they can be disseminated to appropriate individuals who can support similar future research efforts. Moreover, such program evaluation reports can be incorporated into agency annual reports or reaccreditation reports. When possible, these reports can also be prepared for publication in a professional journal so we can enhance our understanding of MFGT, advance the theory development, and provide additional empirical support of this innovative treatment modality. This latter suggestion may require consultation with a researcher, which is one of the benefits of conducting MFGT program evaluation in collaboration with a researcher affiliated with a local university.

RESEARCH DESIGNS

There are a number of research designs that could be utilized when conducting program evaluation of multiple family group therapy. However, only eight of these designs will be delineated in this section since this author has found that they are the more common ones to use when evaluating treatment and process outcomes for multiple family groups.

1. Randomized Pre/Posttest Control Group Design

This type of research requires that all subjects be randomly assigned to either a treatment or control group with an assessment measure administered before and after the completion of a group. Even though this type of research is considered a classic or true experimental design, it is very difficult to conduct in most settings because there are usually not enough families available to assign to the two groups (experimental and control). In addition, many treatment settings do not allow for the use of control groups where clients are receiving no services.

2. Nonequivalent Control Group Design

When ethical concerns or too small a sample size prohibits random assignment of clients to control/experimental groups, the nonequivalent control group design can be utilized. This research design involves the use of a matched group where the members do not receive MFGT but are matched with the treatment group in terms of members' identifying variables. In most settings this type of research would be easier to conduct than the classic research design, but it can still be challenging to find a matched comparison group, particularly when conducting multiple family groups. Readers should remember that the composition of these groups involves a much wider array of ages and genders among the membership than a traditional group. For this reason, identifying a matched group can be very difficult if not impossible.

3. Case-Study Analysis Design

In this type of research design the treatment impact of an intervention is assessed and can usually be conducted with little cost. The analysis is based on records maintained by the facilitator on variables such as behavior of group members in the group, behavior of members reported outside the group, group therapist interventions, and subjective evaluation of members' progress. This type of research can be invaluable in further developing the underlying theory for MFGT. In addition, both treatment variables and process variables can be examined through this type of analysis.

4. Pretest-Posttest Design

In this design a control group is not utilized so the evaluation focuses only on the MFGT members receiving treatment. A single measure (or sometimes multiple standardized measures) is administered pre- and postgroup treatment to the MFGT participants to examine change on one or more areas of functioning. This is one of the research designs that most facilitators can more easily conduct and typically such evaluation does not interrupt the group process.

5. The A-B Design

When following this research design measurement is taken periodically during the pregroup phase and intervention phase. This type of research provides the facilitator ongoing feedback that can inform adjustments to the treatment intervention. One of the challenges with this design is that most standardized measures are not sensitive enough to surface changes over such short periods of time. However, facilitators can determine specific behaviors that will be evaluated during these periodic assessments that can further refine their MFGT intervention and contribute to our knowledge base.

6. Posttest-Only Design

When facilitators do not have the time to evaluate multiple family group members before treatment begins, the posttest-only design can be used. In this research a measure is administered only at the completion of treatment. Even though this design will not allow for a comparison between pre- and post-data, the findings surfaced can complement and add validation to the impressions of a facilitator. In addition, this type of research can inform hypotheses that can be later tested in more rigorous research designs.

7. Qualitative Research Designs

Some group therapists use qualitative research designs because they want their evaluation to focus on understanding the complexity of the group therapy experience. Data surfaced when this design is utilized cannot be as rigorously measured as data surfaced in quantitative research. However, such findings often further elaborate the underlying theory for an approach, inform future quantitative research, and provide more in-depth understanding of a treatment intervention. This type of research is typically not costly but does require the use of a trained focus group facilitator/researcher or interviewer.

8. Process/Treatment Outcome Research Designs

There is a beginning awareness that we need more research designs that examine the connection between treatment outcome and process outcome. For example, do particular identifying variables of the facilitator positively impact treatment outcome? Or do specific approaches used in the group correlate positively with treatment outcomes? These designs typically require the use of a research consultant because evaluation targets treatment outcomes, process outcomes, and the relationship between these two outcomes. Although this research is more involved to design, it yields critical findings in regard to both treatment impact and variables that positively correlate with treatment outcomes. Facilitators will find that this research design will often surface rich findings that specifically inform their practice of MFGT.

Readers are reminded that the material in this section on research designs is intended to provide general information on these evaluation approaches. Facilitators will usually need to consult a researcher and/or textbook on this topic in order to determine the most ideal research design for their MFGT program. In addition, once the design is determined further planning will be necessary in terms of the measurement procedures, obtaining informed consent of participants, securing confidentiality of subject data, analyzing data surfaced, and formulating results and recommendations based on findings. At the end of this chapter readers are provided suggested resources on planning, designing, and carrying out program evaluation of treatment interventions. Material in these books should be used to complement and further delineate the contents of this chapter.

QUANTITATIVE MEASUREMENT PROCEDURES

In this section examples of quantitative measurement procedures that could be used for a MFGT program evaluation are delineated. This list is by no means exhaustive but provides readers with some of the more common standardized scales or methods that could be used to evaluate the treatment outcome of multiple family groups. Facilitators will determine which measures they are going to use in their research based on several variables. For example, the treatment goals of the MFGT program must be considered along with a scale's administration time, intended age group for the measure, availability of funds for purchasing scales, and analysis required once data have been collected. Therefore, facilitators should carefully examine these issues before selecting the quantitative measures for their program evaluation research.

Before listing some of these assessment scales, it is important to differentiate quantitative approaches from qualitative approaches. Bisman and Hardcastle (1999) provide a very simple but clear definition of quantitative approaches when they state, "Numbers are used in quantitative measurements to indicate relationships of intensity, magnitude, severity, duration, and frequency" (p. 79) whereas Sherman and Reid (1994) note that symbols are used in qualitative measurement approaches. For this reason, readers will find that some type of rating or counting system is used in all of the following suggested measures. This list contains quantitative measures specifically for multiple family groups that focus on at risk adolescents due to the focus of this text.

Hopefully, practitioners will be able to add to this list as they continue to conduct evaluations of their MFGT programs.

Standardized Measures for Parents

Measure: Adult-Adolescent Parenting Inventory (AAPI)
Source: S.J. Bavolek, Family Development Associates, P.O. Box 94365, Schaumberg, Illinois, 60194.

Measure: Index of Parental Attitude
Source: Hudson, W. (1992). WALMYR Publishing Company, P.O. Box 24779, Tempe, Arizona, 85285.

Measure: Maryland Parent Attitude Survey (MPAS)
Source: D. K. Pumroy, College of Education, University of Maryland, College Park, MD, 20742.

Measure: Parent-Adolescent Communication Scale (PACS)
Source: D. H. Olson, H. L. McCubbin, H. Barnes, A. Larsen, M. Muxen, & M. Wilson (1982). Minneapolis, MN: University of Minnesota Family Inventories.

Measure: Parenting Social Support Index
Source: Telleen, S. (1985). Chicago: University of Chicago, School of Public Health.

Measure: Parental Strengths and Needs Inventory
Source: Strom, R. & Colledge, N. (1987). Tempe: Arizona State University.

Measure: Stress Index for Parents of Adolescents (SIPA)
Source: P. L. Sheras & R. R. Abidin, Psychological Assessment Resources, 16204 N. Florida Ave., Lutz, Florida, 33549.

Standardized Measures for Adolescents

Measure: Index of Peer Relations
Source: Hudson, W. (1992). WALMYR Publishing Company, P.O. Box 24779, Tempe, Arizona, 85285.

Measure: Revised Behavior Problem Checklist (RBPC)
*Also a Youth Self-Report available by same authors and company
Source: Quay, H. & Peterson, D. Psychological Assessment Resources, 16204 N. Florida Ave., Lutz, Florida, 33549.

Measure: Reynolds Adolescent Adjustment Screening Inventory (RAASI)
Source: W. M Reynolds, Psychological Assessment Resources, 16204 N. Florida Ave., Lutz, Florida, 33549.

Measure: Substance Abuse Relapse Assessment (SARA)
Source: Schonfeld, L., Peters, R., & Dolente, A. Psychological Assessment Resources, 16204 N. Florida Ave., Lutz, Florida 33549.

Measure: The Problem-Solving Inventory (PSI)
Source: Heppner, P. & Peterson, C. (1982). The development and implications of a personal problem-solving inventory. *Journal of Counseling and Psychology, 29*, 66-75.

Standardized Measures for Families

Measure: Family Adaptability and Cohesion Evaluation (FACES III)
Source: Olson, D. H., Family Social Science, University of Minnesota, 290 McNeal Hall, 1985 Buford Ave., St. Paul, MN, 55108.

Measure: Family Assessment Device (FAD)
Source: Epstein, N., Baldwin, M., & Bishop, D. Family Research Program, Butler Hospital, 345 Blackstone Blvd., Providence, RI, 92906.

Measure: Family Awareness Scale (FAS)
Source: Kolevzon, M. & Green, R., Florida International University School of Public Affairs and Services, Social Work Department, North Miami, Florida, 33181.

Measure: Family Functioning Style Scale (FFSS)
Source: Trivette, C., Dunst, C., Deal, A., Hamby, D., & Sexton, D. (1994). In C. Dunst, C. Trivette, & A. Deal (Eds.). Supporting and strengthening families, vol. 1: Methods, strategies, and practices (pp. 132–138). Cambridge, MA: Brookline.

Measure: Family Support Scale (FSS)
Source: Dunst, C., Jenkins, V., & Trivette, C. (1984). Family support scales: Reliability and validity. *Journal of Individual, Family, and Community Wellness, 1,* 45–52.

Measure: Index of Family Relations
Source: Hudson, W. (1992). WALMYR Publishing Company, P.O. Box 24779, Tempe, Arizona, 85285.

Measure: Self-Report Family Instrument (SFI)
Source: Beavers, W. R., Southwest Family Institute, 12532 Nuestra, Dallas, Texas, 75230.

Reference Sources on Clinical Standardized Measures

Fischer, J. & Corcoran, K. (1994). *Measures for clinical practice: Vol. 1, Couples, families and children.* New York: Free Press.

Fischer, J. & Corcoran, K. (1994). *Measures for clinical practice: Vol. 2, Adults.* New York: Free Press.

Jordan, C. & Franklin, C. (1995). *Clinical assessment for social workers.* Chicago: Lyceum.

Self-Anchored Scales

"These are scales where clients are asked to rate themselves on a continuum, usually a 7- or 9-point scale from low to high" (Gabor, Unrau, & Grinnell, 1994, p. 161). Typically clients are asked to provide descriptors for each point on this continuum so the measure truly assesses changes in specific states of functioning relative to the client's expectations. Often this type of measure can be invaluable in obtaining data on a group participant's internal state of functioning. Self-anchored rating scales can either be used alone or in combination with other assessment methods.

Goal Attainment Scaling (GAS)

Goal attainment scaling (Kiresuk, Smith, & Cardillo, 1994) has been used for defining and determining the level of goal attainment for both individual client's goals and groupwide goals. A 5 point scale is used (much less than expected to much more than expected) with a goal area delineated in very specific terms for each of these levels. Typically group goals should be the focus of this measurement when it is used to evaluate a MFGT program.

In-Group or Out-of-Group Observational Data Collection

Facilitators may choose to use a structured observational system either in group sessions or outside as their measurement approach

(Rose, 1998). There are many different types of observational methods, but regardless of the method selected it is imperative that facilitators delineate the specific behavior to be observed. It is also important that the frequency of conducting the observation is clearly outlined along with the counting method used in the recording. Typically structured observations in group are more accurate due to the added control this setting establishes for such recording of behavior.

Knowledge Tests

These tests are either individually designed by a facilitator or developed by the author of a psychoeducational training program. Since therapeutic instruction is often one targeted goal area of a MFGT program, it can be useful to measure the amount of knowledge acquired by group participants. This type of evaluation measure can complement the assessment of members' other areas of functioning. In addition, many studies have reported that MFGT participants often report that increased understanding of a particular problem area was one of the most beneficial parts of this treatment modality experience.

QUALITATIVE MEASUREMENT PROCEDURES

What defines and differentiates qualitative measurement procedures? Royse et al. (2001) provide clear criteria for these measurement procedures when they state "...virtually all qualitative studies—regardless of their epistemological backdrop—share in common a few key ingredients: (1) a focus on naturalistic inquiry in situ; (2) a reliance upon the researcher as the instrument of data collection; and (3) reports emphasizing narrative over numbers" (p. 83). Keeping in mind these defining ingredients, following are the types of qualitative measurement procedures that could be used for a MFGT program evaluation. This list is by no means exhaustive but provides readers with some of the more common qualitative assessment procedures that could be used to evaluate the treatment outcome of multiple family groups. Facilitators will determine which measurement procedures they are going to use in their research based on several variables. For example, the treatment goals of the MFGT program must be considered along with availability of trained professionals to collect data, process the data, and analyze the data. Therefore, facilitators should carefully examine these issues before selecting the qualitative measures for their program evaluation research.

Structured Interviews with Individuals or Family Units

One qualitative method for evaluating a MFGT program is through structured interviews that are conducted at the completion of such a treatment intervention. These interviews can either be with individual group participants or with members of family units. Facilitators will have to determine which type of interview will best address their evaluation needs and surface the most helpful and relevant data. When making this decision, group leaders must also consider their resources because individual interviews will take more time and personnel efforts than family unit interviews. Moreover, the method for recording these interviews will have to be determined ahead of time since relevant equipment or personnel will have to be secured (e.g., tape recorders, trained professional note taker, etc.).

It is very important that facilitators who do not have a research background obtain the consultation of a trained researcher for designing these structured interviews, conducting the interviews, and analyzing the data. Due to the nature of this evaluation method, it is critical that a researcher be involved throughout this type of assessment procedure. Readers are referred to more specifics on the designing of interview questions, coding of data, and data analysis in M. Patton's (1987) book titled *How to Use Qualitative Methods in Evaluation*. This text is a basic resource on this type of program evaluation method and the author provides lots of checklists, scales, and recordkeeping forms as samples.

It will also be necessary that the interviewer for this evaluation method not have been involved in any of the prior treatment group sessions. Also, no treatment professionals involved in a MFGT should be present for these interview sessions. It is essential that group members feel comfortable and safe to respond honestly and openly to the interview questions posed. Interviewers should assure participants that only the data surfaced from the groupwide responses to the questions will be shared with the treatment staff, with no participants' names associated with such data.

The specific questions contained in a structured interview will vary depending on any number of variables. For example, a facilitator will have to determine what type of data he or she wants to surface from this assessment method. Also, the amount of time that can be spent in each interview will determine the number of interview questions and the depth to which they can be explored. In addition, group leaders will have to plan how they can effectively elicit responses to the structured interview questions from all age groups of participants. Readers must remember that one of the challenges of a MFGT program is the wide age range of its members. Therefore, it will be essential that these interview questions are articulated such that they are age-appropriate for the individuals being interviewed. As a result, some interview questions may have to be delineated into two or three different forms such that they can be easily understood by the different age groups of MFGT members.

Focus Groups Sessions

Focus group sessions are also conducted at the last session of a MFGT program and involve all participants. The number and type of questions posed to a group during this type of evaluation method will also vary due to several variables. Facilitators will first have to determine what type of data they want to surface via this method. Also, they will have to consider how much time will be available to conduct this group evaluation session. In addition, the inclusion of all members necessitates that questions can be easily understood by all age groups. Therefore, it is essential that facilitators, in consultation with a researcher, carefully determine their focus group questions. Also, the method for recording and collecting the responses from MFGT participants during these evaluation sessions will have to be planned such that the necessary equipment and personnel can be obtained ahead of time.

One of the unique challenges of conducting focus group sessions with a multiple family group is to equally engage all participants in the discussions that surface once each question has been posed to the group. It will also be necessary that the facilitator of such a group has not been involved in any of the prior treatment group sessions. Also, no treatment professionals involved in a MFGT should be present for these evaluation sessions. It is essential that group members feel comfortable and safe to respond honestly and openly to the focus group questions. Facilitators of these focus groups should assure participants that only the data surfaced from the groupwide responses to the questions will be shared with the treatment staff, with no participants' names associated with such data.

Readers are referred to the following references that provide more extensive guidelines for formulating focus group questions, recording and coding responses, conducting focus group sessions, and analyzing the data.

1. Denzin, N. & Lincoln, Y. (Eds.). (1994). *Handbook of qualitative research.* Thousand Oaks, CA: Sage.
2. Krueger, R. (1994). *Focus groups: A practical guide for applied research.* (2nd ed.). Thousand Oaks, CA: Sage.
3. Padgett, D. (1998). *Qualitative methods in social work research.* Thousand Oaks, CA: Sage.
4. Patton, M. (1987). *How to use qualitative methods in evaluation.* Beverly Hills, CA: Sage.

Facilitators are strongly advised to use a researcher and refer to information in these resources when utilizing this evaluation method. This qualitative method can surface some very rich data and thus it is imperative that these focus groups be effectively planned and conducted.

Group Observation with Field Notes

This qualitative evaluation method involves a trained research observer going into MFGT sessions and recording field notes based on detailed observations. Unlike structured interviews or focus groups, these observations are typically conducted throughout the stages of a group program. The timing of such observations is individually determined by the facilitator depending on the type of data needed and the purpose of such an evaluation method. Also, it is important that the level of involvement this observer has with a MFGT be clarified before such an assessment is conducted. There is great variation in the type of involvement observers have with treatment groups, with some having no interaction while others are almost as fully engaged as the participants.

It is essential that facilitators consult with a researcher when conducting this type of evaluation. A researcher can provide invaluable guidance in identifying a trained observer, determining the type of observations to be noted, delineating the way the observations are recorded, and conducting an analysis of the data surfaced. This is an evaluation method that surfaces some very rich data that will both inform the ongoing treatment of multiple family group therapy and identify ways this modality impacts the participants. As a result, it is imperative that group observations be carefully and effectively planned such that this evaluation method will elicit the most informative data.

FUTURE DIRECTIONS FOR MFGT

Clinical observations and reports have repeatedly indicated the positive impact of MFGT with an increasingly wide array of at risk families. Even more impressive is the success of this intervention modality with some of the most chronic and severe presenting problems and client populations. In addition, these are client groups that have generally not responded well to more traditional forms of treatment. It is truly impressive that many of these reports note similar types of positive impact. In fact, some of the most seasoned group facilitators often are passionate about the changes elicited by this innovative treatment approach. However, very few of these reports are based on well-designed research studies and thus lack the empirical evidence to support these claims of success. As a result, it is imperative that more carefully designed research be conducted on this unique treatment modality.

As indicated earlier in this chapter, the related literature has surfaced some specific types of studies that are needed to provide further validation and support for this group approach. Following are the types of research needed to further develop the underlying theory for this treatment method and provide empirical support.

- More controlled and rigorous studies where MFGT is not an additive to other therapies
- More randomized pre/posttest control group designs
- Follow-up studies to see if the positive changes are maintained
- Research on the usefulness of this treatment modality when com-

pared with more traditional methods
- Studies that focus on the race and ethnicity of group members
- Research that explores the correlation between the training and credentials of facilitators and treatment outcome
- Studies on the cost efficiency of this approach with specific client populations
- More process outcome studies that examine curative factors that are most important to MFGT participants
- Studies that target treatment outcome, process outcome, and the relationship between these two types of evaluation.
- Research that combines qualitative and quantitative evaluation methods within the same study

There are many other types of studies that could be valuable to further understanding this treatment approach and offering empirical evidence of its treatment impact. Readers are strongly urged to consider designing an evaluation of their MFGT during their initial planning stage. Such research will be critical for the ongoing development of this truly unique and impressive treatment modality.

SUMMARY

In this chapter the reader was provided an overview on the current status of research on MFGT. Readers were then provided step-by-step instructions for setting up and carrying out an evaluation of their multiple family group programs. Specifics regarding research designs and quantitative and qualitative evaluation procedures were delineated to further assist facilitators in developing and conducting a well-designed study of their MFGT program. A wide selection of references was also provided in this chapter such that readers will be able to easily identify possible standardized measures to use in their program evaluation. In addition, further material on conducting qualitative evaluation procedures was indicated that will complement the contents of this chapter. The chapter ended with a summary of the types of research still needed to further develop the underlying theory for this approach and provide empirical evidence for its efficacy. It is hoped that the material in this chapter will encourage readers to make program evaluation a standard procedure when they are planning their multiple family group therapy. It will only be through such combined efforts that this treatment approach will receive the recognition and validation it deserves.

APPENDICES

Appendix A
Sample of Multiple Family Group Therapy Contract

We as members of the _____family do hereby agree to participate in the Multiple Family Group Therapy Program being sponsored by _____. This group will meet weekly on _____evenings from _____. The dates of this group program are from _____ to _____. We agree, that except in the case of an emergency, we will attend all sessions that are planned for this group. We also agree to abide by the following rules while participating in this group:

1. All information shared in the group will be held confidential and never shared with anyone outside the group.
2. As parents of this family unit, we agree to be responsible for assisting with keeping our children on task during sessions.
3. Participate in all sessions and share as much as we are comfortable sharing with this group.
4. Be motivated and committed to address problems in our family in regard to:

_____

_____

_____

_____

Please note: The law requires that professionals working in treatment sessions with clients must report any cases where minors (children under 18 years of age) have been or may be victims of abuse or neglect. If such disclosure surfaces in this group then it must be reported to the appropriate authorities.

This contract is being signed on _____(date)

Signature of family members: _____

_____

_____

_____

_____

Signature of Group Facilitator:_____

ccfile

Appendix B
Multiple Family Therapy Group Planning Sheet

Session: _____ Warm-up Technique: _____ Primary theme of session: _____ Main Intervention Plan: _____ Processing Comments: _____	Session: _____ Warm-up Technique: _____ Primary theme of session: _____ Main Intervention Plan: _____ Processing Comments: _____	Session: _____ Warm-up Technique: _____ Primary theme of session: _____ Main Intervention Plan: _____ Processing Comments: _____
Session: _____ Warm-up Technique: _____ Primary theme of session: _____ Main Intervention Plan: _____ Processing Comments: _____	Session: _____ Warm-up Technique: _____ Primary theme of session: _____ Main Intervention Plan: _____ Processing Comments: _____	Session: _____ Warm-up Technique: _____ Primary theme of session: _____ Main Intervention Plan: _____ Processing Comments: _____

Appendix C

Master Listing of Techniques for Initial, Middle, and Termination Phases of Group

Chapter 5: Relationship Building Techniques Target: Process Goals of all group phases	Chapter 6: Psychoeducational Techniques Target: Treatment Goals of Initial Group Phase	Chapter 7: Problem-Solving Techniques Target: Treatment Goals of Middle Group Phase	Chapter 8: Group Termination and Closure Techniques Target: Process and Treatment Goals of Termination Phase
1. Family Drawing	26. A Closer Look at a Family Problem	51. What Do You Visualize?	71. A Profile of a New You and New Family
2. Give us the Family Rap!	27. Trash your Problems	52. 1st Steps to Your Problem Resolution Journey	72. A Work in Progress
3. What's in Style for your Family Members?	28. What Makes Children and Teens Resilient?	53. Believing is Seeing!	73. Before and After Group Pictures!
4. Your Family's Coat of Values	29. Bibliotherapy for Familywide Understanding	54. Dissecting your Family Problem	74. Validation of Members' Progress and Strengths
5. Family Rituals at your House	30. Self-rating on a Standard-ized Scale and Discuss	55. Cut Your Losses and Move On!	75. Group Good-bye Card
6. Words that Describe your Family	31. Fun and Free Family Activities	56. Expectations and Changing Behavior	76. A Vision of your Family 5 Years in the Future!
7. Our Family Cartoon	32. A Recipe for a Resilient Family	57. Weather Report on my Family Life	77. Your Personal Motto for Happiness
8. Good Times and Difficult Times in our Family History	33. Typical Problems of Teenagers and Parents of Teenagers	58. Spring Cleaning for Family Attitude Adjustment	78. Mapping Out your Keys to Success
9. It's on my Mind these Days!	34. How Families can Always be Upset and in Conflict!	59. Concerns and Areas of Control	79. A Family Insurance Plan
10. We Dial...for Support	35. 1-2-3-4 for Family Conflict Resolution!	60. You Should Chill Out When...	80. A Meditation for You and Your Family
11. What's the Radio Playing at your Home?	36. Healthy Grieving for Families	61. Dear Family Consultant	

12. Strengths of our Family!	37. Don't Worry–Act Out your Worst Fear!	62. Alternative Coping Responses for 21st Century Families
13. Tracking the Unique Me	38. Our Family Values versus the Jones' Values	63. How to See the Glass as Half Full!
14. Family Problem Checklist	39. Are you Hearing me Now?	64. Pass the Basket of Problems
15. Good News/Bad News at our Home this Past Week	40. Whose Job is it Anyways?	65. Computer Files to Delete, Add, and Modify
16. Fantasy Family	41. Drawing Boundary Lines for Healthy Family Functioning	66. Scenes from your Family Life to Cut
17. What is each Family Member's Mantra?	42. Brainstorm Ways to Build Family Members' Self-esteem	67. When the Rubber Hits the Road!
18. Rate your Life	43. Living with Change, Challenges, and the Need for New Game Plans	68. Things You Could Do to Help your Family
19. If I Were the Parent/If I Were the Teen	44. Try It Out and Report Back!	69. Coming Home and Feeling Good!
20. Take a Walk in my Shoes	45. Just Record and Watch!	70. Your Bag of Tricks
21. What is Becoming Extinct in your Family?	46. Family Safety Issues	
22. Good-bye Group Letter Completion	47. A...each Week Keeps our Family Okay	
23. Family Poem Completion	48. Family Relapse Prevention: Warning Signs and a Plan	
24. This Group Has Been Like...	49. Report Card on our Family	
25. Our Family Leaves this Group Feeling...	50. Family Challenges in the 21st Century!	

Appendix D
Multiple Family Group Therapy Progress Note Form

Note Form for Family Entering Treatment Group

This family has contracted to be involved in a Multiple Family Group Therapy Program from _____ to _____. This group treatment program will be focusing on the following areas of functioning that will serve as the focus of the treatment goals for this intervention.

List targeted areas of functioning specific to this MFGT Program here:

_____

_____

_____

This family has committed to working specifically on the following problems in this treatment group:

_____

_____

_____

The following family members have agreed to participate in this group program:

_____

_____

Additional Comments:_____

_____

_____

Facilitator(s) of Group: _____

_____

Signature of Clinician:_____

Note Form for Group Members whose Group is ending the Initial Phase of MFGT

This family has been participating in a multiple family group therapy program that has now met for _____sessions. This group has focused on the following initial group phase goals:

Process Goals

1. To create an attractive group setting.
2. To initiate balanced participation among members.
3. To build a trusting relationship among members.

Treatment Goals

1. To delineate more specific treatment goals that are common to the membership.
2. To provide psychoeducation on targeted treatment areas of functioning.

Progress specifically of family in regard to above goals:

_____

_____

_____

_____

_____

Progress of family in regard to specific problems focused on in this group:

_____

_____

_____

_____

Attendance of family to sessions: _____

_____

_____

Signature of Clinician:_____

Note Form for Group Members whose Group is ending the Middle Phase of MFGT

This family has been participating in a multiple family group therapy program that has now met for _____ sessions. This group has focused on the following middle group phase goals:

Treatment Goals

1. To increase members' awareness of their specific problems in regard to targeted treatment areas of functioning.
2. To increase members' awareness of alternative responses to problems.
3. To assist members in selecting alternative responses to their problems and integrating those into their repertoire.

Process Goals

1. To continue building an attractive group setting.
2. To increase member-to-member participation and maintain balanced participation.
3. To continue developing member trust and a cohesive group unit.

Progress specifically of family in regard to above goals:

_____

_____

_____

_____

_____

Progress of family in regard to specific problems focused on in this group:

_____

_____

_____

_____

Attendance of family to sessions: _____

_____

Signature of Clinician: _____

This family has been participating in a multiple family group therapy program that has now met for _____ sessions. This group has focused on the following termination group phase goals:

Process Goals

1. To have members acknowledge value of group and grieve its ending.
2. To have members acknowledge progress they have made in group.
3. To have members identify other sources that will support the changes they have made in group.

Treatment Goals

1. To have members acknowledge attainment of treatment goals in groups.
2. To have members develop a relapse prevention plan for maintaining positive treatment gains.

Progress specifically of family in regard to above goals:

_____

_____

_____

_____

_____

Progress of family in regard to specific problems focused on in this group:

_____

_____

_____

_____

Attendance of family to sessions: _____

_____

Signature of Clinician:_____

Appendix E
Resiliency References for Youth & Families

Anthony, E., & Cohler, B. (1987). *The invulnerable child.* New York: Guilford Press.

Chick, S. (1987). *Push me, pull me.* London: Women's Press.

Christiansen, J., Christiansen, J., & Howard, M. (1997). Using protective factors to enhance resilience and school success for at-risk students. *Intervention School and Clinic, 33*(2), 86–89.

Garmezy, N. (1992). *Saving children at risk: Poverty and disabilities.* Newbury Park: Sage.

Glick, H. (1992). Resilience research: How can it help city schools? *City Schools, 1*(1), 11–18.

Glodich, A., & Allen, J. (1998). Adolescents exposed to violence and abuse: A review of the group therapy literature with an emphasis on preventing trauma reenactment. *Journal of Child and Adolescent Group Therapy, 8*(3), 135–154.

Graham, T. L. (1993). Beyond detection: Education and the abused student. *Social Work in Education, 15*(4), 197–206.

Joseph, J. M. (1994). *The resilient child: Preparing today's youth for tomorrow's world.* New York: Plenum.

McCubbin, H., McCubbin, A., & Thompson, A. (1997). Families under stress: What makes them resilient? *Journal of Family and Consumer Sciences, 89*(3), 2–11.

Richman, J., Rosenfield, L., & Bowen, G. (1998). Social support for adolescents at risk of school failure. *Social Work, 43*(4), 309–323.

Richardson, G. E. (1997). Resilient youth and curriculum. Material available by calling 1-888-667-7934 or e-mail at grichard@phth.health.utah.edu

Tower, C. C. (1987). *How schools can help combat child abuse and neglect.* Washington, D. C.: National Education Library.

White-Hood, M. (1993). Taking up the mentoring challenge. *Educational Leadership, 51,* 76–78.

Appendix F
Bibliotherapy References

Anger Management

Carlson, D., & Mark Lee, R. E., (2000). *Stop the pain: Teen meditations.* Madison, CT: Bick Publishing House.

Cullern, M. C., Wright. J., & Gondles, J. A., Jr., (1996). *Cage your rage for teens: A guide for anger control.* Landham, MD: American Correctional Association.

Fernley, F. (2004). *I wrote on all four walls: Teens speak out on violence.* Toronto, ON: Annick Press.

Gardner, J. (Ed.). (1997). *Runaway with words: Poems from Florida's youth shelters.* Tallahassee, FL: Anhinga Press.

Hemman, L. (2001). *The hidden light.* Lincoln, NE: Writers Club Press.

Mazer, H. (Ed.). (1997). *Twelve shots: Outstanding short stories about guns.* New York, NY: Random House Children's Books.

Seaward, B., & Bartlett, L. (2002). *Hot stones and funny bones: Teens helping teens deal with stress and anger.* Deerfield Beach, FL: Health Communications.

Simmons, R. (2003). *Odd girl out: The hidden culture of aggression in girls.* New York, NY: Harvest Books.

Simmons, R. (2004). *Odd girl speaks out: Girls write about bullies, cliques, popularity, and jealousy.* New York, NY: Harvest Books.

Coping with Losses and Grieving

Allen, J. (2001). *Using literature to help troubled teenagers cope with end-of-life issues.* Westport, CT: Greenwood Publishing Group, Inc.

Bodart, J. R. (2002). *Radical reads: 101 YA novels on the edge.* Lanham, MD: Scarecrow Press.

Bowman, C. A. (Ed.). (1999). *Using literature to help troubled teenagers cope with health issues.* Westport, CT: Greenwood Publishing Group.

Carroll, P. (Ed.). (2000). *Using literature to help troubled teenagers cope with family issues.* Westport, CT: Greenwood Publishing Group.

Joshua, J. M., & DiMenna, D. (2000). *Read two books and let's talk next week: Using bibliotherapy in clinical practice.* Somerset, NJ: John Wiley.

Kapan, J. S. (1999). *Using literature to help troubled teenagers cope with identity issues.* Westport, CT: Greenwood Publishing Group.

Kaywell, J. (2004). *Using literature to help troubled teenagers cope with abuse issues.* Westport, CT: Greenwood Publishing Group.

Tussing, H. L., & Valentine, D. P. (2001). Helping adolescents cope with the mental illness of a parent through bibliotherapy. *Child and Adolescent Social Work Journal, 18*(6), 455–469.

Depression and Suicide

Cobain, B. (1998). *When nothing matters anymore: A survival guide for depressed teens.* Minneapolis, MN: Free Spirit Publishing.

Grimmett, C. D. (1995). *Never cry alone: Someone somewhere knows how you feel, you are not alone.* Woodbridge, VA: Southern Publishers.

Coping with Family Life Changes

MacGregor, C. (2004). *The divorce helpbook for teens.* Atascadero, CA: Impact Publishers.

Price, E. (2004). *Divorce and teens: When a family splits apart.* Berkeley Heights, NJ: Enslow Publishers.

Schuurman, D. (2004). *Never the same: Coming to terms with the death of a parent.* New York, NY: St. Martin's Press.

Trujillo, M. L. (2000). *Why can't we talk?: What teens would share if parents would listen.* Deerfield Beach, FL: Health Communications.

Dealing with Several Issues/Problems

A Taste-Berry teen's guide to managing the stress and pressures of life. (2001). Deerfield Beach, FL: Health Communications.

Goldsworthy, J. L. (2000). *Approaching the crossroads: Four stories of adolescence.* Lincoln, NE: Writer's Showcase Press.

Lynch, C. (2001). *All the old haunts.* New York, NY: HarperCollins Children's Book Group.

Teens write through it: Essays from teens who've triumphed over trouble. (1998). Minneapolis, MN: Sagebrush Education Resources.

Parent Coping Skills

Cheever, S. (2002). *As good as I could be: A memoir of raising wonderful children in difficult times.* New York, NY: Washington Square Press.

Friel, J. C., & Friel, L. D. (1999). *Seven worst things (good) parents do.* Deerfield Beach, FL: Health Communications.

Godfrey, R., & Godfrey, N. S. (2004). *The teen code: How to talk to them about sex, drugs, and everything else—teenagers reveal what works best.* Gordonsville, VA: Rodale Press.

Haffner, D. W., & Tartaglione, A. H. (2004). *Beyond the big talk: Every parent's guide to raising sexually healthy teens—from middle school to high school and beyond.* New York, NY: Newmarket Press.

Kunther, T. (2003). *Gimme your lunch money!: The complete guide to bullies and bullying.* Los Angeles, CA: Mars Publishing, Inc.

Lamb, S. (2002). *The secret lives of girls: What good girls really do—sex play, aggression, and their guilt.* New York, NY: Simon & Schuster.

McCarthy, A. R., & Sweeney, D. B. (2000). *Healthy teens: Facing the challenges of young lives.* Birmingham, MI: Bridge Communications.

Schaefer, C., & DiGeronimo, T. F. (1999). *How to talk to teens about really important things: Specific questions and answers and useful things to say.* Somerset, NJ: John Wiley.

Self-Esteem Enhancement

Benson, P. L., Espeland, P., & Judy, G. (1998). *What teens need to succeed: Practical ways to share your own future.* Minneapolis, MN: Free Spirit Publishing.

Carlson, E. (2000). *Don't sweat the small stuff for teens.* New York, NY: Hyperion Press.

Canfield, J., et. al. (1997). *Chicken soup for the teenage soul.* Deerfield Beach, FL: Health Communications.

Covey, S. (2000). *The 7 habits of highly effective teens.* New York, NY: Simon & Schuster.

Fiorille, M. (2003). *I will be me: Nothing more, nothing less.* Frederick, MD: Publish America.

Friel, J. C., & Friel, L. D. (2000). *Seven best things that smart teens do.* Deerfield Beach, FL: Health Communications.

Palmer, P. & Froehner M. A. (2000). *Teen esteem: A self direction manual for young adults* (2nd ed.). Atascadero, CA: Impact Publishers.

Stedman, G. (2000). *Teens can make it happen: Nine steps for success.* New York, NY: Simon & Schuster.

The secret life of teens: Young people speak out about their lives. (2000). San Francisco, CA: Harper San Francisco.

Handling Issues Related to Sexuality

Lichtenberg, G. (2000). *Playing catch with my mother: Coming to manhood when all the rules have changed.* New York, NY: Bantam Books.

Madaras, L., & Madaras, A. (2004). *My body, my self for boys.* New York, NY: Newmarket Press.

Madaras, L., & Madaras, A. (2004). *My body, my self for girls.* New York, NY: Newmarket Press.

Mather, C. L., & Debye, K. E. (2004). *How long does it hurt?: A guide to recovering from incest and sexual abuse for teenagers, their friends, and their families.* Somerset, NJ: John Wiley.

Potash, M. S., & Fuitman, L. P. (Eds.). (2001). *Am I weird or is this normal?: Advice and info to get teens in the know.* New York, NY: Simon & Schuster.

Addressing and Coping with Substance Abuse Issues

Burgess, M. (1999). *Smack.* New York, NY: Avon Books.

Hyde, M., & Setaro, J. F. (2003). *Drugs 101.* New York, NY: Simon & Schuster.

McClellan, M. (2004). *The big deal about alcohol: What teens need to know about drinking.* Berkeley, NJ: Enslow Publishers.

Pardee, D. (1997). *Find your own path: A workbook for adolescents recovering from chemical dependency.* Soquel, CA: ToucanEd Publications.

Toten, T. (2002). *The game.* Calgary, Canada: Red Deer Press.

REFERENCES

Abraham, T. V. (1953). *Maternal dependency and schizophrenia: Mothers and daughters in a therapy group: A group analytic study.* New York: International Universities Press.

Anderson, C. M., Hogarty, G. E., & Reiss, D. J. (1980). Family treatment of adult schizophrenia patients: A psychoeducational approach. *Schizophrenia Bulletin, 6,* 490–505.

Anderson, C. M., & Reiss, D. J. (1982). Family treatment of patients with chronic schizophrenia: The inpatient phase. In H. Harbin (Ed.), The psychiatric hospital and the family. New York: Spectrum.

Anderson, C. A. (1983). *A psychoeducational program for families of patients with schizophrenia.* New York: The Guilford Press.

Anderson, C. M., Griffin, S., Rossi, A., Pagonis, E., Holder, D. P., & Treiber, R. (1986). A comparative study of the impact of education versus process groups for families of patients with affective disorders. *Family Process, 25,* 185–205.

Anton, R., Hogan, Z., Jalali, B., Riodan, C., & Kleber, H. (1981). Multiple family therapy and naltrexone in the treatment of opiate dependence. *Drug and Alcohol Dependence, 8,* 157–168.

Aponte, H. J., Zarski, J., Bixenstene, C., & Cibik, P. (1991, July). Home/Community–based services: A two-tier approach. *American Journal of Orthopsychiatry, 61*(3), 403–408.

Arnold, L. E., Sheridan, K., & Estreicher, D. (1986). Multifamily parent-child group therapy for behavior and learning disorders. *Journal of Child and Adolescent Psychotherapy, 3*(4), 279–284.

Barcai, A. (1967). An adventure in multiple family therapy. *Family Process, 6,* 185–189.

Bauman, T. A., & James, G. L. (1990). A support group for burn victims and their families. *Social Work with Groups, 12,* 159–184.

Behr, H. (1996). Multiple family group therapy: A group analytic perspective. *Group Analysis, 29,* 9–22.

Benningfield, A. B. (1978). Multiple family therapy systems. *Journal of Marriage and Family Counseling, 4,* 25–34.

Berg, I. K., & de Shazer, S. (1991). Solution talk. In D. Sollee (Ed.), *Constructing the future.* Washington DC: American Association for Marriage and Family Therapy.

Berma, K. K. (1966). Multiple family therapy: Its possibilities in preventing remission. *Mental Hygiene, 50,* 367–370.

Bisman, C., & Hardcastle, D. (1999). *Integrating research into practice.* Boston: Brooks/Cole.

Black, D., & Blum, N. (1992). Obsessive-compulsive disorder support groups: The Iowa Model. *Comprehensive Psychiatry, 33*(1), 65–71.

Bloomfield, O. H. (1972). Groups: The more primitive psychology? A review of some paradigms in group dynamics. *Australian New Zealand Journal of Psychiatry, 6,* 238–246.

Bowen, M. (1972). Principles and techniques of multiple family therapy. In J. O. Bradt & C. J. Moynihan (Eds.), *Systems Therapy*. Washington, DC: Self-published.

Boyd-Franklin, N. (1993). Black families. In F. Walsh (Ed.), *Normal Family Process*. New York: Guilford.

Brennan, J. W. (1995). A short-term psychoeducational multiple-family group for bipolar patients and their families. *Social Work, 40*, 737–743.

Burton, G., & Young, D. (1962). Families crisis in group therapy. *Family Process, 1*, 214–223.

Carlson, C. (1998). Multiple family group therapy. In K. C. Stoiber & T. R. Kratochwill (Eds.), *Handbook of group intervention for children and families.* (pp. 268–279). Boston: Allyn and Bacon.

Cassano, R. D. (1989). Social work with multifamily groups. *Social Work with Groups, 12*(1), 15–39.

Coughlin, F., & Winberger, H. (1968). Group family therapy. *Family Process, 7*, 37–50.

Cox, C., & Ephross, P. H. (1989). Group work with families of nursing home residents: Its socialization and therapeutic functions. *Journal of Gerontological Social Work, 13*(3/4), 61–73.

Cwiakala, C. E., & Mordock, J. B. (1997). The use of multifamily play groups for families with a parent in addiction recovery. *Alcohol Treatment Quarterly, 15*(1), 15–28.

Dennison, S. (1995). The E.S.S.E. group model: A 21st century approach for families at risk. *Journal of Family Social Work, 1*(2), 57–71.

Dennison, S. (1997). *Creating positive support groups for at-risk children*. Austin: Pro-ed.

Dennison, S. (1999). Multiple-family groups: Practice implications for the 21st century. *Journal of Family Social Work, 3*(3), 29–51.

Detre, T., Kessler, D., & Sayers, T. (1961). A socioadaptive approach to treatment of acutely disturbed psychiatric inpatients. *Proceedings Third World Congress Psychiatry, 1*, 501–506.

Donner J., & Gamson, A. (1968). Experience with multifamily, time limited, outpatient groups at a community psychiatric clinic. *Psychiatry, 31*, 126–137.

Duhatscheck-Krause, A. L. (1989). A support group for patients and families facing life-threatening illness: Finding a solution to nonbeing. *Social Work with Groups, 12*, 55–69.

Durrell, V. G. (1969). Adolescents in multiple family group therapy in a school setting. *International Journal of Group Psychotherapy, 19*, 45–52.

Dziegielewski, S. F. (1991). Social group work with family members of elderly nursing home residents with dementia: A controlled study. *Research on Social Work Practice, 1*(4), 358–370.

Edwards, S. (2001). *The essential elements of multi-family group therapy: A DELPHI study.* Unpublished doctoral dissertation, Virginia Polytechnic Institute and State University, Blacksburg, VA.

Fallon, I. R. H., Liberman, R. P., Lillie I. F. J., & Vaughn, I. C. (1981). Family therapy of schizophrenics with high risk of relapse. *Family Process, 20*, 211–221.

Foley, V. D. (1982). Multiple family therapy with urban blacks. In L. A. Wolberg & M. L. Aronson (Eds), *Group and family therapy*. New York: Brunner/Mazel.

Fristad, M. A., Gavazzi, S. M., & Soldano, K. W. (1998). Multifamily psychoeducation groups for childhood mood disorders: A program description and preliminary efficacy data. *Contemporary Family Therapy, 20*, 385–402.

Garrett, K., & Rice, S. (1998). Psychoeducational multiple-family groups. *The Journal of Baccalaureate Social Work, 3*(2), 89–99.

Goldmuntz, P. (1990). *Families experiencing a chronic illness: The effects of a multiple family psychoeducational group on level of functioning and stress*. Unpublished dissertation, Antioch University, New England Graduate School, NH.

Goldstein, M. (1996). Psychoeducational family interventions in psychotic disorders. *New Trends in Experimental and Clinical Psychiatry, 12*(2), 71–79.

Gould, E., & DeGroot, D. (1981). Inter- and intra-family interaction in multifamily group therapy. *The American Journal of Family Therapy, 9*(2), 65–74.

Gould, E., & Glick, I. D. (1977). The effects of family presence and brief family intervention on global outcome for hospitalized schizophrenic patients. *Family Process, 16,* 503–510.

Greenfield, B. J., & Senecal, J. (1995). Recreational multifamily therapy for troubled children. *American Journal of Orthopsychiatry, 65,* 434–439.

Gritzer, P. H., & Okun, H. S. (1983). Multiple family group therapy, In B. B. Wolman, & G. Stricker (Eds.), *Handbook of family and marital therapy.* New York: Plenum Press.

Gurman, A. S., & Kniskern, D. P. (1981). Family therapy outcome research: Knowns and unknowns. In A. S. Gurman, & D. P. Kniskern (Eds.), *Handbook of family therapy.* New York: Brunner/Mazel.

Hardcastle, D. R. (1977). A multiple family counseling program: Procedures and results. *Family Process, 16,* 67–74.

Harrow, M., Astrachan, B., Becker, R., Miller, J., & Schwartz, A. (1967). Influence of the psychotherapist on the emotional climate of group therapy. *Human Relations, 78,* 49–64.

Hes, J., & Handler, S. (1961). Multidimensional group psychotherapy. *Archives of General Psychiatry, 5,* 92–97.

Hyde, A., & Goldman, C. (1993). Common family issues that interfere with the treatment and rehabilitation of people with schizophrenia. *Journal of Psychosocial Rehabilitation, 16*(4), 63–74.

Jarvis, P., Esty, T., & Stutzman, L. (1969). Evaluation and treatment of families at Fort Logan Mental Health Center. *Community Mental Health Journal, 5,* 14–49.

Julian B., Ventrola, L., & Christ, T. (1969). Multiple family therapy: The interaction of young hospitalized patients with their mothers. *International Journal of Group Psychotherapy, 19,* 501–509.

Kaufman, E., & Kaufman, P. (1979). Multiple family therapy with drug abusers. In E. Kaufman, & P. Kaufman (Eds.), *Family therapy of drug and alcohol abuse.* New York: Gardner.

Kimbro, E., Taschman, H., Wylie, H., & Machennan, B. (1967). A multiple family group approach to some problems of adolescence. *International Journal of Group Psychotherapy, 17,* 18–24.

Kiresuk, T., Smith, A., & Cardillo, J. (Eds.). (1994). *Goal attainment scaling: Applications, theory, and measurement.* Hillsdale, NJ: Lawrence Erlbaum.

Klimenko, A. (1968). Multifamily therapy in the rehabilitation of drug addicts. *Perspective Psychiatric Care, 6,* 220–223.

Lang, L.R. (1993). *A multifamily group intervention to facilitate open communication between adopted adolescents and their adoptive parents.* Unpublished dissertation, Rutgers University.

Laqueur, H. P. (1972). Mechanism of change in multiple therapy. In F. T. Sager, & H. S. Kaplan (Eds.), *Progress in group and family therapy.* New York: Brunner/Mazel.

Laqueur, H. P. (1976). Multiple family therapy. In P. J. Guerin (Ed.), *Family therapy, theory, and practice.* (pp. 405–416). New York: Gardner.

Laqueur, H. P. (1980). The theory and practice of multiple family therapy. In L. R. Wolberg, & M. L. Aronson (Eds.), *Group and family therapy.* New York: Brunner/Mazel.

Laqueur, H. P., & LaBurt, H. A. (1962). The therapeutic community on a modern insulin ward. *Journal of Neuro-Psychiatry, 3,* 139–149.

Laqueur, H. P., & LaBurt, H. A. (1964). Family organization on a modern state hospital ward. *Mental Hygiene, 48,* 544–551.

Laqueur, H. P., Wells, C. F., & Agreti, M. (1969). Multiple-family therapy in a state hospital. *Hospital and Community Psychiatry, 20,* 13–19.

Leichter, E., & Schulman, G. (1968). Emerging phenomena in multifamily group treatment. *International Journal of Group Psychotherapy, 18,* 59–69.

Leichter, E., & Schulman, G. L. (1972). Interplay of group and family treatment: Techniques in multifamily group therapy. *International Journal of Group Psychotherapy, 22,* 167–176.

Luber, R. F., & Wells, R. A. (1977). Structured short-term multiple family therapy: An educational approach. *International Journal of Group Psychotherapy, 27,* 43–58.

Manchester Berger, T. (1984). Crisis intervention: A drop-in support group for cancer patients and their families. *Social Work in Health Care, 10*(2).

Mandell, D., & Birenzweig, E. (1990). A model for group work with remarried couples and their children. *Journal of Divorce and Remarriage, 14*(1), 29–35.

Marner, T., & Westerberg, C. (1987). Concomitant group therapy with anorectics and their parents as a supplement to family therapy. *Journal of Family Therapy, 9,* 255–263.

Matthews, K. L., & Cunningham, T. M. (1983). Combination of multiple-family therapy with parallel groups. *American Journal of Psychotherapy, 42*(1), 113–120.

McFarlane, W. R. (1983). Multiple family therapy in schizophrenia. In W. R. McFarlane (Ed.), *Family therapy in schizophrenia.* New York: The Guilford Press.

McFarlane, W. R. (2001). *Multifamily groups in the treatment of severe psychiatric disorders.* New York: The Guilford Press.

McFarlane, W. R. (2002). *Multifamily groups in the treatment of severe psychiatric disorders.* New York: The Guilford Press.

McFarlane, W. R., Link, B., Dushay, R., Marchal, T., & Crilly, T. (1995). Psychoeducational multiple family groups: Four-year relapse outcome in schizophrenia. *Family Process, 34,* 127–144.

McFarlane, W. R., Dushay, R. A., Stastny, R., Deakins, S. M., & Link, B. (1996). A comparison of two levels of family-aided assertive community treatment. *Psychiatric Services, 47,* 744–750.

McKay, M. M., Gonzalez, J. J., Stone, S., Ryland, D., & Kohner, K. (1995). Multiple family therapy groups: A responsive intervention model for inner city families. *Social Work With Groups, 18*(4), 41–56.

McKay, M. M., Gonzales, J., Quintana, E., Kim, L., & Abdul-Adil, J. (1999). Multiple family groups: An alternative for reducing disruptive behavioral difficulties of urban children. *Research on Social Work Practice, 9*(5), 593–607.

Meezan, W. M., & O'Keefe, M. (1998). Evaluating the effectiveness of multifamily group therapy in child abuse and neglect. *Research on Social Work Practice, 8*(3), 330–353.

Meezan, W. M., & O'Keefe, M. (1998). Multifamily group therapy: Impact on family functioning and child behavior. *Families in Society, 79*(1), 32–44.

Meezan, W., O'Keefe, M., & Zariani, M. (1997). A model of multi-family group therapy for abusive and neglectful parents and their children. *Social Work with Groups, 20*(2), 71–88.

Nash, K. B. (1990). Self-help concepts: An empowerment vehicle for sickle cell disease patients and their families. *Social Work with Groups, 12,* 81–97.

O'Shea, M. D., & Phelps, R. (1985). Multiple family therapy: Current status and critical appraisal. *Family Process, 24,* 555–582.

Ostby, C. H. (1968). Conjoint group therapy with prisoners and their families. *Family Process, 7,* 184–201.

Papell, C. P., & Rothman, B. (1989). Preface. *Social Work With Groups, 12*(1), xi–xiii.

Parker, T., Hill, T. W., & Miller, G. (1987). Multiple family therapy: Evaluating a group experience for mentally retarded adolescents and their families. *Family Therapy, 14*(1).

Parloff, M. B. (1976). The narcissism of small differences—and some big ones. *International Journal of Group Psychotherapy, 26,* 311–319.

Parmenter, G., Smith, T. C., & Cecic, N. A. (1987). Parallel and conjoint short-term group therapy for school-age children and their parents: A model. *International Journal of Group Psychotherapy, 37*(2), 239–254.

Parsonnet, L., & O'Hare, T. (1990). A group orientation program for newly-admitted cancer patients. *Social Work, 35,* 37–40.

Pasnau, R., Meyer, M., Davis, L., Lloyd, R., & Kline, G. (1976). Coordinated group psychotherapy of children and parents. *International Journal of Group Psychotherapy, 26,* 89–103.

Pattison, E. M. (1973). Social system psychotherapy. *American Journal of Psychotherapy, 1,* 396–409.

Paul, N. L., & Bloom, J. D. (1970). Multiple family therapy: Secrets and scapegoating in family crisis. *International Journal of Group Psychotherapy, 20,* 37–47.

Pellman, R., & Platt, R. (1974). Three families in search of a director. *American Journal of Orthopsychiatry, 44,* 224–225.

Polcin, D. (1992). A comprehensive model of adolescent chemical dependency treatment. *Journal of Counseling and Development, 70,* 376–382.

Pomeroy, E. C. (1984). *A psychoeducational group intervention for family members of persons with AIDS: An effectiveness study.* Unpublished dissertation, University of Texas at Austin.

Powell, M. B., & Mohahan, J. (1969). Reaching the rejects through multi-family group therapy. *International Journal of Group Psychotherapy, 19,* 35–43.

Quinn, W. H., Bell, K., & Ward, J. (1997). Family solutions for juvenile first offenders. *The Prevention Researcher, 4*(2), 10–12.

Raasoch, T. W. (1981). Multiple family therapy. In R. T. Corsini (Ed.), *Handbook of innovative psychotherapies.* New York: John Wiley.

Rabin, C. (1995). The use of psychoeducation groups to improve marital functioning in high risk Israeli couples: A stage model. *Contemporary Family Therapy, 17,* 503–515.

Reiss, D., & Costell, R. (1977). The multiple family group as a small society: Family regulation of interaction with nonmembers. *American Journal of Psychiatry, 134,* 21–24.

Reiss, D., & Costell, R. (1979). The multiple family group as a small society: Family regulation of interaction with nonmembers. In T. G. Howells (Ed.), *Advances in family psychiatry,* New York: International Universities Press.

Rhodes, R. M., & Zelman, A. B. (1986). An ongoing group in a women's shelter. *American Journal of Orthopsychiatry, 56*(1), 120–130.

Rose, S. (1998). The role of research in group therapy with children and adolescents. In K. C. Stoiber, & T. R. Kratochwill (Eds.), *Handbook of group intervention for children and families.* (pp. 47–67). Boston: Allyn & Bacon.

Royse, D., Thyer, B., Padgett, D., & Logan, T. (2001). *Program evaluation: An introduction.* Toronto: Brooks/Cole.

Schaffer, D. S. (1969). Effects of frequent hospitalization on behavior of psychotic patients in multiple family therapy program. *Journal of Clinical Psychology, 25,* 104–105.

Sherman, S., & Reid, W. (Eds.). (1994). *Qualitative research in social work.* New York: Columbia University Press.

Singh, N. (1982). Notes and observations on the practice of multiple family therapy in a adolescent unit. *Journal of Adolescence, 5,* 319–332.

Springer, D. W., & Orsbon, S. H. (2002). Families helping families: Implementing a multi-family therapy group with substance-abusing adolescents. *Health and Social Work, 27*(3), 204–207.

Steinglass, P., Gonzalez, S., Dosovitz, L., & Reiss, D. (1982). Discussion groups for chronic hemodialysis patients and their families. *General Hospital Psychiatry, 4,* 7–14.

Strelnick, A. H. (1977). Multiple family group therapy: A review of literature. *Family Process,* 307–325.

Tunnard, T. (1989). Local self-help groups for families of children in public care. *Child Welfare, 68,* 221–227.

Wamboldt, M. Z., & Levin, L. (1995). Utility of multifamily psychoeducational groups for medically ill children and adolescents. *Family Systems Medicine, 13,* 151–161.

Wellisch, D. K., Mosher, M. B., & Van Scoy, C. (1978). Management of family emotional stress: Family group therapy in a private oncology practice. *International Journal of Group Psychotherapy, 28,* 225–231.

Wilmer, H. A., Marko, I., & Pogue, E. (1966). Group treatment of prisoners and their families. *Mental Hygiene, 50,* 380–389.

Yalom, I. D. (Ed.) (1985). *The theory and practice of group psychotherapy.* New York: Basic Books.

Zarski, J. J., Aponte, H. J., Bixenstine, C., & Cibik, P. (1992). Beyond home-based family intervention: A multifamily approach. *Contemporary Family Therapy, 14*(1), 3–14.

INDEX

Out-of-group observation data, 271–272

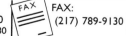